Shuln Kntn

D1603015

On the Celebrated *and* Neglected Poems *of*
Andrew Marvell

On the
Celebrated
and
Neglected Poems
of
Andrew
Marvell

Edited by Claude J. Summers
and Ted-Larry Pebworth

University of Missouri Press
Columbia and London

Copyright © 1992 by
The Curators of the University of Missouri
University of Missouri Press, Columbia, Missouri 65201
Printed and bound in the United States of America
All rights reserved

5   4   3   2   1   96   95   94   93   92

Library of Congress Cataloging-in-Publication Data

On the celebrated and neglected poems of Andrew
    Marvell / edited by Claude J. Summers and Ted-Larry
    Pebworth.
        p.   cm.
    Includes index.
    ISBN 0–8262–0795–2
    1. Marvell, Andrew, 1621–1678—Criticism and
    interpretation.   I. Summers, Claude J.   II. Pebworth,
    Ted-Larry.
    PR3546.05   1992
    821'.4—dc20   91–26174
                                                      CIP

∞™ This paper meets the requirements of the
American National Standard for Permanence of Paper
for Printed Library Materials, Z39.48, 1984.

Designer: Kristie Lee
Typesetter: Connell-Zeko Type & Graphics
Printer and Binder: Thomson-Shore, Inc.
Typeface: Palatino Display and Palatino

For
Ernest W. Sullivan, II
and
Achsah Guibbory

Contents

A Note on the Text

Unless otherwise noted, all quotations from Marvell's poetry follow the text of H. M. Margoliouth, ed., *The Poems and Letters of Andrew Marvell,* 3d ed., rev. by Pierre Legouis and E. E. Duncan-Jones, 2 vols. (Oxford: Clarendon Press, 1971), with line numbers cited parenthetically in the text.

On the Celebrated *and* Neglected Poems *of*
Andrew Marvell

Claude J. Summers
and Ted-Larry Pebworth

Introduction

ANDREW MARVELL remains the most enigmatic of major seven-teenth-century literary figures; he resists generalizations and eludes categorization. The Restoration satirist is very different from the social analyst of "An Horatian Ode," the Cromwellian apologist seems incompatible with the royalist who wrote the verses to Lovelace and the elegies on Hastings and Villiers, and none of these manifestations of the political Marvell is perfectly consonant with the lyric poet who celebrates solitude. Not only does Marvell appear internally inconsistent, but he is notoriously difficult to place on the map of seventeenth-century poetry. Claimed as an heir to both Donne and Jonson and as a disciple of Milton, he is in fact very distinct from each of them. In so many ways, he is finally *sui generis.* His uniqueness results not from his insusceptibility to literary influences, but, quite to the contrary, from his self-conscious absorption, transcendence, and transfiguration of literary traditions of the most subtle and erudite kinds. Moreover, the qualities that most fully characterize Marvell's lyric poetry—balance and equipoise, suggestiveness and delicacy, intelligence and playful-ness—contribute to his celebrated elusiveness.

These characteristics also help create the apparent simplicity that conceals astonishing depth and the impression of lightness that masks philosophical weightiness. Marvell's poems are unsettling precisely because their placid surfaces so frequently belie barely concealed ambiguities, ironies, and expansiveness. Marvell's signature as a poet is a complexity conveyed so lightly as to be a "Mosaique of the Air," a phrase that perfectly captures the poetry's teasing wit and imaginative evasiveness. Much of the pleasure of reading Marvell's poetry resides in the constantly shifting parameters of its meaning, in the stubborn refusal to yield all its secrets, and in the persistent discrepancy between its ostensible accessibility and its actual resistance to critical approaches of all kinds.

The essays collected in this volume seek to explore both the unity and the diversity, the brilliance and the depth reflected in Marvell's poetic canon. They originated as submissions to the eighth Biennial Renaissance Conference at the University of Michigan–Dearborn, " 'The Mosaique of the Air': The Achievement of Andrew Marvell," held on October 21–22, 1988.[1] The original (though abbreviated) versions of all the essays were presented there. They were written independently and without consultation among the authors, but the final versions printed here have benefited from the stimulating exchanges and responses afforded by the conference, and they intersect, reinforce, and challenge each other in significant ways. Together, they reflect the aims of the conference: to explore the range and variety of Marvell's art, not only in his celebrated lyrics, Cromwell poems, and "Upon Appleton House," but also in the neglected poems of his canon. As here placed in a variety of biographical and generic and intellectual contexts and seen from a number of vantage points, Marvell and his poetry continue to inspire fascination and interest.

The two essays that open the volume are wide-ranging in scope and seek to find patterns of order and unity in the Marvell canon. Donald Friedman's subject is the reflection of a new kind of music in Marvell's poetry. Possibly inspired by the innovative song settings of Henry Lawes, Marvell abandoned the older Orphic concept favored by Milton, which sees music as "concord between hierarchically articulated sounds" that has the power to govern nature, in favor of a "revisionary presentation of the poetics of music." This new poetics, Friedman argues, invokes not Orpheus but Amphion, who "is a builder of cities, a harper whose music can command intractable and insensate stones and can move them to form strong and stable wholes out of adamant

---

1. Selected papers from the first seven Dearborn conferences have been published: those from the 1974 conference as *"Trust to Good Verses": Herrick Tercentenary Essays*, ed. Roger B. Rollin and J. Max Patrick (Pittsburgh: University of Pittsburgh Press, 1978); those from the 1976 conference on seventeenth-century prose as a special issue of *Studies in the Literary Imagination* 10, no. 2 (1977), ed. William A. Sessions and James S. Tillman; those from the 1978 conference as *"Too Rich to Clothe the Sunne": Essays on George Herbert*, ed. Claude J. Summers and Ted-Larry Pebworth (Pittsburgh: University of Pittsburgh Press, 1980); those from the 1980 conference as *Classic and Cavalier: Essays on Jonson and the Sons of Ben*, ed. Claude J. Summers and Ted-Larry Pebworth (Pittsburgh: University of Pittsburgh Press, 1982); those from the 1982 conference as *The Eagle and the Dove: Reassessing John Donne*, ed. Claude J. Summers and Ted-Larry Pebworth (Columbia: University of Missouri Press, 1986); those from the 1984 conference as *"Bright Shootes of Everlastingnesse": The Seventeenth-Century Religious Lyric*, ed. Claude J. Summers and Ted-Larry Pebworth (Columbia: University of Missouri Press, 1987); and those from the 1986 conference as *"The Muses Common-Weale": Poetry and Politics in the Seventeenth Century*, ed. Claude J. Summers and Ted-Larry Pebworth (Columbia: University of Missouri Press, 1988).

and unconnected parts." It is this new concept of music, Friedman concludes, "both more varied and more variously political" than the Orphic model, that informs and connects such apparently dissimilar poems as "The First Anniversary," "Musicks Empire," and the "Two Songs at the Marriage of the Lord Fauconberg and the Lady Mary Cromwell."

Stella Revard's essay explores the classical influences that unify Marvell's various canon. More specifically, Revard locates a pervasive influence on Marvell's style in the epigrams of the Greek Anthology. She considers in detail how the subject matter, language, and technique of the Greek epigrammatists and their Renaissance imitators left their mark on some of the most famous of Marvell's lyrics in Latin and English, notably "To His Coy Mistress" and the Latin and English counterparts "Ros"/"On a Drop of Dew" and "Hortus"/"The Garden." Arguing that Marvell weds epigrammatical vividness and wit to the lyrical tradition, Revard concludes that "it is hard to believe that Marvell did not profit from the collective wit and wisdom that made the Greek Anthology so popular in the sixteenth and seventeenth centuries."

Utilizing several different critical approaches, the next five essays in the collection consider individual lyrics. In a stimulating discussion, Dale Randall examines afresh a famous textual crux in "To His Coy Mistress." With a formidable magazine of scholarly ammunition, he defends the William Popple emendation of "gates" to "grates" in the folio reading of "the Iron gates of Life." Evoking the "restricting, naysaying, pleasure-thwarting iron grates" of castles, tombs, prisons, cages, traps, convents, and Renaissance tennis courts, Randall finds that the lady's "coyness" at the beginning of the poem is reiterated in the "grates" at its end in that both are impediments to the life force. Perception is the concern of the essay that follows on "Eyes and Tears." Joan Hartwig examines the poem in the contexts of the emblem book tradition and the popular religious literature of tears. She argues that "Eyes and Tears" is not as disjointed as it seems and that in it Marvell affirms weeping as a way of comprehending the mysteries of existence. When properly perceived, she concludes, apparent dualities yield their essential unity.

Two essays engage one of Marvell's most problematic poems, "The Nymph Complaining for the Death of her *Faun*." In very different ways both are concerned with genre. Paul Sellin, after noting the inadequacy of the various generic identifications of Marvell's poem to explain its content and action, and after surveying the problems of interpretation that arise because its precise genre remains elusive, offers as a possibility an ancient Greek genre, an aulic song that focuses on maidens and

youths who literally die for love. Although no examples of the genre
survive, Sellin finds in Scaliger's description of the lost *calyca* of the
poet Stesichorus—a virgin's song of unrequited love that immediately
precedes her suicide—a telling similarity to the situation of Marvell's
nymph; and he finds in that generic identification a key to understanding Marvell's poem. Barbara Estrin, on the other hand, reconsiders the
relationship of "The Nymph Complaining" to the revenge genre. From
a feminist perspective she finds in the poem not one revenge and one
story, as formerly noticed, but two: "the story of the nymph's triumph
over Sylvio's dismissal (her re-creation of his gift) and the story of the
nymph's triumph over the soldiers (her de-creation of the world she
made)." The nymph's first revenge, Estrin explains, lies in her success,
while her second revenge consists of a deliberate failure.

Sexual politics is also the major concern in Eugene Cunnar's illuminating essay on "The Garden." In the carving of the trees' own
names into their bark, rather than the names of mistresses, Cunnar
contends that Marvell subverts and implicitly criticizes Petrarchism.
This critique of male dominance is then resolved in an interpretation of
the Hermaphroditus myth that reflects the poet's "desire for a return to
an Edenic time when signifier and signified, male and female were
united without division or tension . . . a return to nature as the model
for human love."

The next several essays examine concerns more traditionally thought
of as political. In a fascinating discussion that distinguishes between
the two conflicting appeals of the Gothic past in Marvell's time—as an
argument for liberty by the republicans and as a sentimental antiquarian interest reflected in such works as the *Monasticum Anglicanum*—
Douglas Chambers demonstrates the political significance of the di-
gression about the convent in "Upon Appleton House." In rejecting
Gothic antiquarianism and espousing nature, Chambers argues, Marvell identifies Lord Fairfax's withdrawal from public affairs as "a withdrawal from the debate about Gothic liberty to an interest in antiquarian Gothicism."

In his essay, M. L. Donnelly probes the rhetoric of political encomium
and, more specifically, Marvell's representation of Cromwell at a time
when the traditional symbolic systems had been thrown into confusion
by a violent change in government. Cut off from the use of images,
symbols, types, and figures that had been long associated with Stuart
absolutism, Marvell had to find a new repertoire of models to represent
and legitimize Cromwell's rule. Donnelly finds that in contrast to imagery of presence and stasis applied to the Stuart kings, in "An Horatian
Ode" Marvell chose for Cromwell images reflecting "relentless commit-

ment to activity and movement"; and in contrast to the Christocentric imagery appropriated by the partisans of the dead King Charles, in "The First Anniversary" he adopts for Cromwell the "fiercely active images of chiliasm, moving history relentlessly toward its culminating acts."

Two of Marvell's least-discussed political poems are addressed by Richard Todd and Diana Benet. Todd seeks to rescue Marvell's 1653 satire "The Character of Holland" from the frequent complaint that it lacks intellectual rigor and complexity by detailing the control and distinctively Marvellian balance that characterize the poem. Marvell sees Holland as a paradox, Todd contends, a developed land that is at the same time ceaselessly in the process of being created; and he recognizes the Dutch state as the chief rival of the fledgling English republic. By analyzing the bilingual puns in the satire, Todd shows how Marvell forces "the Dutch language itself into participating in the act in which the providential histories of the rival republics meet." Benet also considers an occasional political poem, "The Loyall Scot," written in support of the union of Scotland and England proposed in 1669–1670; but she does so to point out that even in such a topical work Marvell pursues one of the most pervasive nonpolitical concerns of his poetry: "the problem of a cohesive, stable self." Focusing on the figures of the Actor and Narcissus in the poem, she examines from a Lacanian perspective the images, themes, and techniques that Marvell uses to explore the fragmented self and to express the relationship of art to this fragmentation. She discovers that Marvell characteristically seeks to reconstitute a disintegrating subject by inscribing it, giving "a paradoxical substance and unity to what he insists is fluid and manifold."

The final essay in the volume is extensive in the poems it considers and in its implications. In it, John Rogers explores Marvell's persistent concern with historiography in a number of the pastoral works, including especially "Upon Appleton House." He identifies Marvell's view of history as materialistic in its conception of providence and redemption; but, significantly, it is a Christian materialism that "reconciles the theological notion of the imminent eschaton with the recently propounded scientific view that physical change is the result of matter in motion." As a consequence, Rogers concludes, Marvell represents the apocalypse not as the transcendent event toward which zealous reformers seek to drive the state, but as a gradual redemptive process of nature. If "Upon Appleton House" implies that purposive human action might elicit divine intervention, the shorter pastoral lyrics insist on the redemptive potential of a radical passivity.

The volume concludes with excerpts from a panel discussion by John

Klause, Ann Baynes Coiro, and Michael Schoenfeldt on the achievement of Andrew Marvell. All three panelists agree that the total of
Marvell's achievement has not yet been recognized and articulated. An
intensely private encoding of experience, Marvell's poetry eludes the
categorizations of experience implicit in most of the critical approaches
so far applied to it. Yet in the panelists' complementary concerns with
the vexed biographical question, with Marvell's ambiguous attitude
toward print, and with the notion of his work as a poetry of concealment, new approaches emerge, at least in shadowy outline, that might
render Marvell whole or at least allow us to accept with greater equa-
nimity his purposeful evasions.

The essays in this volume attempt to illuminate Marvell's achievement by exploring from various perspectives individual poems, pervasive ideas, and characteristic influences and techniques. Each essay
contributes to a fuller understanding of the "Mosaique of the Air" that
is Marvell's poetry. Yet the volume as a whole reaches no firm consensus about the achievement of Andrew Marvell. This is partly because of
the focus of the essays on particular works at the expense of others, the
neglect of some areas of the canon, and the failure to pose overarching
questions. But it is preeminently because Marvell's achievement itself
resolutely resists generalization and because his poetry continues to
elicit markedly divergent responses from readers. Not only are Marvell's works notably disparate and perhaps irreconcilable, but even his
lyric poetry—apparently all of a piece—teases us out of thought. Perhaps the only meaningful consensus about Marvell's achievement that
can be reached is that it is impressive. As evidenced by this volume,
Marvell and his works remain vital in their ability to excite scholarly
admiration and critical interest. If this collection provides no neat summary of Marvell's achievement or of his place in seventeenth-century
poetry, it does illuminate important areas of the canon—both the widely admired anthology pieces like "To His Coy Mistress," "The Nymph
Complaining for the Death of Her *Faun*," and "The Garden" and neglected poems like "The Loyall Scot" and "The Character of Holland"—
explores significant aspects of Marvell's art, and furthers our understanding and informed appreciation of Marvell's genius.

* * *

This book and the scholarly meeting from which it originated have
profited from the great effort, wide learning, and professional generos-
ity of the conference steering committee. Donald M. Friedman, Achsah
Guibbory, Robert B. Hinman, Judith Scherer Herz, John R. Roberts,
and John T. Shawcross helped referee the submissions to the con-

ference and offered valuable suggestions for revision. Their contributions have been extensive, and we join the authors of the essays in expressing gratitude for their insights and devotion. It is also our happy duty to acknowledge the support of the Horace H. Rackham Graduate School of the University of Michigan and the Campus Grants Committee of the University of Michigan–Dearborn. We are particularly grateful for the support of John H. D'Arms, Dean, Rackham Graduate School, and of the following administrators at the University of Michigan–Dearborn: Christopher C. Dahl, former Chair, Department of Humanities; James A. Foster, Dean, College of Arts, Sciences, and Letters; and Eugene Arden, former Vice Chancellor for Academic Affairs and Provost.

Donald M. Friedman

Marvell's Musicks

WHEN, IN "MUSICKS EMPIRE," Marvell is about to show how the "Empire of the Ear" was gained by combining the powers of the several "harmonious Colonies" of numbers, the phrase he turns to describe, or to define, music is entirely characteristic. To imagine a "Mosaique of the Air" is to make the insubstantial solid, to interlace the terminologies of different arts, to make an image of a sound; all these are habits of the Marvellian mind. So is the discovery of the etymological root shared by "music" and "mosaic" in the Greek word for "muse,"[1] a coincidence—or concinnity—that would have delighted him. Beyond the morphological or even the allegorical dimension of etymology, the web of implications that tie music to mosaic is woven of conceptions of composition that are intrinsic both to Marvell's thought and to his poetry. Further still, the multivalent puns that form the substrata of meaning in the phrase, "the Mosaique of the Air," are generated by the unsettling, at a particular moment of history, of ancient ideas of music itself, of the nature of harmony, and of the relationships between the words of the poetic text and their setting in musical form. Marvell could not have been unaware of that unsettling; his awareness is reflected in the many allusions to musical concepts and technical terms in his poems.

The very phrase, "Mosaique of the Air," is an invitation to muse on music, to toy with the embodied echoings of melody in the accompanied (and accompanying) air, the lyric form that was in Marvell's lifetime coming to displace the polyphonic forms of the earlier century. It is to air in the mind those resonances between composed airs and the actual currents of air that carried their concatenated sounds, to celebrate the marriages of "bright aerial spirits" and the formal harmonies of voice and verse, those solemnities of music hymned by Milton, which Marvell recognized as transcending, in *Paradise Lost*, the "old

---

1. John Hollander, *The Untuning of the Sky: Ideas of Music in English Poetry, 1500–1700* (New York: Norton, 1970), 313. The entire discussion of "Musicks Empire" is of interest, as is the book's general consideration of changes in concepts of music during the period.

song," by finding a way to sing with both "gravity and ease" a music
created "so strong, so equal, and so soft" by its founding in "number,
weight, and measure" (*"On Mr. Milton's Paradise Lost"*). And this is not
to speak of the conceptual polyphony of "mosaic" in its biblical register, its connotations of prophecy and narrative, its freight of divine
truth—nor the underlying thought of revealing that truth by telling a
story, constructing a destined reality out of a sequence of events, the
pieces of history.

The phrase also calls up the tesselated vision of the word "mosaique," its focus on visible patterns made of sharp-sided, isolated pieces
of color and form,[2] patterns dependent for their existence on monads
held together in meaning by an idea greater than each yet discernible in
none; patterns dependent equally on perceptions themselves dependent on separation, distance, and perspective. The images of a mosaic
are made up of parts not themselves images and are conveyed to the
mind through the senses by organizations that deceive the perceiver
while revealing unreservedly the atomized materials out of which they
are made. How much more tantalizing and improbable in its insub-
stantiality, then, is a mosaic made of air.

Such speculation and meditation on the narrative histories embedded in words are always attractive to Marvell. In "Musicks Empire,"
and in other poems that allude to music, it is stimulated by his consciousness of the unsettling of established ideas of music, and by the
understanding, both practical and metaphoric, of the principles of harmony as it existed during the lifetimes of Milton and Marvell, particularly during the middle years of the seventeenth century, and even
more particularly during the years of the Commonwealth and the Cromwellian Protectorate.[3]

Among the many reasons for invoking Milton's name beside Marvell's is their shared, passionate, and pervasive alertness to the powers
and the processes of music. This is not a matter only of their informed
mastery of the technicalities of practical, performed music, which in
itself is not unusual. Crashaw's "Music's Duel," for example, is only
one of a number of late Renaissance poems that are nearly tissues of
technical musical terminology. A more noteworthy link between the

---

2. Cf. Michael Craze, *The Life and Lyrics of Andrew Marvell* (London and Basing-
stoke: Macmillan, 1979), 255.

3. For an extended and brilliant consideration of this mental habit in Marvell, see
Marshall Grossman, "Authoring the Boundary: Allegory, Irony, and the Rebus in
'Upon Appleton House,'" in *"The Muses Common-Weale": Poetry and Politics in the
Seventeenth Century,* ed. Claude J. Summers and Ted-Larry Pebworth (Columbia:
University of Missouri Press, 1988), 191–206.

two secretaries for foreign tongues is their frequent and easy resort to
the discourse of universal harmony, mathematical and macro-micro-
cosmical theories that mutate from the unrecoverable practices of Greek
sung poetry to Christian doctrines of the two cities, and which find
their way into the Renaissance accompanied primarily by the music of
the spheres. But what is more striking is, rather, the divergence between
the two men who, although they begin with and maintain a store of
such cosmologically correspondential figures of music, deploy them to
represent and comment on their inherited ideology in ways that reflect
significant personal and historical differences.

Within their shared tradition Milton may be allowed, for sake of
argument, to stand for the received Renaissance understanding of the
relationship between what Boethius fixed as *musica instrumentalis* and
musica humana and the organization of the created cosmos according to
principles of harmony, which he called *musica mundana*.[4] The concepts
that hold that relationship together may be epitomized in the imagined
concordance of the notes sounded by the moving spheres of the heavens and the perfection of the aural harmony of the octave, which in
itself is grounded in the tables of rational proportions drawn up by
Pythagoras to describe the resonances of a divided string. Cosmology
and sense perception thus agree, and the agreement is taken as a sign
of the rational mathematical structure of the seen and unseen worlds.
From here it is an easy step to other, corollary definitions of concord,
ranging from the political to the psychological; indeed, to think of a
"range" in this case is to admit twentieth-century distortions of perspective, since in such a system the tempering of the four bodily
humours is governed by the same basic laws of harmony that control
the tuning or tempering of a stringed instrument.

In order to illustrate the normative treatment of harmony in this
period, one can cite the centrality of such ideas and figures in Milton's first major English poem, the Nativity Ode, the extraordinary
poetic conceit of "At a Solemn Music," and the provocative presences
and absences of musical thinking in the epics and *Samson Agonistes*.
Throughout his career Milton turned to this set of signs when he wanted
to explain the facts of life that both separated human beings from their
creative origins and held forth the best promise of reconciliation with
them. The Nativity Ode is almost exactly divided by his meditation on
the second sounding of the heavenly music, and characteristically that
imagined sound strikes for him a note of exhortation, a plea for the

4. For a concise account of these fundamental formulations, see Hollander, *Untuning of the Sky*, 24–26.

spheres to "Ring out"[5] loud or clear enough to bless, by touching, senses made insensitive by sin. Only this would suffice to inspire the base earth to sound the lowest note in creation's organ and thus to make up the full—and since the Fall, incomplete—harmony of nine. The exhortation is itself a response to the imagination of the spheres' music, the poet's muse-given version of the corresponding resonance he wishes for by describing. It is also a highly sophisticated mimesis of the symbolic phenomenon in which a string of one instrument resounds sympathetically with its congener when it is struck or otherwise sounded.

But even in this first work of his poetic maturity, Milton characteristically shapes materials of deeply traditional cast to fit the mold of his personal and ideological needs; before he invokes the "ninefold harmony" of the music of the spheres he defines the "angelic symphony" as "Divinely-warbled voice / Answering the stringed noise," as they play their harps in "loud and solemn quire." The lines outgo the particularity of the "multitude of the heavenly host, praising God," mentioned in Luke 2:13. In Job 38:4–8 the morning stars sing together, and the sons of God shout for joy, but there is no string symphony.[6] But in book 7 of *Paradise Lost* Raphael describes the "celestial choirs," as they "hymning praised / God and his works . . . with joy and shout" while touching "their golden harps" (ll. 254–59). For Milton the fullness of harmony is conceived as the interinanimation of vocal and instrumental melody, or even more idiosyncratically, as the fusion of verbal and nonverbal music, the sound of the human voice and the rhythmic turning of numerous verses, the word and the note, the music of meaning carried on metered sound. That he knew the aural effects of polyphony—in domestic madrigal and churchly anthem—we may perhaps infer from the intimacy of L'Allegro's invocation of the "melting voice through mazes running" / "With wanton heed and giddy cunning." Or Nan Cooke Carpenter may be right in arguing that those phrases show that Milton was thinking of the aria, which was becoming popular amongst Italian or Italian-influenced musicians during his youth.[7] In

5. Quotations from "On the Morning of Christ's Nativity" are taken from John Carey and Alastair Fowler, eds., *The Poems of John Milton* (London: Longmans, Green, 1968), 101–13. All subsequent quotations from Milton's poetry are taken from this edition.

6. As the *OED* entry for "symphony" shows, its primary meanings in Milton's time and for long before apply to the concerted sounds made by a group of instruments; it is also used figuratively for various kinds of harmonious behavior or utterance. Its application to verse, or to sung or spoken utterance, is least common, but it is precisely verse Milton focuses on.

7. See "The Place of Music in *L'Allegro* and *Il Penseroso*," *University of Toronto Quarterly* 22 (1953): 355.

any case, while the fundamental tropes of the poetry of universal harmony consist comfortably with late Elizabethan and Jacobean polyphony, Milton's concern with the internal harmonies of music and
poetry is more obviously consonant with the development of the monody, a term somewhat awkwardly applied to the English accompanied
air, but one which he felt sufficiently clear about to use in the Trinity
manuscript to specify the genre of *Lycidas*. The term occurs in the first
line of the epigraph to *Lycidas*, which does not appear in the 1638
version of the poem published in *Justa Eduardo King naufrago*, and was
added, presumably, after Milton's return from his European journey in
1639. Gretchen L. Finney argued some time ago that Milton was aware
of the developments in Italian opera that advanced the *recitativo* style as
a re-creation of Greek *mousike* before his Italian trip, if only because of
his association with Henry Lawes and the latter's interest in these
matters.[8]

Thus Milton's role in this context as the conserver of traditional
assumptions and forms, rather than as the revisionist of all conventions that he most often seems, presents an apparent anomaly. Although
his intense concentration on the interdependency of "voice and verse"
is patent, he continued throughout his career to rest on the much more
expansive metaphoric vocabulary of universal harmony. Moreover, his
association with Henry Lawes in the production of *Arcades* and *Comus*
introduced him to the most radical advances in the Caroline period of
expressive vocal writing and innovative harmonic style. It is clear from
the admiring sonnet drafted in 1645 and first published in the composer's 1648 volume of *Choice Psalmes* that Milton was moved primarily
by Lawes's acknowledgment of the primacy of song texts; he praises
him for scanning "with just note and accent" the verse he "honours."
Milton seems relatively unaware of the characteristics of Lawes's songs
that most impressed his contemporaries: expressive subtlety and
declamatory power. In short, while he responds gratefully to Lawes's
sensitivity to poetry, he seems to scant the distinctive departures from
prior musical norms to which that sensitivity leads.[9]

---

8. "*Comus, Dramma per Musica*," *Studies in Philology* 37 (1940): 482–500; and the
summary discussion in James Holly Hanford and James G. Taaffe, *A Milton Hand-
book*, 5th ed. (New York: Appleton-Century-Crofts, 1970), 334–36 (Appendix F,
"Milton in Italy"). Lee A. Jacobus was kind enough to allow me to read in manuscript his "Milton Hero: The Rhetorical Gesture of Monody" and "Lycidas and the
Rhythms of Italian Monody," both forthcoming, which have been very helpful in
guiding my thinking about music and poetry in the 1630s.
9. Peter le Huray, "The fair musick that all creatures made," *The Age of Milton*, ed.
C. A. Patrides and Raymond Waddington (Manchester: Manchester University
Press, 1980), 241–72.

Marvell, by contrast, while knowing, and speaking, and singing the poetic language of musical correspondence with comparable familiarity, is more conscious of great morphological shifts taking place during his lifetime, in that he seems to register in his own metaphoric practice what is happening in the actual practice of musical performance. Coming to maturity more than a decade after Milton, he was if anything more familiar with the music of the generation of Lawes; his experience of English monody is reflected in Marvell's typical references to music, its nature and its powers, and in *his* poetic resorts to the figures and doctrines of cosmic harmony.

What Eve was for Milton, music was for Marvell; that is, the representation of each reveals mingled feelings of attraction and apprehension. Neither the epitome of the female nor the idea of harmonious sound could have appeared as they do respectively in their works if the poets had not experienced the overwhelming attraction expressed by both their praises and their condemnation. In "The Fair Singer" Marvell fashions something like a parallel to "At a Solemn Music," attributing the defeat of the lover to the combined forces of "both beauties" of eye and voice that Love has "composed" in "fatal harmony." Going further, he confesses that even if he had been able to save himself from the "trammels of her hair," he could not have avoided being caught in the "fetters" the fair singer has forged from the "very air" he breathes. Nevertheless, that enslavement is not of the senses, as we learn when the beloved's voice is said to threaten to "captivate" the mind. The same point is made by the rejoinder of the Soul to Created Pleasure when in their dialogue it insists, "None can chain a mind / Whom this sweet chordage cannot bind," referring to the "charming airs" prepared by music for the soul's temptation ("A Dialogue Between the Resolved Soul, and Created Pleasure"). It is not only the mind that conducts the resistance to that temptation, but the mind that is its peculiar target; its power is consonant with its vulnerability, a perception about the ties between the senses and moral consciousness that Milton shares with Marvell. Yet within that common sense there is a fine distinction to be made: like the soul in Marvell's "Dialogue between the Soul and the Body," "manacled in hands," the Lady in *Comus* nevertheless insists that the tempter cannot touch the freedom of her mind; but Marvell's mower, having been overcome by Juliana, accuses her of having conquered not by sensual appeal but by having "displaced his mind," cutting down his thoughts and him— indivisible—like the scythe he knows so well ("The Mower to the Glo-Worms" and "The Mower's Song"). The mind in Marvell is not only the irreducible core of identity it is for Milton, but also the fragile, delicately poised interpreter of the world it perceives, giver of names and prober of essences, and above all scanner of its own processes, interrogator of its own reports on the environment. The obvious differences between the personalities of the two poets, which we infer from their different voices and personas in their poems, are consonant with these views of what they call "mind." They are also understandable in terms of their presentation of music and the idea of harmony throughout their work.

If Milton's music is usually closely tied to images of concord between hierarchically articulated sounds or entities—and is in this respect conceptual and ethical—Marvell's musics are both more varied and more variously political. Perhaps another way to put the point is to note that of the two egregious figures in the classical mythology of music, Milton, as is well known, invokes Orpheus often and at crucial junctures, and that Marvell turns to Amphion at comparable moments in his poetry. It may be worth noting, too, given the prominence of the two legendary musicians in literary mythology, that the name of Amphion occurs nowhere in Milton's entire English corpus, and that Marvell never mentions Orpheus. Both played the lute (or, more properly, the lyre), but the Orphic aura is composed of ideas about the power of poetry to govern nature. Poetry, as in one of the original meanings of Greek *mousike*, is made of sung words, the distinction between the two carriers of meaning as yet unimagined. This may be why the poetry of Orpheus was also understood as the embodiment of eloquence, and therefore as the foundation of human civility, despite the fact that the poet-musician is most often recalled exercising his semidivine powers by controlling animals and trees. Amphion, son of Zeus rather than Apollo, emerges dimly from the mists of the legends of Cadmus and the dragon's teeth; he earned his place in memory by charming the scattered stones of a destroyed city to form the walls of Thebes, his music rousing them to ordered and creative motion (Ovid, *Metamorphoses*, VI). Amphion is neither poet-priest nor possessor of the power to raise dead things; in short, he is not Orphic. Rather, he is a builder of cities, a harper whose music can command intractable and insensate stones and can move them to form strong and stable wholes out of adamant and unconnected parts.[10]

And so he appears in Marvell's "The First Anniversary of the Government under O.C." where "indefatigable Cromwell," as he tunes

10. In *Ad Patrem*, defending the importance of poetry to song, Milton argues that Orpheus ruled nature *carmine, non cithara*.

"the ruling Instrument,"[11] is compared to the founder of Thebes in an extended passage whose underlying metaphor is the implicit comparison between music and the art of political architecture. Amphion's gentle hand on the lute makes the "rougher Stones" dance "up in order from the Quarreys rude," "hew'd . . . unto his Measures." In this instance, the architect whose hewing of green trees was so poignantly deplored by the Body in its dialogue with the Soul is seen as the divine creator by "number, weight, and measure," as musical rhythm is equated with the useful shaping of participants in a complex society. Unlike the "Forrain *Architect*" in "Upon Appleton House" who is execrated for making caves of quarries in order to build extravagant country houses, Amphion is praised for bringing order to "the Quarreys rude" by leading their dancing stones to form the walls of a city. Amphion's versatility, later easily and fully transferred to Cromwell, is demonstrated as he turns his instrument to martial, sweet, or grave sounds, thereby teaching the stones how to become a tower, a palace, or a temple. And all the while, Marvell notes, he observes the "listning Structures" with a wondering eye. The phrase nicely captures the serious comedy of sentient formal creations, the *things* that are made by the many kinds of harmony that poets—that is, makers—command. Here, harmony is not an abstract mathematical reality but a living principle of cooperative action. It is in a plausible sense political, if we take the art of politics to be that of forming capable structures out of isolated and even competitive single elements. Marvell plays on the idea of a music that can coordinate difference without relying on an ideal consonance (such as that epitomized in the octave and its eternally valid proportions) by describing Amphion applying "new Stopps to various Time," a phrase made up of technical musical terms that do not apply to each other in normal usage. Stops, or frets, are literally applied—or brought to bear—on strings;[12] they produce different sounds by cutting off other sounds, by dividing strings according to Pythagorean formulas. "Various Time" is in itself oxymoronic, but points to the interplay between expressive variation and underlying rhythmic structure, comparable to the relation between melodic vocal line and a figured bass. The entire phrase imitates in its semantic and grammatical dislocations the effects we can hear when pitch and note values alter in unfamiliar patterns; they are

---

11. The phrase refers to the Instrument of Government, the document by which the office of Lord Protector was created in 1653 after the Long Parliament had been dissolved by Cromwell.

12. The term is also applied to finger holes or keys on wind instruments, but here Amphion is playing a stringed instrument.

expressive, but not in ways that can be accounted for by traditional harmonic theory. But this music is about creative power rather than that "undisturbed song of pure concent" Milton sings of in "At a Solemn Music" (l. 6). That is, music is depicted here as a process by which harmony is made, through the purposeful command over disparate parts, rather than as a reflection or embodiment of a preexistent ideal of concord. Amphion's "harmonious City of the seven Gates" is founded on a new definition of harmony; and Marvell unfolds it in the lines that follow as Cromwell appears as "our *Amphion*."

The Commonwealth is implicitly compared to Thebes, the "listning Structures" translated into "the willing Frame," as the mythic city becomes the "House" that stands for the truly invented government brought into being in 1653 by the document called the "Instrument." Cromwell's achievement may be said to surpass Amphion's because "who the Minds of stubborn Men can build? / No Quarry bears a Stone so hardly wrought." The stones of Thebes were easy to move compared to the entrenched and contradictory forces of the Protectorate Parliament. But Cromwell's skill, the "Musique" he has learned to "tune this lower . . . Sphere," creates a harmony within which "the crossest Spirits . . . do take their part"; indeed, their very crossedness is converted by his "attractive Song" into the source of their collective strength, since he draws opposing parties into positions where they find themselves "Fast'ning the Contignation which they thwart." In so doing, they "throng" into the "Animated City" this second Amphion has created; like the "listning Structures" of the Theban walls, Cromwell's society is a living architectural construct, held together by stresses cunningly marshalled to support each other by the opposition of force. The idea of harmony acquires a new dimension, the possibility of building with dissonances as solidly as with the more familiar and comforting materials of proportional, mathematically predictable, and concordant parts. When the fallen angels sing to the harp "their own heroic deeds" in book 2 of *Paradise Lost*, Milton admits that though "Their song was partial" (l. 552), its harmony was still ravishing enough to suspend Hell. But Marvell is concerned to find and declare the harmony of partiality and of partial music, a harmony which for him is embodied in the figure of Amphion/Cromwell, a figure that does not draw upon the Orphic myth for its vision of the power of music.[13]

13. Interestingly enough, it is in the prose *Areopagitica* that Milton uses an extended architectural figure to design the construction of the reformed church and state; there he emphasizes the need to include and reconcile opposing forces in the building of an earthly institution: *Complete Prose Works of John Milton*, ed. Douglas Bush et. al., 7 vols. (New Haven: Yale University Press, 1953–1982), 2:555. See also

A similar perspective on the harmony of partiality shapes "Musicks Empire," a poem which is less patently the *laus musicae* it purports to be than a mythic history of the progressive conquest of sound; that is, the title can be pronounced with the strong stress on either of its two nouns. There has been disagreement about the scope of Marvell's initiating myth and about the hierarchical order of meanings he erects between "the World" and "Heavens quire."[14] But it is clear that in gaining "the Empire of the Ear," music suffers from belatedness, like Zeus among the Giants, or Alexander among the Homeric heroes. The "victorious sounds" that Marvell ends by celebrating begin as jarring echoes struck by unordered forces out of isolated and inhuman natural forms. It is Jubal rather than Orpheus or Amphion who summons the anarchic sounds; but characteristically he builds a city, figured here as an organ. The sounds themselves, now wedded by their opposition and procreating through the resultant harmonies, form colonies by choosing the instruments best suited—or attuned—to their specific qualities. It is only at this point that music appears in order to prepare the "solemn noise" that will conquer all "between the Earth and Sphear." Thus, music is not a sensible version of a preexistent mathematical ideal, nor is it motivated and dominated by the imperative to imitate a higher music that can only be imagined, not heard. It is presented as a power that knows how to employ differing and highly individualized sounds in a common enterprise of conquest; it gives shape and purpose to what otherwise would still be colonies, however harmonious within themselves. It is in this sense "the *Mosaique* of the Air," an audible image made of aural monads. We know that in "The First Anniversary" it is Cromwell's Amphionic magic that underpins his ability to convert contention into cooperation, but nothing in "Musicks Empire" explains how music makes a noise of separate instruments. There is no antecedent power, only music itself, which thus becomes its own explanation and justification. Music is that which brings disparate energies together to produce something they could not have made alone. In Marvell's version it seems to draw its own creative force as much from the powers it organizes as from its own nature; indeed, that force is inherently directed toward the act of organization, since only thus can the original "solitary sound" become the "solemn noise" that in ultimate conquest can be hailed as "Victorious sounds!" In this respect

Margarita Stocker, *Apocalyptic Marvell: The Second Coming in Seventeenth-Century Poetry* (Brighton, England: Harvester, 1986), 14.

14. Cf. Hollander, *Untuning of the Sky*, 310ff., and Legouis's comments in *Poems and Letters* 1:266.

"Musick" looks downward toward its component elements rather than above to a Pythagorean model.

In attempting to account for Marvell's revisionary presentation of the poetics of music, questions of temperament and of political attitude are inevitably invoked. But we should not ignore Boethius's third category, *musica instrumentalis*, or practical music. There was, after all, actual music composed and played in England during Marvell's lifetime. Musical performance was disrupted during the climactic years of the civil wars, but the Commonwealth saw the revival of private recitals, even if church music was severely curtailed. Cromwell was well known as a lover of music, and concerts were one of his particular domestic delights. He had the organ of Magdalen College, Oxford, moved to Whitehall, and John Hingston, his Master of Music, played upon it regularly for the Protector and his family.[15] The Protectorate Court itself, especially in the period after 1653, began to take on some of the airs and ceremonies of the Stuart monarchy it had dispossessed, including the occasional performance of a masque, and some fairly lavish entertainments, such as the consort of fifty trumpets that made up part of the celebration of the marriage of Cromwell's daughter Frances at Whitehall Palace in 1657. Only a week later, his daughter Mary was married to Thomas Bellasis, Lord Fauconberg, in a ceremony carried out perhaps more decorously but certainly more modestly at Hampton Court (in part because the bridegroom requested that the expenses of the wedding be allocated to the dowry, a becoming prudence that further endeared him to his new father-in-law).[16] For the second wedding Marvell composed two pastoral dialogues, called "Songs" in the 1681 Folio; it seems reasonable to assume that they were performed on that occasion, and that Marvell would at least have heard the musical settings for his words and might even have had occasion to work cooperatively with the composer, whose identity remains unknown, as do the settings themselves. These facts set the "Two Songs at the Marriage of the Lord Fauconberg and the Lady Mary Cromwell" apart from the musical history of the "Dialogue between Thyrsis and Dorinda," the only other poem by Marvell which we can be sure was set, although several others have been advanced as strong candidates for musical transformation.

15. Sir John Hawkins, *A General History of the Science and Practice of Music*, ed. C. Cudworth, 2 vols. (New York: Dover, 1963), 1:577. Cf. Percy Scholes, *The Puritans and Music in England and New England* (London: Oxford University Press, 1934), 142; and Roy Sherwood, *The Court of Oliver Cromwell* (London: Croom Helm, 1977), 135–38.
16. For a full account of the weddings, based on a wide sampling of contemporary reports, see Antonia Fraser, *Cromwell. The Lord Protector* (New York: Dell, 1975), 735–38. Cromwell is said to have been so eager to obtain Fauconberg's hand for Mary that he provided a dowry of fifteen thousand pounds.

Three settings of "Thyrsis and Dorinda," by three different composers—
William Lawes, John Gamble, and Matthew Locke—have survived, the
earliest, by Lawes, in a manuscript that probably dates from the
mid–1630s, so that some editors find it hard to accept the text as Marvell's; the poem's authenticity has been challenged on other grounds as
well.[17]

"Thyrsis and Dorinda" is in the form of a pastoral dialogue that ends
with a chorus, a form that was widely popular for musical entertainments in the later years of Charles I's reign. Whether he wrote "Thyrsis
and Dorinda" or not, Marvell revived the form in the late 1650s on the
occasion of Mary Cromwell's marriage, and in doing so was making
anachronism his choice.[18] What had changed in the interim, however,
was the manner of setting such dialogues, a change epitomized by
developments from the songs written for Milton's *Mask* by Henry Lawes
in 1634, his settings for lyrics by Thomas Carew in later years, and in
revisions Lawes made in his work as he prepared his *Ayres and Dialogues* for publication in the 1650s.[19]

Marvell's actual colleague composer is unknown. But solely to suggest the nature of the interaction between the poet's words and the
music that accompanied his marriage songs, we may consider what is
known about other compositions of the time. Theatrical presentations
never disappeared entirely during the Commonwealth; the best known
are the musical-dramatic performances Davenant was allowed to mount
during the Protectorate. The texts have survived, but not the music, for
the "Entertainment at Rutland House" and *The Siege of Rhodes* (1656).
The latter included songs but consisted mainly of what Davenant called
"declamations" and "*Recitative* music." George Hudson, Henry Cooke,
and Charles Coleman contributed music for the "Entertainment"; Cooke
was noted primarily as a singer, Hudson and Coleman for their instrumental works. For *The Siege of Rhodes* the instrumental music was again
composed by Coleman and Hudson, while Cooke wrote vocal parts for
two of the "Entries" and Matthew Locke vocal music for another. Lawes
contributed to the "Entertainment" and wrote vocal music for two of
the "Entries" of *The Siege*.[20]

17. There is a full discussion in *Poems and Letters* 1:247–49.

18. Hollander, *Untuning of the Sky,* 368; Ian Spink, *English Song: Dowland to Purcell*
(New York: Taplinger, 1974), 46ff.

19. E. F. Hart, "Introduction to Henry Lawes," *Music and Letters* 32:3 (July 1951):
217–25, argues that Lawes's progressive interest in declamation, beginning with the
songs for *Comus*, achieves its "final development . . . in the early 1650s when he was
preparing his songs for the press."

20. A. M. Gibbs, ed., *Sir William Davenant: The Shorter Poems, and Songs from the
Plays and Masques* (Oxford: Clarendon Press, 1972), xxxii–iv; *A transcript of the regis-*

The single example of a masque from the Commonwealth period is James Shirley's *Cupid and Death*, first performed in 1653 for the Portuguese Ambassador, and again in 1659, in a revised version. Orlando Gibbons's son Christopher wrote the music for the first performance; Matthew Locke composed the later one, and it is his score alone that has survived. Locke's writing for *Cupid and Death*, in the view of Murray Lefkowitz, "did not make any advances on earlier masques by, for example, William Lawes. . . . [H]is most original contribution lay in his recitatives, more numerous and longer than in earlier masques, which combine an angular English declamatory style with a more emotional Italian idiom. The effect of intense parlando and wide-ranging, disjunct, almost erratic lines is intensely dramatic." E. J. Dent says of *Cupid and Death:* "The long recitatives are in regular common time, but declaim the words with complete freedom according to their sense, disregarding the formal metre of the verse entirely. . . . It will be noted that Locke almost invariably places . . . florid passages on monosyllables of no importance such as the articles 'a' or 'the,' and never on a word of dramatic significance, as is the usual practice of Italian and German composers."[21]

Although Locke can in some ways be taken as representative of the development of *stilo recitativo*, the song compositions of Henry Lawes exemplify more comprehensively and illuminatingly the characteristics of late Caroline and Commonwealth vocal music. Moreover, although Lawes, like his brother William, had been an ardent supporter of King Charles, Cromwell was extraordinarily forgiving of Royalists who accepted the establishment of the Commonwealth, and he employed many of them in responsible positions. While the theaters, masquing-halls, and other public entertainments fell with the monarchy, Cromwell maintained not only a Master of Music but also a group of performers comparable to the Chapel Royal. Lawes was active in offering musical instruction to a wide and loyal circle and in holding very popular concerts in his home. Milton's nephew Edward Philips attended often.[22]

ters of the worshipful Company of stationers: from 1640–1708, ed. G. B. Eyre, 3 vols. (London: Privately Printed, 1913–1914), 2:157. December 7, 1657, records "A Poem to my Lord Broghill Epithalamium upon the marriage of the Lady Mary daughter to his Highness, with the Lord Viscount Ffalconbridge, to bee sung in recitative musick"; the poem has been lost. Broghill was Roger Boyle, Lord Orrery, a Royalist who nevertheless served as a member of Cromwell's council.

21. Lefkowitz, "Locke, Matthew," *The New Grove Dictionary of Music and Musicians*, ed. Stanley Sadie, 20 vols. (London: Macmillan, 1980), 11:13; Dent, *Musica Britannica* (London, 1951), 2:xv.

22. Sherwood, *Court of Oliver Cromwell*, 170; Willa McClung Evans, *Henry Lawes:*

Thus, it is not altogether inconceivable that Lawes was asked to set Marvell's songs. Hingston, Cromwell's master musician, was primarily an organist and wrote mainly church music. Lawes had long been famous for his skills in the composition of court masques (*Comus* being in this instance, as in others, the anomaly) and for his unparalleled sensitivity to poetry. He would surely have been known to Marvell by his reputation alone, even if his connection with Milton were not taken into consideration. Perhaps the best reasons to imagine that he might have been Marvell's composer for the two wedding songs are that Cromwell knew him to be the best musician of his time, that Cromwell loved music, and that he was generous with his children and fond of Fauconberg.

Other oddities surround this obscure episode: Marvell's interest in the marriage of his employer's daughter—for it was in 1657 that he was appointed finally to the co-secretaryship for foreign tongues that Milton had sought for him years earlier—was manifold. Viscount Fauconberg, known also as the Lord Falconbridge, was a Yorkshireman, grandson of the daughter of Sir Thomas Fairfax of Denton, ancestor of Marvell's famous patron. The first Viscount Fauconberg, the bridegroom's grandfather, fought on the King's side in the civil wars. Both bore the given name of Thomas. There is a tantalizing letter, written in 1647 and cited by Lawes's biographer to prove the composer's presence in London in that year, that is addressed to Capt. Thomas Falconbridge, asking that some money be paid to a surrogate for Lawes.[23]

What kind of music would Lawes have written? Milton's praise of Lawes's ability "not to scan / With Midas' ears, committing short and long" (ll. 2–4), glancing back to the experiments of Campion and others in setting quantitative verses, alludes to a new understanding of the long-sought-for goal of an equal-tempered harmony between text and melodic line.[24] The ideal formed part of the humanist revival of classical learning and had hovered over the notion of Greek *mousike* from the time when knowledge of the actual practice of Greek music was lost. Aspirations toward it had arisen again in the activities of the Italian academies, and at the turn of the century became a central impulse in the creation of the operatic form by Monteverdi, Peri, and others.

Karl Fellerer distinguishes between the "derived" monody of these Italian composers, which aimed at achieving greater emotional expressiveness than was possible in polyphonic settings by emphasizing rhe-

Musician and Friend of Poets (New York: Modern Language Association, 1944), 212–13.
23. Evans, *Henry Lawes*, 171.
24. "Sonnet 13," *The Poems of John Milton*, ed. Carey and Fowler, 292–93.

torical declamation of text, and the monodic experiments of the Florentine Camerata and its associates, whose goal was the revival of the sung
drama of the Greeks. These initiatives in musical style were known in
England from the early decades of the seventeenth century, but not
perhaps the cultural motives behind them.[25]

English responses to the new movement in Italy were fairly swift, in
part because of the prominence in London musical circles of Italian-
born or Italian-trained composers. But it has been argued convincingly
that the English monodists of the later Caroline period were not in fact
merely imitating Monteverdian attempts to achieve emotional musical
effects by declamatory settings of poetic texts. Elise Jorgens, for example, believes that changes in seventeenth-century musical rhetoric were
largely determined by changes in poetic style, the "impersonal complimentary" Elizabethan lyric giving way to the Cavalier poem of persuasive argument, which needed less in the way of conventional ornament to achieve its rhetorical purposes. The creation of a colloquial,
personal voice presents new problems for musical setting, and monody replaces polyphony because "argument is best represented
through its own words; the best way to set it to music is in a style that
will make it fully intelligible and not detract from its force with ornament." Ian Spink suggests that, with the possible exception of Alfonso
Ferrabosco, English musicians did not remain closely in touch with
Italian musical activities during the early part of the century, and that
the *stilo rappresentativo* was virtually unknown in England until quite
late. Lawes in particular sought, rather, a way to set words that would
follow English accentual rhythms as faithfully as the Italians matched
syllables and quantities, and which at the same time would draw its
expressive force primarily from the poetry it served. R. J. McGrady
points a contrast between Dowland's mode of achieving continuity "by
melodic and harmonic means," and Lawes's musical continuity based
on "rhythmic means." He describes Lawes's music as "highly rhetorical
in style; lyric grace is abandoned in favour of an argumentative tone in
which rests and rhythmic variety emphasize the meaning of the verse."[26]

25. *The Monody,* trans. Robert Kolben (Cologne: Arno Volk, 1968). I owe this reference to Lee Jacobus. See also Elise B. Jorgens, *The Well Tun'd Word* (Minneapolis:
University of Minnesota Press, 1982), 175–77.

26. Jorgens, *Well Tun'd Word,* 241, see also 250 for a helpful discussion of the differing demands made upon composers by the syllabic meters of French and Italian and
the basically accentual meters of English; Spink, "English Cavalier Songs,
1620–1660," *Proceedings* of the Royal Musical Association, 86th Session, 1959–1960,
61–78. His thesis is given expanded treatment in *English Song: Dowland to Purcell*
(New York: Taplinger, 1974); McGrady, "Henry Lawes and the Concept of 'Just Note
and Accent,'" *Music and Letters* 50:1 (January 1969): 86–102.

In short, English song settings of the midcentury, sometimes called monodies, and sometimes subserving texts divided into lyrical and discursive parts and thus described as *stilo recitativo* or *stilo rappresentativo*, subjected the musical line to the poetic text; it is little wonder that poets were delighted with Lawes.[27] It may be worth noting that whereas in Dowland's many collections of songs the authors of most of the texts are not named, Lawes's collections were always liberally supplied with attributions to the leading poets of the day.[28]

The typical lyric setting of the midcentury, then, whether we call it baroque continuo song or declamatory "ayre," is one that exhibits a relationship between melodic structure and poetic text very different not only from that characteristic of the great lutenist airs of a half-century earlier, but also from the ideal of the divine marriage of voice and verse cherished by Milton and enshrined in the figures of corresponding celestial and earthly harmonies. Insofar as the continuo song as practiced by Lawes represents a peculiarly English development, it may have something to do, as Ian Spink suggests, with the special circumstances of the performance of the court masque. In the crowded and noisy Jacobean and Caroline masquing-halls, the delicate contrapuntal accompaniments of the lutenists would have been swallowed up. Elise Jorgens, among others, has argued very persuasively that as the Caroline lyric poem moved further toward an argumentative structure and away from the formulaic, rhetorical ornamentation of Elizabethan complimentary verse, the love lyric came more and more to rest on a musical structure that highlighted the dramatized persona and the logical propositions being advanced, and thus tended to deprive itself of the resources of purely musical emphases and embellishments. However partial these explanations may seem individually, they combine to support the notion that the kind of music available to Marvell for the settings of his pastoral dialogues—whether by Lawes or not—would have been such as to underline their fanciful, ironic, and undoubtedly self-conscious texts as its primary purpose. The resources and achievements of harmony, symbolic or otherwise, would not be very prominent.[29]

The basic meter of both songs is Marvell's favored iambic tetrameter, richly salted with trochaic inversions. The second dialogue is con-

27. One of Hollander's major arguments in *Untuning of the Sky* is that during the European Renaissance the ancient concepts of *musica universalis* gave way to criteria of emotional expressiveness; nevertheless, he observes that "the seventeenth-century English poets take immediately to the newer notions of affective music, while yet clinging to the imagery of Christian speculative music, notably that of the heavenly harmony, the singing of the angel-spheres," etc. (202).

28. Jorgens, *Well Tun'd Word*, 256.

29. Spink, "English Cavalier Songs, 1620–1660," 65; Jorgens, *Well Tun'd Word*, 240ff.

ducted mainly in heptasyllabic lines; the choruses in every case are
stanzaic forms that vary from lines of one or two iambic feet to full
pentameters. Most of the individual speeches are in quatrains, but
others vary from half-lines to six lines. Davenant's songs in the "Entertainment" tend to be more regular, in octasyllabic quatrains; the solo
song in *The Siege of Rhodes* follows the same pattern, but the choruses,
particularly the satiric ones sung by "women" and "wives," show more
rhythmic and metrical variety. In *Cupid and Death* Locke sets the dialogue mainly in recitative form; the occasional songs are almost
entirely in regular octasyllabics. Immediately before the "grand dance"
that concludes the reconciliation and the masque, Mercury sings:

> Open bless'd Elysium grove,
> Where an eternal spring of love
> Keeps each beauty fair; these shades
> No chill dew or frost invades.
> Look how the flowers, and every tree
> Pregnant with ambrosia be;
> Near banks of violet, springs appear,
> Weeping out nectar every tear;
> While the once-harmonious spheres,
> (Turn'd all to ears)
> Now listen to the birds, whose quire
> Sing every charming accent higher.[30]

While this offers, in the third and tenth lines, some occasion for rhythmic
variation and in the last couplet for mimetic expressiveness, the form is
essentially regular, allowing for repeated motifs and phrasing. The concluding choral song of Marvell's second dialogue reads rather differently:

> Joy to that *happy Pair,*
> Whose Hopes united banish our Despair.
> What *Shepheard* could for Love pretend,
> Whil'st all the *Nymphs* on *Damon's* choice attend?
> What *Shepherdess* could hope to wed
> Before *Marina's* turn were sped?
> Now lesser Beauties may take place,
> And meaner Virtues come in play;
>> While they,
>> Looking from high,
>> Shall grace
> Our Flocks and us with a propitious Eye.

30. *Cupid and Death*, ed. B.A. Harris, in *A Book of Masques* (Cambridge: Cambridge
University Press, 1967), 398–99.

> But what is most, the gentle Swain
> No more shall need of Love complain;
> But Virtue shall be Beauties hire,
> And those be equal that have equal Fire.
> *Marina* yields. Who dares be coy?
> Or who despair, now *Damon* does enjoy?
> Joy to that happy Pair
> Whose Hopes united banish our Despair.
>   (29–48)

The celebratory theme is colored by the demands of a conscious, allegorized topicality: the political implications of the marriage are touched on in the delicately complimentary assertion that "those [shall] be equal that have equal Fire," and by the wry observation to the assembled courtiers that "lesser Beauties" and "meaner Virtues" may now "take place" and "come in play." Marvell exploits the domestic situation of the masque or entertainment, and his verse therefore calls for supple, responsive musical setting, one that can catch oblique allusions and stagy, ironic texts.

The "Two Songs," however occasional or slight they may appear, pick up themes and manners from many better-known poems, particularly the pastoral and religious dialogues. The first represents the wooing of Endymion and Cynthia (of course, the wooer and the wooed are here decorously reversed); the other the rejoicing of two rustics, Phillis and Hobbinol, largely because now, as they say, since "Marina yields. Who dares be coy? / Or who despair, now Damon does enjoy?" The knowing, almost arch tone is struck in the first line of the first dialogue when the Chorus sings, "The astrologers' own eyes are set," to indicate that it is late at night. Endymion is encouraged to woo boldly, on the grounds that "Anchises was a Shepheard too," Anchises in this case being the aptly named Lord Rich, who had become the husband of Cromwell's younger daughter Frances only the week before. And later Jove is praised for giving his approval to this match between a goddess and a mortal because "he did never love to pair / His Progeny above the Air." This is a nice way to defuse surprise at Cromwell's marrying Mary to a prominent nobleman with Royalist associations, by alluding to the marriage two months earlier of Marvell's former pupil Mary Fairfax to the Duke of Buckingham, a much more egregious example of mating erstwhile supporters of Parliament and the Royalist faithful.[31] In any

31. Rumors were current, too, that the future Charles II was interested in assisting his return to the English throne by a marriage to Frances Cromwell, but that Cromwell had scotched the proposal because of Charles's already reputed debauchery.

case, the calculated naivete of the singers and the overall pseudo-pastoral courtliness of the arguments suggest that the musical declamation might be as pointed as the in-group jokes themselves. Introduced like Damon the Mower—"Heark how he sings, with sad delight"—Endymion is presented not only as a woeful lover but as a thoroughly Marvellian rhetorician, skilled in turning arguments (and words) back upon themselves, and alert to the veiled assumptions beneath ostensibly rational attitudes. A comic version of the Resolved Soul, he rebuts Cynthia's snobbish rejection of a mortal, and a shepherd, by pointing out "Nor merits he a *Mortal's* name / That burns with an *immortal Flame*"; as soon as Cynthia claims to be too busy taking care of the "Waves that Ebb and flow" to attend to him, Endymion proposes that she extend her definition of "Sublunary things" to include "these double Seas, / Mine Eyes uncessant deluges." When he complains that even atop Latmos he cannot reach to Cynthia's height, she wittily and dismissively rejoins, " 'Tis needless then that I refuse, / Would you but your own Reason use"; reasonably, her suitor replies, "Though I so high may not pretend, / It is the same so you descend." Endymion's ultimate triumph is signalled by a divided line, in which Cynthia hints at a hitherto-denied interest, and her lover capitalizes on it by clinching the argument with both practical and ontological demonstrations:

> *Cynthia*   That Cave is dark.
> *Endymion*   Then none can spy:
> Or shine Thou there and 'tis the Sky.

The second "Song," a pastoral rather than a mythological dialogue, displays a decorously different kind of wit, glancing at actualities of the occasion, such as the time of year ("They ha' chosen such an hour / When *She* is the only flow'r." The wedding took place on November 19). Cromwell, who had figured in the first dialogue as "serenest" Jove, now appears as Menalcas, who "when Young as we did graze, / But when Old he planted Bayes"; Marvell thus recalls his early praise of Cromwell in the "Horatian Ode" for leaving his "private Gardens" to follow the call of "industrious Valour," and at the same time gestures toward his present status as patron of arts, a role he is at the moment fulfilling as sponsor of the song he listens to. The shepherd Tomalin admires the bride in a mode reminiscent both of the mower's love laments and of the conversation of Clorinda and Damon: " 'Twas those Eyes, I now dare swear, / Led our Lambs we knew not where." The Phillis of this dialogue is a worldly cousin to Dorinda and the others;

she is sure that the bridegroom "so looks as fit to keep / Somewhat else then silly *Sheep.*"

To this kind of personified declamation—delivered in quotation marks, so to speak—Lawes's technique in song composition was admirably suited. Wilfrid Mellers notes that "the Caroline ayre habitually . . . involves an element of rhetorical self-dramatization." Of Lawes in particular Mellers says that his "most successful songs of the through-composed or declamatory type are his settings of poems that have a highly developed intellectual rather than emotional content"; in contrast to Dowland's lyricism and Purcell's later development of drama in his music, Lawes provides "a musically unobtrusive setting that exaggerates the manner in which a reciter would declaim the poem before an initiated audience." Manfred Bukofzer's description of Lawes's style in the *Comus* songs may also serve to convey the impression made by his music: "They are quasi-recitatives characterized by incisive marking of the rhyme, and an erratically moving bass. The melody is carried forward mainly by the prosody of verse fragments. The musical rhythm is, however, not derived from the regular meter of the verse, but is achieved by emphatic repeats of single words or phrases." Bukofzer notes also the "tension between the regularity of the poetic meter and the discontinuous cadential falls of the music," a quality that would reinforce the playfulness of Marvell's highly-wrought octasyllabics. The characteristics of Lawes's *Comus* settings are, if anything, refined and intensified in his later vocal settings of the Caroline and Protectorate years, as is suggested by the revisions he undertook while preparing his songs for publication in the 1650s.[32]

The marriage between that compositional style and the poems it served was one of clear subordination of melody to word. That subordination was achieved at the expense of older ideas of mutual support, ideas which themselves were rooted in figures and beliefs that saw harmonic invention as a mimesis of principles of concordance intrinsic to the structure of the human psyche and of the visible and invisible universe. Continuo song did not destroy the idea of universal harmony, but it did make it more difficult to believe in—or to hear—evidence of such harmony in practical, performed music. The turn of music toward the expressive word and away from formulaic musical rhetoric brought into focus much more prominently the individual components of the sung text, highlighting and emphasizing rhymes, line-ends, and particular points of argument rather than strophic, repeated, or ornamen-

32. Mellers, *Harmonious Meeting* (London: Dennis Dobson, 1965), 115; Bukofzer, *Music in the Baroque Era* (New York: Norton, 1947), 185.

tal elements. The baroque continuo song is in this respect much more like a pattern made up of highly-defined parts than it is like a contrapuntal or polyphonic composition. In emphasizing the rhetorical structure of the song text, these compositions, even while highlighting emotive content, worked a division between words and notes; the custom of printing only a figured bass for instrumental accompaniment, thus calling for improvisation, is a sign of the conceptual change from Milton's ideal of the marriage between voice and verse, a marriage to be consummated in the poet-singer's mind. Thus, although words and sounds work together in the continuo song, primarily to affect an audience, they cooperate as unequal partners, yoked by a common functional goal. Like "Musick" in "Musicks Empire," their victorious union is the consequence of their choosing and seeking each other out, rather than the exemplification of an Idea of harmony which exists apart from, and prior to, any particular harmonic realization. Like Amphion/ Cromwell, the practical musician whose songs Marvell heard worked with disparate and even recalcitrant materials, creating an affective pattern out of words, notes, and rhetorical manipulations of both. In this sense, Marvell's ear was true when he thought to name music "the mosaique of the air."

Stella P. Revard

Intertwining the Garland of Marvell's Lyrics
The Greek Anthology and Its Renaissance Heritage

HANDED DOWN FROM antiquity both in the fifteen books of the Roman poet Martial and in the heterogeneous collection called the Greek Anthology, the epigram not only flourished in the Renaissance in its own right in Latin and vernacular translations and imitations, but also exerted considerable influence with its pithy elegiac couplets, which so readily and brilliantly render summary comment on many other genres of poetry, even on the lyric, which might at first appear far removed from its domain. In the work of Andrew Marvell, we find the influence of the epigram tradition, both directly on his Latin epigrammatical poetry and indirectly on his English lyrics. An accomplished Latin epigrammatist, Marvell translated many of the habits of composition used for the Latin epigram to his composition of his lyric poetry, particularly to those so-called lyrics of his middle period, "Hortus"/"The Garden" and "Ros"/"On a Drop of Dew," that exist in both Latin and English versions. As Rosalie Colie has observed, the nine stanzas of "The Garden" and the nine sections of its companion piece, "Hortus," read like a sequence of epigrams on pastoral and amatory topics.[1] Similar epigrammatical strategies can be noted in "Ros"/"On a Drop of Dew" and in "To His Coy Mistress."

Marvell's predilection for the couplet in his English verse may in part be linked to the epigram tradition. The elegiac couplet was the standard form for the epigram in Greek or Latin from the Alexandrian period through the Renaissance. Its counterpart for vernacular English translators and imitators of the epigram was the iambic pentameter or tetrameter couplet, a favorite form for Marvell in his English lyrics. Although Marvell has few English epigrams, his fondness for the epigram and for elegiac couplets is particularly pronounced in the Latin poetry. Nine out of Marvell's sixteen Latin poems are epigrams; all but

---

1. Colie, *"My Ecchoing Song": Andrew Marvell's Poetry of Criticism* (Princeton: Princeton University Press, 1970), 163.

four of the Latin poems use elegiac couplets.[2] Marvell's interest in the
epigram continued throughout his life. His first published poem was a
Greek epigram, composed when he was an undergraduate and published in a collection celebrating the birth of Princess Anne, Charles I's
fifth child. Among his late poetry is a series of inscriptional Latin
epigrams on the Louvre. Marvell's epigrammatical poetry exhibits the
lively wit, the compression of statement, the use of extravagant figure
that are the signatures of the epigram tradition. Those very qualities are
also manifest in many of Marvell's lyrics. I believe that Marvell's knowledge of the best practitioners of ancient and Renaissance epigram and
his own training as an epigrammatist contributed much to what we
most admire in his lyric poetry.

As a seventeenth-century poet who wrote both Latin and English
verse, Marvell, like his contemporaries, Milton, Herbert, Crashaw, and
Cowley, looked back to a tradition that began when the first humanist
poets started to turn the epigrams of Martial and of the Greek Anthology
into Latin. This practice of Latin translation and imitation was widespread, and it included not only school-boy exercises but also the work of
the leading humanists. Thomas More, for example, composed a large
number of epigrams, many of which are direct translations of the Greek
Anthology. Johannes Secundus imitated both Roman and Greek epigrammatists. Other Neo-Latin poets, such as Michael Marullus, use
Greek epigrams as models for their own epigrammatical poetry. As
James Hutton documents in his studies of the Greek Anthology in Italy
and France, fifteenth- and sixteenth-century continental poets, writing
in Latin and the vernaculars, produced many versions of the epigrams
from the Greek Anthology, both close translations and free adaptations
of the originals.[3] Early in the Renaissance tradition the Greek epigram
was preferred as a model to its Roman counterpart, being considered
more refined. Although a poet like Jonson imitated both Martial and the
Greek epigrammatists, many seventeenth-century writers preferred the
Greek to the Latin, as is attested by the following citation of Rene Rapin's
remarks on the epigram by an English critic.

> The *Greek Epigram* runs upon the *turn* of a
> Thought that is natural, but fine and subtle.

2. *The Latin Poetry of Andrew Marvell*, ed. William A. McQueen and Kiffin A. Rockwell (Chapel Hill: University of North Carolina Press, 1964), 3. Both the text and the
translation of Marvell's Latin lyrics are cited from this edition.

3. *The Greek Anthology in Italy to the Year 1800* (Ithaca: Cornell University Press,
1935); *The Greek Anthology in France and in the Latin Writers of the Netherlands to the Year
1800* (Ithaca: Cornell University Press, 1946). Hutton includes a useful index of
Renaissance translations and adaptations.

> The *Latin Epigram* by a false taste that sway'd
> in the beginning of the decay of the pure *Latin*
> *Stile,* endeavours to surprise the Mind by some
> *nipping Word* which is call'd a Point. . . .
> Catullus wrote after the Greek style, for he
> endeavours to close a Natural Thought within
> a delicate turn of Words, and within the
> simplicity of a very soft Expression.[4]

Marvell with his subtle wit would seem to be an exponent of the Greek style.

The Greek Anthology, as Marvell and most Renaissance writers knew it, was a collection of epigrams drawn from the fourteenth-century manuscript of Maximus Planudes. Although Salmasius had discovered in 1606 the larger and fuller Palatine manuscript, and although some apographs of this manuscript circulated, it is the Planudes version that was the basis of all printed editions of the Greek Anthology from 1497 on and was probably the one Marvell knew, either in Estienne's authoritative text, first printed in 1566, or in another of its many printings. The collection is best described as heterogeneous, and its variety probably made it appeal to a poet like Marvell. It contains epitaphs, amatory pieces, convivial invitations to eat, drink, and enjoy the pleasures of life, humorous observations and satirical attacks, complimentary verses to friends, princes, poets, philosophers, laments on the instability of fortune and life's brevity, descriptions of unusual objects in art and nature, and many curiosities. Marvell's own poetry, like the Anthology, is full of variety and full of curiosities, containing, like it, descriptive pieces, complimentary poems to persons, parodies, epitaphs, brief gnomic sayings, longer philosophical expositions, poems on love, nature, the soul, the dangers of soothsaying, the evils of writing books, the praise of monarchs and of eunuchs, addresses to houses and to mountains. In his Latin poetry Marvell often follows directly in the tradition of the Greek Anthology. The inscriptional epigram, invented by the poets of the Greek Anthology and imitated by Martial and later by Renaissance epigrammatists, directly influences that set of inscriptional distichs that Marvell wrote for the frontispiece of the Louvre. Marvell's complimentary Latin poems to Cromwell and Queen Christina employ the pattern of the laudatory epigram, much practiced in the Renaissance and ultimately indebted to such laudatory epigrams as those of Callimachus to Queen Berenice included in the Anthology. His epigram to Maniban debunking graphol-

---

4. Sir Thomas Pope Blount, *De Re Poetica* (London, 1694), 71–74.

ogy follows a tradition, also popular in the Anthology, of satirizing sooth-
sayers who pretend to divine the future. In his Latin verse Marvell gives
us many indications that he admires the techniques and the range of
subject matter that the Greek Anthology bequeathed to the Renaissance.
But what about the English poetry? Here too, I believe, we may discover
the imprint of the epigram and may trace some influences of both ancient
and more modern epigrammatists.[5]

First, let us look at one of Marvell's most celebrated lyrics, "To His
Coy Mistress." Both in style and subject matter "To His Coy Mistress"
has definite affinities to the epigram tradition. Each of its three sections
is self-contained and employs the epigram's characteristic understate-
ment, compression, and antithesis. Its well-compacted couplets in each
section march to a witty summation. The middle section, moreover,
lines 24–32, exploits one of the favorite subjects of epigram, the vanity of
preserving virginity, and is similar to a famous and much imitated
epigram from the Greek Anthology. Within the longer lyric it almost
functions as an embedded epigram.

> Thy Beauty shall no more be found:
> Nor, in the marble Vault, shall sound
> My ecchoing Song: then Worms shall try
> That long preserv'd Virginity:
> And your quaint Honour turn to dust:
> And into ashes all my Lust.
> The Grave's a fine and private place,
> But none I think do there embrace.

Marvell's would-be seducer's warning has a long and dishonorable
heritage; to trace it to a single epigrammatical model might be fool-

5. For an account of the composition and transmission of the Greek Anthology see
the following: *Select Epigrams from the Greek Anthology,* ed. and trans. J. W. Mackail
(London: Longmans, 1911), esp. 2–28; *The Greek Anthology: Hellenistic Epigrams,* ed.
A. S. F. Gow and D. L. Page (Cambridge: Cambridge University Press, 1965); *The
Greek Anthology: The Garland of Philip, and Some Contemporary Epigrams,* ed. A. S. F.
Gow and D. L. Page (London: Cambridge University Press, 1968); Hoyt Hopewell
Hudson, *The Epigram in the Renaissance* (Princeton: Princeton University Press,
1947); Hutton, *The Greek Anthology in Italy* and *The Greek Anthology in France.* Recent
studies of the impact of the epigram tradition on England include Ann Baynes Coiro,
Robert Herrick's Hesperides and the Epigram Book Tradition (Baltimore: Johns Hopkins
University Press, 1988); Mary Thomas Crane, "*Intret Cato:* Authority and the Epi-
gram in Sixteenth-Century England," in *Renaissance Genre, Essays on Theory, History, and Interpretation,* ed. Barbara Kiefer Lewalski (Cambridge: Harvard University
Press, 1986), 158–86. For a discussion of Marvell's Latin epigrams, see Carl Bain, "The
Latin Poetry of Andrew Marvell," *PQ* 38 (1959): 436–49.

hardy, had not a good many critics before me remarked on the striking similarity of Marvell's words to his coy mistress and Asclepiades's advice to a reluctant virgin, composed almost two thousand years earlier in the third century B.C.[6] I quote the original, followed by a translation in Marvell's own meter.

φείδη παρθενίης. Καὶ τί πλέον; Οὐ γὰρ ἐς ᾅδην
ἐλθοῦσ' εὑρήσεις τὸν φιλέοντα, κόρη;
Ἐν ζωοῖσι τὰ τερπνὰ τὰ Κύπριδος. ἐν δ' Ἀχέροντι
ὀστέα καὶ σποδιὴ, παρθένε, κεισόμεθα.

(5.85)

You'll stay a virgin? to what end?
Hades holds no loving friend;
Among the living we must know
Cyprian sweetness—there below
In the darkness when we die,
Bones and ash uncoupled lie.[7]

In the sixteenth century this epigram was a favorite of Neo-Latin and vernacular poets. Both Secundus and Ronsard produced versions of it. Ronsard, in fact, translated it once as an epigram and later paraphrased it as a sonnet, where the original of Asclepiades functions more as subtext than text. It is in this capacity that Marvell also, I believe, uses it. It remains the shadowy presence beneath his own lines. Both Asclepiades and Marvell court a reluctant virgin with grim wit by creating for her that inescapable world beyond the grave, where beauty exists no more and an eager lover is mere bones and dust. And both conclude with a triumphant quip that no one makes love in that dark bed. Marvell not only captures the gist of Asclepiades's epigram, but he duplicates in his own way its ironic nonchalance. Like Asclepiades's epigram, Marvell's lyric poses a proposition and then moves succinctly to a summation in the briefest number of lines. By identifying the central section of Marvell's lyric as an embedded epigram, we can read the lyric in a different way, savoring a wit that has its source in an ancient tradition.

6. J. B. Leishman, *The Art of Marvell's Poetry* (London: Hutchinson, 1966), 76; Donno, ed. *Andrew Marvell: The Complete Poems* (1972; rpt. New York: Penguin, 1985), 234; Jules Brody, "The Resurrection of the Body: A Reading of Marvell's *To His Coy Mistress,*" *ELH* 56 (Spring 1989): 53–79.

7. All epigrams cited by book and number are from *The Greek Anthology,* ed. W. R. Patton (London: William Heinemann, 1917). Translations, unless otherwise indicated, are mine. Hutton in *Greek Anthology in France,* 361–62, 599, cites a number of translations of this epigram, among them versions in Latin by Secundus and Dousa and in French by Ronsard.

The phenomenon of the embedded epigram is not peculiar to "Coy Mistress" alone. "The Garden" and its companion Latin piece, "Hortus," both draw on the epigram tradition. The loosely connected stanzas of both lyrics develop a number of familiar epigrammatical topics in typical epigrammatical fashion, forming, in fact, minianthologies on a miscellany of subjects: the vanity of ambition, the delight of rural quietness, the praise of trees, the dispraise of love. Rosalie Colie has studied the influence of the Renaissance emblem tradition on Marvell's garden poems. Certainly, the emblems vividly illustrate many of the topoi that Marvell develops, but to look at the emblems alone is only to see half the picture. The texts that usually accompanied the emblems were epigrammatical in form; frequently the epigrams were adapted from those in the Greek Anthology. Alciati particularly made ample use of the Anthology, adapting and translating its epigrams. To look more closely at the epigrams themselves is merely to explore what lay beyond the emblems. Besides, though Marvell draws pictures for us in his poetry, his wit is preeminently verbal, like the wit of the epigrammatists. To trace Marvell then to the epigram tradition is to understand more clearly yet another source of his poetry.

In adapting topics from this ancient source, Marvell sometimes echoes, sometimes playfully inverts that very tradition he follows. The overall theme of the garden lyrics may have been suggested by an epigram of Meleager, where the poet, praising the song of the cicada and noonday quiet, seeks to escape love.

ἀλλά, φίλος, φθέγγου τι νέον δενδρώδεσι Νύμφαις
παίγνιον, ἀντῳδὸν Πανὶ κρέκων κέλαδον,
ὄφρα φυγὼν τὸν Ἔρωτα, μεδημβρινὸν ὕπνον ἀγρεύσω
ἐνθάδ᾽ ὑπὸ σκιερᾷ κεκλιμένος πλατάνῳ.

(7.196)

But, friend, sing some new sportive song for the wood nymphs,
Weaving an antiphonal tune for Pan,
That, fleeing from love, I may take some noon-time sleep,
Here reclining under a shading plane-tree.

The Anthology also offers us some specific models. Marvell's treatment of trees, for example, may go back to the anthropomorphic trees of the Greek Anthology who speak for themselves and castigate human beings that abuse them. A walnut tree complains that it has been planted by the side of the road where boys passing by strip it of twigs and use its own fruit to pelt it (9.3). An olive tree repines that a grapevine has encircled her and threatens her sobriety, she a chaste follower of Pallas and not a drinker (9.130). A poplar pleads not to have her bark stripped and an oak for respect due her age (9.706,2.312). A pine, in an epigram that Thomas More translated (9.30), protests about being cut down for ship timber. It is almost as though Marvell has heard these complaints, for he promises the leafy denizens of his garden that no one will cut their bark, except to carve their own names on it. Not mistresses, but trees shall be honored. In "Hortus" he replaces a catalogue of human mistresses—Neaera, Chloe, Faustina, Corynna, names familiar in classical and Neo-Latin love literature—with a catalogue of trees—"O charae Platanus, Cyparissus, Populus, Ulmus!" The trees, his preferred loves, are, ironically, masculine rather than feminine in grammatical gender. Perhaps Marvell is enjoying a typical epigrammatical joke. Trees treated as symbolic entities may be found in Renaissance emblems, as for example in Alciati's emblem books, where the cypress, oak, poplar, and laurel—all trees of Marvell's garden—are designated certain moral qualities.[8] But the trees of Marvell's garden are not moral symbols, but mistresses, who, even though they do not speak, take on human qualities; they are trees far closer to the speaking trees of the Greek Anthology than to those of the Renaissance emblematists.

The wry, detached attitude toward love that Marvell adopts in "The Garden" and the appearance of the boy-god Amor in "Hortus" may also owe something to the epigrammatists of the Greek Anthology. The god Love makes only an oblique appearance in Marvell's English garden: "When we have run our Passions heat, / Love hither makes his best retreat" (25–26). In the Latin garden, however, the little god, disarmed and pastoralized, occupies an entire stanza. The Latin poem seems particularly close to its epigrammatical sources. In his portrayal of Amor, Marvell looks back to a long tradition that probably had its genesis with the third-century B.C. Alexandrian epigrammatists, who turned Aphrodite's child Eros into a mischievous boy-god. Both Asclepiades and Posidippus depict Love and his company as disarmingly innocent children who have gotten the better of them. In frustration, Posidippus cries out in one epigram: shoot at me, Loves, so that you may become famous for archery among the immortals (12.45). Asclepiades, in a similar mood, accuses the little Loves who cause him to perish of merely playing like children at knucklebones (12.46). Summing up the themes of the earlier epigrammatists, Meleager calls Love both an infant, whose play inadvertently destroys the soul (12.47), and a fierce tyrant, whose arrows wound and whose torch consumes the

---

8. More, *Latin Epigrams*, ed. Leicester Bradner and Charles Arthur Lynch (Chicago: University of Chicago Press, 1953), 17; Andrea Alciati, *Emblemata* (Leiden, 1548).

heart (12.48). A heartless god, he laughs at the injuries his arrows cause
and hides in the lady's eyes to inflict his wounds (5.176).

One of the earliest Renaissance poets to recapture the Eros of the
Greek epigrammatists was Michael Marullus, a fifteenth-century Ital-
ian Neo-Latin poet of Greek heritage, who was much indebted to the
recovery of and interest in Byzantine manuscripts in Florentine circles.
His epigrams recreate for the Renaissance the prankish Eros of the
Greek Anthology. In "De Amore et Mercurio" (1.38), Marullus shows us
Love accusing Mercury of trying to steal his quiver; in another epigram
(1.3), the little god weeps because Neaera has stolen his darts; in "De
Amore" (1.47) he is triumphant, once more wreaking devastation on
human and divine hearts.[9] By the time Marvell comes upon the tyrannical little Amor, he is to be found everywhere, not just in epigrams,
but in lyrics, in emblems, and in all genres of literature and in art. It is
to escape the tyranny of Amor that Marvell retreats to the garden, and
though in "Hortus" he permits Amor to enter the garden, it is only on
condition that he give up his rage ("deferuescente tyranno" [38]). Amor
has laid aside his bow and arrows, inverted his torch and either walks
around without his wings or lies asleep on his quiver, deaf to the call of
his mother Cytherea, and forgetful in his dreams of past iniquities.

> Hic Amor, exutis crepidatus inambulat alis,
> Enerves arcus & stridula tela reponens,
> Invertitque faces, nec se cupit usque timeri;
> Aut exporrectus jacet, indormitque pharetrae;
> Non auditurus quanquam Cytherea vocarit;
> Nequitias referunt nec somnia vana priores.
>
> (32–37)
>
> Here Love, his wings cast aside, walks about in sandals,
> Laying aside his nerveless bows and hissing arrows,
> And inverts his torches, nor does he wish to be feared;
> Or he lies stretched out and sleeps on his quiver;
> Nor will he hear, although Cytherea call;
> Nor do idle dreams report previous iniquities.

Marvell has inverted the tradition of the tyrannical Love, just as he has
inverted Amor's torch and made it harmless. There is precedent for this
inversion, too, in the Greek Anthology. The epigrammatist Plato depicts
Love asleep in the woods among rose blossoms, his quiver hanging in a
tree and smiling in his dreams, while the bees sprinkle him with honey

---

9. *Carmina*, ed. Alessandro Perosa (Zurich: Thesaurus Mundi, 1951).

(16.210). In "Hortus," Marvell has created a self-contained passage that much resembles Plato's epigrammatical portrait of the sleeping Love.

Marvell's famous quips in "The Garden" on the transformations of Daphne and Syrinx may also have been suggested by some ancient epigrams on these nymphs. One epigram on Daphne wittily remarks that the honors she denied to Apollo as a nymph, she confers on Caesar as a laurel tree; as a laurel she consents to grow luxuriantly, the epigrammatist observes, right out of the stone of Caesar's altar (9.307). Another epigram on Syrinx applauds her transformation from nymph to reed to pen; from being a useless plant, the epigrammatist remarks, Syrinx has become as a pen the inspired medium for uttering the mysteries of Helicon (9.162). The Renaissance epigrammatist Marullus has given us the transformed Daphne's retort to the frustrated Apollo:

> "Nunc," ait, "exulta, ramos complexus inanes:
> Ut tua sim, coniunx non ero, nempe tua."
>
> (4.3)
>
> "Now," she said, "rejoice, though you embrace my branches
> In vain, that I am yours, not your wife, but truly yours."

Like the epigrammatists, Marvell shapes his stanza in "The Garden" to lead up to a final quip; he too, contrary to our expectation, makes the transformation of the nymphs the desired end, not the mere thwarting of the gods' passion.

> The Gods, that mortal Beauty chase,
> Still in a Tree did end their race.
> *Apollo* hunted *Daphne* so,
> Only that she might Laurel grow,
> And *Pan* did after *Syrinx* speed,
> Not as a Nymph, but for a Reed.
>
> (27–32)

Culling the flowers of his predecessors, Marvell has decorated the borders of his own Renaissance garden.[10]

The best epigrammatists of the Greek Anthology—the Alexandrian masters of the third century B.C.—had more to offer Renaissance poets than merely a heterogeneous number of topics treated wittily. Epigram does not turn on clever wordplay alone. Often it is through an image

---

10. The Greek Anthology also includes epigrams on sundials (see 9.780, 806, 807).

that an epigrammatist makes his point. Sometimes the image is simple and understated, sometimes contrived and highly developed. We tend to trace Marvell's striking conceits to Donne and the influence of the Metaphysical School. In so doing, we have not paid enough attention to the influence of the ancient epigram that often used highly developed and striking conceits to make its mark. When Asclepiades wishes us to see the beauty of the black girl he loves, he likens her to a coal, which, when lit, glows red like the hearts of roses (5.210). The sweetness of love he compares to the sudden joy that sailors, winter-bound, feel when they first sight the constellation of Ariadne that promises the spring. Callimachus uses a series of images to suggest the effect of secret love—it is a fire under ashes, a quiet river that undermines a wall, a silent vine that creeps alone slowly but engulfs all (12.139). When Asclepiades wishes to evoke the memory of the dead courtesan Archeassa, he does so by contrasting the cold ashes that her tomb holds with the fire with which the living woman once scorched her lovers.

> ἁ νέον ἥβης ἄνθος ἀποδρέψαντες ἐρασταὶ
> πρωτοβόλου, δι᾽ ὅσης ἤλθετε πυρκαιῆς.
>   (7.217)

You lovers who reaped the first flower of her youth
with its lightning flashes; through what a conflagration you passed.

Simply through this contrast of fire and ashes, its inevitable product, Asclepiades has defined for us the difference between the living and the dead courtesan.

If we look at Marvell's epigram on Mary Magdalene, we can note similar manipulations of image. Marvell has suggested the difference between the lascivious and the penitent Magdalene through the contrast of fire and water—the fiery eyes with which the courtesan held her lovers bound and the watery eyes from which the penitent dropped tears that bound Christ's feet with liquid chains.

> Magdala, lascivos sic quum dimisit Amantes,
>   Fervidaque in castas lumina solvit aquas;
> Haesit in irriguo lachrymarum compede Christus,
>   Et tenuit sacros uda Catena pedes.

> Thus, when Magdalene dismissed her wanton lovers,
>   And dissolved her sultry eyes into chaste waters,
> Christ stood fixed in a flowing bond of tears,
>   His sacred feet held in a liquid chain.

As in Asclepiades's epigram, contrasting images of fire and, in this case, water convey the difference between the woman as she was and as she is. With the fire of her lust she bound her lovers; dissolving that bond, she now binds Christ in the watery tears of her penitence. Marvell's technique in this Latin epigram, as in the longer English poem, "Eyes and Tears," is usually connected with the baroque extravagance that marked the end of the Renaissance tradition of tear poetry.[11] Yet there is nothing in the manner in which Marvell develops the conceit of fire and water that could not equally have come out of the ancient epigram tradition.

A similar case exists for Marvell's paired Latin and English poems on the drop of dew. Rosalie Colie makes a strong argument for connecting the dew poems with Henry Hawkins's *Partheneia Sacra* (1633), a Catholic emblem book devoted to meditations on the Virgin (pp. 115–17). While I by no means dispute the influence of Hawkins's emblems, I believe that a more complex combination of influences is in operation. For Marvell's dew poems are not about the Virgin but about the soul; moreover, both secular and sacred influences inform the central image of the poem—the dew-sprinkled cluster of roses. In concept, Marvell's dew is probably Neo-Platonic. But in developing the image of dew on roses Marvell owes much to the secular love tradition and to a number of epigrammatical sources, both ancient and Renaissance.

To begin with, we detect, I believe, Neo-Platonic terminology both in Marvell's description of the dew and in the notion that the dew, the pure soul exiled from heaven, longs instinctively for return. The dew is, in English, "the Soul, that Drop, that Ray / Of the clear Fountain of Eternal Day" (19–20); in Latin, "Fontis stilla sacri, Lucis scintilla perennis" (A drop of the sacred fountain, a glimmer of eternal light [27]). Like the Neo-Platonists, Marvell describes it both in terms of water and light, its essence being part of the pure essence above. We find striking resemblances between Marvell's dew-soul and the descriptions of the soul found in the third hymn of the fourth-century A.D. Greek Christian Neo-Platonist Synesius, a writer readily available in the Renaissance and undoubtedly known to Marvell, as to the Cambridge Platonists.[12] In the hymn Synesius prays that his soul, exiled and fallen from heaven, like a drop of water, may be reunited to the heavenly fountain.

11. Donno, *Complete Poems*, 36.
12. Synesius's hymns were first printed by Aldus in 1499 and were reprinted throughout the sixteenth century, in editions, for example, by Oporinus in Basel in 1567 and by Estienne in Geneva in 1568. Synesius is included also in Roviere's edition of the Greek poets, printed in 1614. Henry More translated two of Synesius's hymns: one into Latin, the other into English.

Grant to me to escape the destiny of the body and to spring
swiftly even to Thy courts, to Thy bosom, whence floweth
forth the fountain of the soul. A heavenly drop, I am shed
upon the earth. Do thou restore me to that fountain whence
I was poured forth, a wanderer who comes and goes.[13]

Conceptually, Marvell's dew owes much to Neo-Platonism. It encloses
within itself the light of the heavenly fountain, it rejects an earthly
habitation, and it longs to return above.

In identifying a possible Neo-Platonic source for Marvell's dew-soul,
we have only solved part of the problem, however. Unlike the Neo-
Platonic hymn, Marvell's lyric expatiates on the dilemma of the exiled
dew-soul. Further, Marvell complicates the dew-soul's dilemma, for it
has fallen into a cluster of roses that "tempt" it to dissolve into them
and nourish them with its otherworldly moisture. That the dew-soul
denies the roses makes for a religious lyric with interesting erotic overtones. The rose or flower is in itself both a secular and a religious
symbol. It can be the symbol in the erotic epigram for the ultimate
earthly beloved or in the sacred epigram tradition for Mary, the ultimate divine-human lady. The flower can even be a symbol for the soul
itself—in its earthly habitation. In a garland or a coronet, the rose can
be a gift of the lover to the beloved. In his own poem "The Coronet,"
Marvell dismantles the garland he had woven for a beloved in order to
present it to Christ. The flowers of "Ros"/"A Drop of Dew" belong, like
those of "The Coronet," both to the secular and to the sacred tradition.
And, as in the other lyric, Marvell weaves both traditions together.

Let us begin with the ancient erotic tradition and a pair of dew-filled
garlands in the works of Asclepiades and his contemporary, Apollonius of Rhodes. The first garland occurs in a simile from Apollonius's
Argonautica, which describes in erotic terms a process important for
Marvell's dew lyrics—the evaporation of dew from the roses when the
sun strikes it. Apollonius tells us how Medea, in first responding to her
lover Jason, is like a dew-filled rose warmed by the sun.

$$\text{ἰαίνετο δὲ φρένας εἴσω}$$
$$\text{τηκομένη, οἶον τε περὶ ῥοδέῃσιν ἐέρση}$$
$$\text{τήκεται ἠῴοισιν ἰαινομένη φαέεσσιν.}$$
$$\text{(3.1020–21)}[14]$$

13. *The Essays and Hymns of Synesius of Cyrene*, trans. with introduction and notes
by Augustine Fitzgerald (Oxford: Oxford University Press, 1930), 2:383.
14. Apollonius Rhodius, *The Argonautica*, ed. R. C. Seaton (London: William
Heinemann, 1912).

> Dissolving, she is warmed
> In her heart, just as within roses
> The dew, warmed by the morning light, dissolves.

Apollonius conveys the effect of erotic warming, as he directs our attention first to the girl, then to the dew-filled roses, repeating the same words, *warm* and *dissolve,* as he describes both. In Marvell's dew lyrics, the sun, acting the part of a lover, warms and dissolves the dew, drawing it to itself. In "On a Drop of Dew," the warm sun pities the pain of the dew and exhales it back to the skies (17–18); the soul, similarly warmed, is compared with the manna, that "does, dissolving run / Into the Glories of th' Almighty Sun" (39–40). In the Latin version of the lyric, "Ros," Marvell makes explicit the erotic comparison, only implied in the English. The dew is compared to an inexperienced girl, who with trepidation returns home late at night; like her, Marvell says, the drop of dew with virginal modesty is fearful until the engendering sun ("sol genitale"), exercising its procreative sexual powers, draws the dew to it. In using the word *genitale,* Marvell is suggesting that the sun, like a divine lover, is warming the dew, just as a human lover might warm an inexperienced girl to her first sexual awakening. So, exploiting a comparison familiar in erotic literature, he contrasts the dew-soul's acceptance of the heavenly lover with its rejection of the earthly roses.

The second garland occurs in an epigram by Asclepiades and offers us a different kind of exercise in ancient eroticism, throwing an interesting light on Marvell's techniques in developing the imagery of "Ros"/ "On a Drop of Dew."[15] In this epigram Asclepiades describes a garland hung above a door. He addresses the garland directly and tells it to remain there and not to shake loose the tears he has sprinkled on it until the beloved appears and opens the door.

> Αὐτοῦ μοι στέφανοι, παρὰ δικλίσι ταῖσδε κρεμαστοὶ
>   μίμνετε, μὴ προπετῶς φύλλα τινασσόμενοι,
> οὓς δακρύοις κατέβρεξα, κάτομβρα γὰρ ὄμματ᾽ ἐρώντων.
>   Ἀλλ᾽ ὅταν οἰγομένης αὐτὸν ἴδητε θύρης,
> στάξαθ᾽ ὑπὲρ κεφαλῆς ἐμὸν ὑετόν, ὡς ἂν ἄμεινον
>   ἡ ξανθή γε κόμη τἀμὰ πίῃ δάκρυα.

(5.145)

> Here, my wreaths, above these double-doors suspended,
> Remain, not shaking precipitously these petals,
> Watered by my tears; for the eyes of lovers are rainy.

---

15. The epigram was much imitated in the Renaissance. Hutton cites versions by Ronsard, Morisot, and Angeriano in *The Greek Anthology in France,* 104ff.

But when the door opens and you see him,
Sprinkle my dew upon his head, so that
His yellow hair may better drink my tears.

Everything in Asclepiades's epigram is conveyed through the central image of the tear-bedewed garland hung above the beloved's door. Everything moves toward the symbolic event that does not actually happen, the opening of the door that will cause the dewlike tears to fall. Asclepiades tells us nothing about the actual situation. We infer from the manner in which he addresses and describes the garland that we have here a poem of exclusion and complaint. The garland itself we assume to be a love token; its suspension outside the door implies the speaker's exclusion from the dwelling. The tears sprinkled on the garland seem to plead the case of a sorrowful and rejected love. The anticipated opening of the door and shaking loose of the tears are the consummating events toward which the poem tends; the events are both uncertain and ambiguous and lend the poem its own peculiar tension. For when the tears fall upon the beloved's head and his hair drinks the tears, the beloved will symbolically accept the lover, condole his sorrow, and solace him. Then, the tears, the very emblem of sorrow, will become that of success. Part of the effect of this epigram depends on the way in which the tears are identified with watery dew and rain; thus, the shedding of the tears, the fall of dew, the sprinkling of rain, and the desired sexual consummation become all one natural process. Like dew or rain, the tears first fall on the garland, watering it with life-giving moisture; when they fall next on the beloved's head and his hair drinks them, as the thirsty earth drinks the rain, another union will take place. Metaphorically, the lover will be one with the beloved.

What makes Asclepiades's epigram interesting as a possible model for Marvell's "Ros"/"On a Drop of Dew" is its artistry in creating a highly detailed but static picture through which a complex relationship is suggested. Marvell creates a comparable picture in the first stanza of "On a Drop of Dew" and suggests through his description the fears and longings of the soul, excluded from heaven.

See how the Orient Dew,
    Shed from the Bosom of the Morn
    Into the blowing Roses,
Yet careless of its Mansion new
For the clear Region where 'twas born,
    Round in its self incloses:
    And in its Globes Extent,

Frames as it can its native Element.
How it the purple flow'r does slight,
Scarce touching where it lyes,
But gazing back upon the Skies,
Shines with a mournful Light;
Like its own Tear,
Because so long divided from the Sphear.
Restless it roules and unsecure
Trembling lest it grow impure:
Till the warm Sun pitty it's Pain
And to the Skies exhale it back again.
(1–18)[16]

Marvell's picture of the dew-drop among the roses, quoted here from the English version, recalls visually the dewy tears on Asclepiades's suspended garland. The dew, trembling and rolling restlessly, is compared to a tear about to fall. The tearlike dew in Marvell's poem, like the dewlike tear in Asclepiades's, is an emblem of exclusion. Marvell, like Asclepiades, is using descriptive detail to explore the inner reality of the picture he gives us. Just as Asclepiades hints at the feelings of the excluded lover by describing the restlessly rolling tears, so Marvell shows us in the trembling dew the soul's fear of the luxuriant "blowing" roses, its attempt, on the threshold of experience, to remain secure—not to fall or dissolve into the roses but to return pure to the skies. In the Latin "Ros" Marvell makes even more explicit the dewsoul's fear of being tainted by the world of the roses. The flowers seem to solicit it with their petals, and the dew on the flowers is compared to a tear on the rosy cheeks of a fearful girl ("uti roseis Lachryma fusa Genis" [14]). The Latin even personifies the dew as an inexperienced girl. In both Latin and English poems Marvell, through the details of a single static picture, creates a world of inner experience and feeling. Like Asclepiades, he also takes this static picture and seems to make it move. But at the beginning and the end of the poems, however, the dew remains on the roses, just as Asclepiades's tears remain on the garland. As Asclepiades makes us anticipate an event, so does Marvell. As the anticipated fall of the tears will bring about a symbolic union that the lover longs for, so the anticipated evaporation of the dew will make possible its return to the skies and his union once more above. Both events are connected with natural processes—the fall of tears with the

16. For discussions of "A Drop of Dew," see Donald R. Dickson, *The Fountain of Living Waters* (Columbia: University of Missouri Press, 1987), 2–8; Colie, *"My Eccho-ing Song,"* 113–17, 120–21.

precipitation of rain, the rise of the soul with evaporation. Never in either poem does the anticipated event happen, but the very fact that what is anticipated is a natural process makes the event seem inevitable and, thus, the hoped-for union assured.

That Marvell should distill the tears of a pagan lover to produce a Christian drop of dew is perhaps astonishing, but Marvell is the kind of eclectic writer who deliberately draws on many traditions. Even as we consider the contribution of the ancient erotic epigram, however, we must not overlook the humanist epigram that itself drew on classical inspiration and was, like Marvell's own lyrics, an effort to transmute the pagan classical into the Christian. The humanist epigrammatist of the sixteenth-century stood immediately behind Marvell and behind emblematists such as Hawkins and his meditations of *Partheneia Sacra*. Two of these Christian humanists— both sixteenth-century poets who wrote in Latin—are Marc-Antonio Flaminio and Ippolito Capilupi, both of whom exploit the imagery of the erotic epigram tradition to produce Christian poems. The ingredients of their poems are, not unexpectedly, dew and flowers.

Capilupi, an Italian bishop and friend of Bernardo Tasso, makes Mary the flower and the dew, by implication, the inseminating power of God himself that fills her womb with divine light.

> Cum ros vere rosam penetrat fulgentibus astris,
> Tum rosa (gemma velut) rore referta nitet.
> Sic postquam Deus ipse tuam delapsus in aluum est,
> Sole magis, era luce repleta micas.[17]

> When dew from the shining stars in spring penetrates
>   The rose, then like a gem the rose shines, filled with dew;
> So after God himself had slipped into your womb,
>   Brighter than the sun you beam, filled with true light.

Although Mary here is the rose, as she often is in Christian iconography, she is also the beloved of the erotic epigram tradition—a flower, the object of the lover's desire, a flower filled with dew, who visually resembles the rose of Apollonius's simile, symbolically the shy girl first responding to her lover's advances. Capilupi's treatment of dew and roses not only looks backward but also forward to the similes of Marvell's "Ros," where the dew is compared to an inexperienced and fearful girl. Both Capilupi and Marvell are attempting to describe a phenomenon of divine love by adopting imagistically similes connected

17. Hippolytus Capilupus, *Capiluporum Carmina* (Rome, 1590), 3. In an epigram on Mary Magdalene, Ippolito compares her tears to celestial dew shining in a rose (p. 9).

traditionally with human love, thus bringing the mystery down to their readers and making it vivid and immediate.

Something similar happens in Marc-Antonio Flaminio's poem on the soul. In that we are dealing with the soul's longing, we approach even closer to the subject of Marvell's dew lyrics. For Flaminio the soul is the flower and the dew the spiritual nourishment that sustains it in an alien world.

> Vt flos tenellus in sinu
> Telluris almae lucidam
> Formosus explicat comam,
> Si ros & imber educat
> Illum; tenella mens mea
> Sic floret, almi spirtus
> Dum rore dulci pascitur;
> Hoc illa si caret, statim
> Languescit, vt flos arida
> Tellure natus, eum nisi
> Et ros & imber educat.[18]

> As a delicate flower in the bosom
> Of the nourishing earth, a beautiful one,
> Spreads out its shining petals,
> When the dew and rain sustain it;
> So my tender mind flourishes,
> When the spirit feeds
> On sweet, nourishing dew;
> But, if it is in want, immediately
> It languishes, as a flower
> Born in dry earth, unless
> Both dew and rain sustain it.

18. Flaminio, *De Rebus Divinis Carmina* (Paris, 1550), 11; Julius Caesar Scaliger's anacreontic on dew and rain is worth comparing to Flaminio's and Capilupi's lyrics:

> Serum mihi est diei,
> Tibi mane. ros tibi ergo.
> Mihi imber ex ocellis.
> Tibi flos in rore turget.
> Cur ego fructu carebo?
>   (Iulius Caesar Scaliger,
>   "Anacreontica," in *Poemata* 1574.)

> It is late in the day for me.
> You, wait; there is dew for you;
> For me rain from my eyes.
> For you the flower swells with dew;
> Why should I lack the fruit?

Flaminio's poem is interesting not only in adopting the language of erotic literature to describe the longing of the soul, but also in using the metaphor of natural process—the distillation of dew on the flower—to move from the secular to the sacred context. The longing of the flower for dew or rain that so readily suggests the desire of the lover for the beloved becomes in Flaminio's poem the soul's desire for sustenance from God. The dew responds to the desire of the flower, dissolving into it, and so the soul attains a union with God comparable to what Marvell's dew-soul attains when, through the opposite process—evaporation—it returns to the skies. Through the traditional description of dew and flowers, Marvell and the sixteenth-century Latin poets before him suggest erotic relationships that far transcend those that the amorous wits of the third century B.C. entertained. Their sacred eroticism, however, would hardly be possible without the model of the ancient epigrammatists that come before them.

It is difficult to sum up in a simple way the influence of the Greek Anthology on a poet such as Marvell. To say that its heterogeneous subject matter stimulated a poet who himself thrived on heterogeneity, that its wit made the witty poet yet more witty, or that its density and complexity of image inspired some of the lofty conceits he builds may seem adventurous claims. But so many topics, themes, poetical anecdotes, quips, and sharply realized images in Marvell's lyrics are so close to those that we find in the Greek Anthology that it is hard to believe that Marvell did not profit from the collective wit and wisdom that made the Greek Anthology so popular in the sixteenth and seventeenth centuries.

Dale B. J. Randall

Once More to the G(r)ates
An Old Crux and a New Reading of
"To His Coy Mistress"

AS ONE OF THE most admired poems in the English language, Andrew Marvell's "To His Coy Mistress" has called forth a veritable library of criticism. Although the gist of the work is perfectly clear, Marvell has managed its development so suggestively that readers have been moved to explicate virtually every element in it, and none more often than those in the following passage (according to the definitive edition of Margoliouth, Legouis, and Duncan-Jones):

> Let us roll all our Strength, and all
> Our sweetness, up into one Ball:
> And tear our Pleasures with rough strife,
> Thorough the Iron gates of Life.
>
> (41–44)

The various elements here function together cumulatively and must ultimately be viewed within the matrix that they all help to constitute, but I will concentrate on what Ann E. Berthoff has termed "that superb allegorical metaphor, 'the Iron gates of Life.' "[1] In his notes to the Margoliouth edition Legouis cites Davison's suggestion that Marvell uses "gates" metaphorically for the labia, but he then complains that Marvell's adjective *iron* for such fleshly gates "makes the *double entendre* less than likely."[2] Legouis himself, on the other hand, ranges far abroad

---

1. *The Resolved Soul: A Study of Marvell's Major Poems* (Princeton: Princeton University Press, 1970), 223–24.

2. *Poems and Letters* 1:254, citing Dennis Davison, "Notes on Marvell's 'To His Coy Mistress,' " *N&Q* 203 (1958): 521. Some readers, nonetheless, find Davison's suggestion plausible. Bruce King writes, "The 'rough strife' refers to the motions of love making, while the 'gates of Life' include a passing allusion to the woman's sexual organs" (*Marvell's Allegorical Poetry* [New York: Oleander, 1977], 72). Others who accept the suggestion might like to consider a professional opinion from *The Whore's Rhetorick* (1683) advising against rendering "the gate of Love so wide as the Pas-

to find that " 'the gates of Life' where the sexual strife is waged suggest the well-known narrow reach of the Danube."[3] Neither suggestion has been universally accepted, and both proceed by ignoring the fact that we have here a textual crux. Although the 1681 Folio of Marvell's *Miscellaneous Poems* reads "gates," there is a strong possibility—which this essay is intended to advance to a probability—that the "right" reading is "grates."

Elizabeth Donno in her 1972 edition is unusual for expressing a reluctance to retain the Folio-authorized "gates." She observes that that word has led to "a somewhat desperate search for signification," and that "in terms of literary tradition, the adjectives most commonly associated with gates are *horn* and *ivory*, whereas *iron* is commonly used with *grates* (see *OED*)."[4] Like others earlier, Donno also recalls Tennyson's remark that a switch to the word *grates* would intensify Marvell's metaphor.[5] In fact, against the authority of Marvell's 1681 Folio, *Miscellaneous Poems*, she chooses to print "grates." This is a brave and convention-breaking choice.[6] In order to make it, however, Donno or indeed anyone writing after 1945 has had the authority of a previously forgotten manuscript reputed to have belonged to Marvell's nephew William Popple (the "Dearest Will" of Marvell's letters). Moreover, as George deForest Lord has written, when it comes to Marvell's text "there are only two witnesses with any pretence to authority: *Miscellaneous Poems* (1681) and 'Popple.' "[7] Now at the Bodleian (MS. Eng.

senger may enter without a touch of either side" (facsimile with introduction by J. R. Irvine and G. J. Gravlee [Delmar, New York: Scholars' Facsimiles, 1979], 122; from Ferrante Pallavicino, *La Retorica delle Puttane* [1642]). In fairness one should add that in *The Poetry of Andrew Marvell* (London: Arnold, 1964), 27, Davison appears to have backed off from his earlier stand.

3. *Poems and Letters* 1:254. Near Orsova, the "Iron Gates" of the Danube is the river's last defile as it flows southeastward over the Prigada rock. In Marvell's day it was unnavigable for three months or so each year. For the record it should be noted that Margoliouth himself included no note at all on "gates" in either his first edition (Oxford: Clarendon, 1927) or his second (Oxford: Clarendon, 1952).

4. *Andrew Marvell: The Complete Poems* (Baltimore: Penguin, 1972), 235.

5. The reference appears among the "Personal Recollections" of E. T. Palgrave in Hallam Tennyson's *Alfred Lord Tennyson: A Memoir* (London: Macmillan 1897), 2:501.

6. Others have declined to follow Donno. Robert Wilcher, who bases his *Andrew Marvell* (Cambridge: Cambridge University Press, 1985) on her edition, goes out of his way to say that in "Coy Mistress" he prefers "gates" to "grates" (11), but he offers no reasons.

7. *TLS*, August 3, 1984, 869. In his edition, Lord nevertheless rejects "grates" because "the Folio's *gates* presents no difficulties" (*Andrew Marvell* [New York: Random House, 1968], xxxiii). The Popple manuscript is discussed by Hugh MacDonald, "Andrew Marvell's Miscellaneous Poems, 1681," *TLS*, July 13, 1951, 444; Thomas Clayton, " 'Morning Glew' and Other Sweat Leaves," *ELR* 2 (1972): 356–75; Hilton Kelliher, comp., *Andrew Marvell* (London: British Museum Publications, 1978), 63–64; and Warren Chernaik, *The Poet's Time* (Cambridge: Cambridge University Press, 1983), esp. 206–7. It is partially reproduced in a Scolar Facsimile of *Miscellaneous Poems* (Menston: Scolar, 1969), second page 20.

poet. d. 49), "Popple" consists in part of handwritten corrections (from whose hand we do not know) placed on printed sheets of the 1681 volume. And all of this is pertinent at present because it does, indeed, change "gates" to "grates."

In exploring some possibilities inherent in the thought that "grates" may serve the poem better than "gates," one might begin by asking whether Marvell uses either "grates" or "gates" elsewhere, and if so, how. In "Upon Appleton House," where one of the *Suttle Nunns* in the "gloomy" cloister attempts to entice the "blooming Virgin *Thwates*" as a conscript (94, 89, 90), she explains that while the convent walls of Nun Appleton protect the nuns' "Liberty," "the Cloyster outward shuts its Gates" in order to lock out those dangerous "wild Creatures, called Men" (100, 103, 102). To "inclose" the men, she says, engaging in some major perceptual inversion, the convent "locks on them the Grates" (101, 104). In other words, Marvell deploys here some Romish sleight-of-hand regarding incarceration and excarceration but nevertheless utilizes both "gates" and "grates" for essentially the same purpose. As Osric might say, "Nothing, neither way."

On the other hand, while gates and grates may both be locked (to enclose inward *or* outward, as Marvell suggests), gates normally provide a means of entry and exit, whereas iron grates normally constitute obstacles to both. Iron grates are by nature usually setters-off, confiners, restricters—and tonally in keeping with the "rough strife" that (according to "To His Coy Mistress") is necessary if one is to proceed through them. Of course, a gate can itself be made either in whole or part of iron and either in whole or part of a grate, but it will be more helpful here to distinguish between these things than to blend them. By sorting such matters and considering some specific types of iron grates, I hope to show here that the presence of the phrase "Iron grates" in "To His Coy Mistress" may be perceived as a strikingly efficient device for helping to unify the major themes of the poem.

* * *

During many of the long years before windows were glazed in England, fixed window grates or grilles (Fr. *grilles*)—which basically were rectangular bars woven together at right angles—served for protection. Despite the strength of this tick-tack-toe form, and probably as a means of conveying iconographically the still greater strength of his love, a fourteenth-century manuscript pictures Sir Launcelot breaking through a window grate to reach his lady.[8] Down to the close of the

---

8. Facts in this sentence and the next are drawn mainly from J. Starkie Gardner, *English Ironwork of the XVIIth & XVIIIth Centuries* (London: Batsford, 1911), 268.

Tudor period such grates continued to be placed in many English dwellings (for instance Compton Wynyates, Penshurst, and Knole), including, of course, the royal palaces (Henry VIII in 1534 paid John à Guylders for grates at Hampton Court), and Christopher Wren and others at the close of the 1600s were still finding varied uses for them.

After something of an aesthetic decline in the sixteenth century, in fact, English ironwork enjoyed a revival in the seventeenth century, probably partly because increasing numbers of Englishmen were discovering handsome examples on the Continent during the time of the civil wars and Interregnum.[9] Such a one was Thomas Killigrew, who in his 1654 *Thomaso I*, set in Madrid, has the courtesan Angelica notice "how the poor Girls [of the local nunnery] crowded to the Grates when we came in."[10] Even early in the century, however, we may find an occasional reference such as that in Thomas Tomkis's *Albumazar* (1615), where one Trinculo tells of hearing in Barbary "A pretty song the Moores sing to a gridiron" at such times as their mistresses are coy.[11] Marvell himself, of course, traveled in France, Italy, and Spain in the 1640s, and found occasion in "Appleton House" to mention such relatively exotic places as Aranjuez and the Buen Retiro. On the other hand, though window grates are especially common in France, Italy, and Spain, one should not lose sight of the fact that Marvell need never have left home to see them.

Moreover, Marvell is almost sure to have carried images of iron grates in his pocket. The great portcullis of early days—massive iron basketry that could be drawn upward by chains into the chamber over the gate of a castle—was one of the insignia of the Tudor and Stuart monarchs. As the badge of the Beauforts (Margaret Beaufort was the grandmother of Henry VIII), and doubtless also because it figured strength and power, the portcullis appeared on the so-called "Portcullis Groat" of Henry VII and thereafter in the coinage of Henry VIII, Edward VI, Elizabeth, James, and Charles.[12] In fact, James insistently

9. Raymond Lister, *Decorative Wrought Ironwork in Great Britain* (Rutland, Vt.: Tuttle, 1957; rpt. 1970), 84; and John Harris, *English Decorative Ironwork from Contemporary Source Books* (Chicago: Quadrangle, 1960), 3.

10. *Comedies and Tragedies* (1664), where *Thomaso I* has a separate title page (1663), 333.

11. *Albumazar* (London: for W. Burre), G2v.

12. In 1633-1634, during the reign of Charles, the portcullis was to be found on the crown, half-crown, shilling, sixpence, twopence, and penny (Herbert Allen Seaby, ed. *Notes on English Silver Coins, 1066-1648* [London: B. A. Seaby, 1948], 1:68). I have found helpful information in George C. Brooke, *English Coins*, 3d ed. (London: Methuen, 1950; rpt. 1955); J. J. North, *English Hammered Coinage*, 2 (London: Spink, 1960); and C. H. V. Sutherland, *English Coinage 600-1900* (London: Batsford, 1973).

31   *Protegere Regium .*

W HILE deadly foes , their engines haue prepard;
with furie fierce , to batter downe the walles ,
My dutie is the Citie gate to guard ,
And to rebate their Rammes , and fierie balls :
  So that if firmely , I do stand without ,
  Within the other , neede no daunger doubt

Dread Soveraigne *I A M E S*., whose puiffant name to heare ,
The Turke may tremble , and the Traitor pine :
Belou'd of all thy people , farre and neere :
Bee thou, as this Port-cullies , vnto thine ,
  Defend without , and thou within fhalt fee ,
  A thoufand thoufand , liue and die with thee .

Obfeffis ut opem certo munimine præftem,
Quæ non fuftineo damna creata mihi.
Sis catarafta tuis (animofe Monarcha) Britannis,
Intus et invenies pectora firma tibi .

Si ftatus Imperii, aut falus provinciarum
in difcrimen vertatur, debebit (Princeps) in acie ftare.   Tacit : 4. Hift .
                                                                        Dies

Fig. 1
The portcullis as emblem in Henry Peacham, *Minerva Britanna*
(1613), 31. Courtesy of the Rare Book Department,
Perkins Library, Duke University.

traced his lineage to Henry VII and his wife Elizabeth, and the Henrician sign with which the Scottish king reinforced his claim to the English throne is still to be seen on the pennies of Elizabeth II.

Unlike a castle gate, which is always visible, a raised portcullis disap-
pears and a lowered one invariably becomes an imposing obstacle, an
eloquent visual statement. Henry Peacham's *Minerva Britanna* of 1613
makes explicit both visually and verbally some of the emblematic
meanings of the portcullis (see Fig. 1). Designed primarily for protection and defense, the iron grate that Peacham provides can readily
"rebate" an attacker's "Rammes, and fierie balls." Conceivably such
military violence as is implicit here helps lend some impetus to Marvell's image of the ball with which the lovers are to "tear" their "Pleasures with rough strife, / Thorough the Iron grates of Life." In any case
it is beyond doubt that the portcullis was used as a sexual image, as
when James Shirley has Lord Bonville say in *Hide Park*,

> no woman could
> Deny me hospitality, and let downe,
> When I desire accesse, the rude Portcullice.[13]

For a more vivid parallel we may turn to a passage in Samuel Holland's
mock-romance, *Don Zara del Fogo* (1656):

> By this time the Sunne was sunk neer his Evening Region, to *Glau-
> cus* infinite joy, who thought each minute an Age, till she had
> tasted those Oily sweets (which she resolved to retalliate with
> Amber-Suds) that every Errant Knight prostrates at the Port-Cullis
> of his Paramour.[14]

However we finally decide to deploy such information, we may safely
say that the grate *qua* portcullis proves to be a ubiquitous seventeenth-
century image, and its range of implications worth considering.

At this point perhaps one should acknowledge also the multitudi-
nous imagery in early writing wherein the lady is herself a castle, fort,
or tower that is subject to the militantly amorous approaches of her
lover. "Now will I invade the fort," says Philip Sidney's Astrophil of the
sleeping Stella.[15] Nathaniel Whiting, speaking of his leading lovers in
Albino and Bellama (1638), observes at one point that Albino has not

13. *Hide Park* (London: for A. Crooke and W. Cooke, 1637), C2v.
14. *Don Zara* (London: for Tho. Vere, 1656), 78–79.
15. *Astrophil and Stella*, Song II, in *The Poems of Sir Philip Sidney*, ed. William A.
Ringler, Jr. (Oxford: Clarendon Press, 1962), 202.

yet attempted "To scale the fortresse of her virgine-tower."[16] In *Appius and Virginia* John Webster has Clodius advise Appius that if other methods to win Virginia fail, "then siege her Virgin Tower / With t[w]o prevailing engines, feare and power."[17] The fact is that Marvell himself was demonstrably aware of the tradition. In his "Daphnis and Chloe" Nature has burdened and constrained Chloe with a frustrating coyness such that the girl knows neither how to enjoy Daphnis nor how to let him go, and

> He, well-read in all the wayes
> By which men their Siege maintain,
> Knew not that the Fort to gain
> Better 'twas the Siege to raise.
> (17–20)

Obviously several elements that are operative in "Daphnis and Chloe" serve Marvell also in "To His Coy Mistress," and from each poem we may learn something about the other. We need to be careful, however. The danger in pursuing the woman-as-castle theme too far in "To His Coy Mistress" is that it may lead to a reading like Davison's.

In any case, just as the portcullis was used to protect the inhabitants of a castle or city, so iron grates—sometimes woven and sometimes made of vertical bars—were placed in churches and cathedrals. Thus in More's *Dialogue Concerning Heresies* (1528) we read of a prior who

> brought pryuely a straunge wenche in to the chyrche that sayd she was sente thyther by god and wolde not lye out of the chyrche. And after [i.e., later] she was grated within yron grates aboue in the rode lofte.[18]

Normally, however, grates in churches were intended to protect the contents of tombs and shrines. First used widely in England after the Norman Conquest, these artful safeguards were to be found nearly everywhere. One notable example of a grille dating from about 1290 is in

16. *The Most Pleasante Historie of Albino and Bellama* (London: for C. Greene, 1638), 132.

17. *Appius and Virginia* (ca. 1608–1634?; earliest surviving text, 1654), 1.3.59–60, in *The Complete Works of John Webster*, ed. F. L. Lucas (New York: Oxford University Press, 1937), 3:162. See also, Anne Lancashire, "The Emblematic Castle in Shakespeare and Middleton," in *The Mirror Up to Shakespeare*, ed. J. C. Gray (Toronto: University of Toronto Press, 1984), 223–41.

18. In *The Complete Works of St. Thomas More*, vol. 6, pt. 1, ed. Thomas M. C. Lawler, Germain Marc'hadour, and Richard C. Marius (New Haven: Yale University Press, 1981), 87.

St. Albans Cathedral at the monument of Humphrey, Duke of Gloucester. "In construction and design," writes Lister, "this grille is reminiscent
of lattice work (*mashrabiyyah*) from the Middle East and it is possible that
the design was made by a smith who had seen service as an armourer on
one of the later Crusades."[19] Also notable among many exemplars are the
"great Eleanor grille," likewise of the late thirteenth century, made by
Thomas de Leghtone and erected at the tomb of Eleanor of Castile,
Queen of Edward I, in Westminster Abbey, as well as that serving in
Newbattle Abbey to protect the marble effigy of Marie de Courcy.[20]
    As for Marvell's poem, one presumably might find hints of a saint's
shrine in the lines on what promises to be the lady's exasperatingly
"long preserv'd Virginity" (28) and what for a moment might appear to
be a parodic adoration of her *membra disjecta*:

> An hundred years should go to praise
> Thine Eyes, and on thy Forehead Gaze.
> Two hundred to adore each Breast:
> But thirty thousand to the rest.
>
>   (13–16)

    The larger point here, however, is that death and the tomb are vital
elements in the argument and imagery of Marvell's poem. Partly to
shock his lady out of her coyness, to induce her to take action, the
speaker describes a future when her beauty shall have passed:

> Thy Beauty shall no more be found;
> Nor, in thy marble Vault, shall sound
> My ecchoing Song . . .
>
>   (25–27)

The adjective "ecchoing" here catches exactly what one cannot avoid hearing either in a stone church set about with marble monuments or (presumably) inside a burial vault, and it suggests what will never be heard in the
present lady's tomb because her lover will not be singing, in fact will not be
in the tomb at all, and most of all because she will be utterly alone.

> The Grave's a fine and private place,
> But none I think do there embrace.
>
>   (31–32)

19. *Decorative Wrought Ironwork*, 73.
20. Ibid., 79; Harris, *English Decorative Ironwork*, 20. See also Katharine A. Esdaile,
English Church Monuments 1510 to 1840 (London: Batsford, 1946).

Let me help you come forth, the speaker might be said to urge, *come forth from a life that is too like death, come through the grates and into a life where sensuality and sexuality are still possible* (I am "not the figure cut in alabaster / Kneels at my husband's tomb," says the Duchess of Malfi),[21] *a life in which it is still possible to take action in time.* Perfectly in keeping with this suggestion is Marvell's idea in "Appleton House" that grates may not only safeguard those within, but also ward off the life outside.

A grated tomb with its mouldering contents is, furthermore, no ill trope for a prison. In fact, the meaning of "grates" itself is multiple even insofar as it relates literally to imprisonment. Grates may themselves be places of confinement for animals or people, or they may be but one feature of such a place. It is the first meaning that John Ford's Perkin Warbeck has in mind when he tries to rally his friends with the claim, "The lion faints not / Lock'd in a grate."[22] And it is the second that Old Wengrave speaks of in Thomas Dekker and Thomas Middleton's *Roaring Girl* (1608) when threatening Trapdoor with prison: "Varlet, I'll make thee look through a grate!"[23] The use of iron grates for imprisonment receives more extreme comic treatment and for good measure brings in a lady in Robert Anton's romance-mocking *Moriomachia* (1613). Here the pygmy Andromago leads Moriana

> as his prisoner towards a castle he had not far off, which was double-grated with huge iron bars, not much unlike the mighty strong barricadoed windows of a monstrous over-grown mouse-trap.[24]

And mingling at least three of the kinds of grates that we have thus far considered here, in fact drawing also on the subject of love, is the passage in John Marston's *Antonio's Revenge* (1600) where Antonio kisses the fair Mellida's hand through the iron grates of a castle vault that serves as a prison.[25]

For a more figurative reference, and therefore one that may be closer still to what Marvell's poem implies, we might consider Samuel Tuke's

21. John Webster, *The Duchess of Malfi*, ed. John Russell Brown (Cambridge: Harvard University Press, 1964), 1.1.454–55.

22. *Perkin Warbeck*, ed. Donald K. Anderson, Jr. (Lincoln: University of Nebraska Press, 1965), 4.5.26–27.

23. *The Roaring Girl*, ed. G. K. Hunter (Lincoln: University of Nebraska Press, 1965), 3.3.50.

24. Charles C. Mish, ed., *Short Fiction of the Seventeenth Century* (New York: Doubleday, 1963), 60.

25. *Antonio's Revenge*, ed. W. Reavley Gair (Manchester: Manchester University Press, 1978), 2.3.122.

The Adventures of Five Hours (1663). Here a native Spaniard complains of the plight of women, the

> miserable Sex amongst us here,
> Born onely to be honorable Prisoners;
> The more of Quality, the Closer kept;
> Which Cruelty is reveng'd upon our selves,
> Whil'st by Immuring those whom most we Love,
> We sing and sigh onely to Iron Grates.[26]

Written several decades after the similar passage already cited from Tomkis, this one, too, serves to remind us that pain may be suffered by lovers on either side of iron grates.

Though each of the meanings of "grates" discussed here thus far is consonant with the main argument of Marvell's poem, and though each gains strength when imped with the others, I will now make two additional suggestions. These two as well as the elements previously considered may be arranged in different patterns (as when one gives a slight shake to a kaleidoscope), but I view the first as subsuming all that we have seen earlier, and the second as an intriguing appendage of a related but rather different sort.

The first is quite simple: Marvell's poem gains considerably if the "Iron g[r]ates" of line 44 are perceived in terms of a nunnery. A nunnery is at once a dwelling (protective and seclusive), a tomb (for those dead to worldly ways), and a cage or prison (which inflicts a sentence for life). It also has grates whose specific function is to separate certain women from what Marvell has the wily nun in "Appleton House" refer to as "those wild Creatures, called Men." Marvell, in fact, says specifically that the nuns in "Appleton House" are "in prison" (206).

Analogues are easy to find. *The Whore's Rhetorick*, for instance, points to the sort of "young Female that is cloystered up in a Monastery, who has renounced the World, put on a new dress, new manners, new thoughts, and who is become (as the Lawyer has it) a person dead in Law."[27] In *Albino and Bellama* Nathaniel Whiting writes of a nunnery as a "Virgine-cage."[28] For yet another and particularly interesting example from a few years earlier we have in Francis Beaumont and John Fletcher's *King and No King* (1611) a passage that is anticipatory of some of the figures and implications in "To His Coy Mistress." The lines are

26. *The Adventures of Five Hours* (London: for Henry Herringman, 1663), 2. The play was adapted from Antonio Coello's *Los empeños de seis horas*.
27. *Whore's Rhetorick*, 221.
28. *Albino and Bellama*, 72.

spoken by Arbaces (the king who is not a king) and his father Gobrius concerning the incarceration of the Princess Panthea:

> *Arb.* She is in prison, Gobrius, is she not?
> *Gob.* She is, sir, till your pleasure do enlarge her,
> Which on my knees I beg. Oh, 'tis not fit
> That all the sweetness of the world in one,
> The youth and virtue that would tame wild tigers
> And wilder people that have known no manners,
> Should live thus cloister'd up.[29]

Finally, one might cite the popular old *chansons de nonnes,* which often had depicted the cloister as both grave and prison. "All over western and southern Europe," writes Eileen Power, "this theme was set to music, now with gaiety and insouciance, now with bitterness."[30] And among other samples she cites:

> Mariez-vous, les filles,
> Avec ces bons drilles,
> Et n'allez jà, les filles,
> Pourrir derrièr' les grilles.[31]

Marvell's knowledge of such matters need not have been extensive, but we should bear in mind that he thought and wrote about nuns in "Appleton House" because the home of his patron, Thomas Lord Fairfax, stood at Appleton on the grounds of an old Cistercian priory some nine miles from York. Nearly four hundred years old at the time of its dissolution in 1539, Nun Appleton had been one of the largest of ten Cistercian nunneries in Yorkshire—where the Cistercians were more firmly entrenched than anywhere else in England. Presumably the Cistercians were contemplative, committed to silence and abstinence, and cloistered with unusual strictness. It was claimed that "the Cister-

---

29. *A King and No King,* ed. Robert K. Turner, Jr. (Lincoln: University of Nebraska Press, 1963), 4.2.195–201.

30. Power, *Medieval English Nunneries c. 1275 to 1535* (Cambridge: Cambridge University Press, 1922), 504. See also Graciela S. Daichman, *Wayward Nuns in Medieval Literature* (Syracuse: Syracuse University Press, 1986).

31. Power here quotes Jerome Bujeaud, *Chants et chansons populaires des provinces de l'Ouest,* 2 vols. (Niort, 1865–1866). The lines may be loosely translated:

> Get married, girls,
> To these good fellows,
> And never go, girls,
> To rot behind grates.

cians were so closely immured that . . . no bird could pierce the closures."[32] From various injunctions that survive, nonetheless, it appears that during certain periods, "there were no more quarrelsome nunneries in the kingdom" than those in Yorkshire.[33] Worse, it was necessary to issue repeated warnings to the nuns "That no Sister bring in any Man, religious or secular, into their Chamber or any secret place day or night, &c."[34] Whether the clouded record of the Yorkshire nunneries may be traced mainly to the Scottish invasions, the boarding of secular women, the acceptance of too many girls with no sense of vocation, or some other cause, we need not attempt to decide. Suffice it to say that, like some other idealistic institutions, convents usually fell short of their goals, and falling rather shorter than most were the convents in Marvell's own Yorkshire.

To protect the nuns of any convent from the outside world (from "those wild Creatures, called Men"), safeguards of various sorts were required, and naturally these included the installation of iron grates. Wherever else they might prove useful, grates were a necessity for separating nuns from outsiders in the convent parlor. *The Rewle of Sustris Menouresses Enclosid* affords us a glimpse of how the device worked:

> Neuerþeles whan any of þe Sustris wole confesse her, bi þe perloure make her confessioun in privite alone to one. . . . None of hem schal speke bi þe grate of yryn bi þe whiche þey schullin be huslid & here diuine office & sermones, but be auenture þat it be for cause resonable & necessarie & wiþ compani. . . . This grate of yren be hanging wiþin a blacke cloþe, so þat bi resoun none suster may be seyne þer þorw & þat none bodi may see none þinge wiþ inne . . . & þis gratis schullyn haue doris of yren bund & naylid whoche schall be alwey closid.

The passage even goes on to suggest how communion could be administered despite such impediments:

> Allegatis in one of þe sydis of þe forseyde grate be a smalle wyndow I-made wiþ a goget of yrin, bi þe whiche þe preest, whan he schal heue vp his honde, may mynistre to þe Sustris goddis bodi,

32. Mackenzie E. C. Walcott, *Church Work and Life in English Minsters* (London: Chatto and Windus, 1879), 2:24. Other sources include John Burton, *Monasticon Eboracense* (York, 1758), George Lawton, *The Religious Houses of Yorkshire* (London: Simpkin, 1853), J. S. Fletcher, *The Cistercians in Yorkshire* (London: Macmillan, 1919), and David Knowles and R. Neville Hadcock, *Medieval Religious Houses: England and Wales* (New York: St. Martin's, 1971).
33. *Medieval English Nunneries*, 597.
34. William Dugdale, *Monasticon Anglicanum* (1693), 107.

and þat none bodi may putte his honde wiþinne þe grate be ani partie of þe grate. And þe forseyde goget alwey schal be closid wiþ two keyis.[35]

Iron grates, in short, were an integral part of convent life.

Strong as they might be, however, such barriers sometimes proved insufficient to the task assigned them. "In the sixteenth, seventeenth and eighteenth centuries," writes Power, "the convents of France and Italy were the haunts of young gallants, *monachini*, who specialised in intrigues with nuns."[36] Since archival history furnishes many references to such convents and lovers, it is no surprise that other kinds of writings do likewise, and in the process provide some references to grates. Here is Whiting again, this time describing the moments immediately after his heroine has been initiated into nunnery life:

> These rites perform'd, behinde an iron grate
> Appeared breathing cowles, and walking copes.[37]

Nor is this smirking indirection allowed to remain obscure: there is never any doubt here that "a Nun without a man, is more than rare." In contrast, and slightly closer to life, Killigrew's heroine in *Thomaso II* is dismayed at the thought of being placed in a convent: "A Monastery! I am like to make a good Nun, this passion is an excellent ingredient for a Grate."[38] His Edwardo vows, "I had as li[e]ve take her as a Cag'd Nymph, a mew'd Maid from a Grate in a Nunnery that acts what she can, and wishes the rest; whose Maiden-head is a prisoner at the best." And expressing his own brand of Cavalier cynicism, Killigrew has Thomaso himself exclaim of nuns, "'tis not honour, nor conscience binds; double grates can only keep them from breaking of their vows." A somewhat similar but more figurative reference occurs in Margaret Cavendish's strange closet drama called *The Religious* (1658), where a conversation spoken by Lord Melancholy "*as at the Grate of the Cloyster of the Lady* Perfection" leads to one of the more striking stage directions of the period. In a sort of would-be *Liebestod*, "*Whilst he speaks, he puts one end of the Sword through the Grate,* [and] *she takes hold of it.*"[39]

There are also references to the singing of bawdy and erotic songs at

---

35. *Two Fifteenth-Century Franciscan Rules*, ed. Walter W. Seton, Early English Text Society, O.S. 148 (London: Kegan Paul, 1914), 88–89.
36. *Medieval English Nunneries*, 446.
37. *Albino and Bellama*, 31, 103.
38. *Comedies and Tragedies*, 403, 453, 458.
39. *Playes* (London: for John Martyr, James Allestry, and Tho. Dicas, 1662), 550, 553.

the grates, to meetings of novices with monks at the grates, and to mock marriages between nuns and friars at the grates. With participants on opposite sides, the grates are said, understandably, to have made sexual intercourse difficult. Roger Thompson retells one story about a certain Abbess, known as the "Patroness of the lascivious Knights of the Grille," who encounters notably bad luck with one of her clients.[40] It seems that in his amorous heats—or what, borrowing from Marvell, one might term "rough strife"—this "over-ardent visitor wrenched away part of the grille only to become embarrassingly stuck as he tried to wriggle through to his beloved." Such a story from the later seventeenth century is striking and useful on its own, surely, but its force is strengthened when one recalls that it is something of a reincarnation three centuries later of that fourteenth-century picture of the noble Launcelot tearing his way through iron grates in order to be with *his* beloved. In any case, it should be clear that the iron grates of a convent constitute a multifaceted symbol that probably should be considered as we reflect on the gate/grate crux and "That long preserv'd Virginity" mentioned in "To His Coy Mistress."

The promised appendage to these remarks on grates and the cloistered life concerns tennis. Any student of the English Renaissance is likely to recall encountering occasional comparisons of life to a tennis game. Because the drama itself is studied so frequently, the most famous of these may be that in *The Duchess of Malfi*, where Bosola says, "We are merely the stars' tennis-balls, struck and banded / Which way please them" (5.4.54–55). Another well-known example occurs in Peacham's *Minerva Britanna* (see Fig. 2). Comparisons of life to a tennis game go back, in fact, to what may be the first mention of tennis in English—in a poem by Gower to Henry IV: "Of the Tenetz to winne or lese a chace, / Mai no lif wite er that the bal be ronne" (ll. 295–96).[41] Contrarily, knowing that the indoor tennis courts in Renaissance England were always painted black (in 1653 Henry More wrote that the uvea of the human eye "is *black'd* like the wals of a Tennis-court"),[42] one might suppose them capable on occasion of suggesting the dark enclosure of a tomb. It is neither the game/life metaphor nor the color of the court

40. *Unfit for Modest Ears* (Totowa, N.J.: Rowman and Littlefield, 1979), 152.

41. "In Praise of Peace," *The English Works of John Gower*, ed. G. C. Macaulay, Early English Text Society, no. 82 (London: Oxford University Press, 1901; rpt. 1957), 2:490. See Joseph Strutt, *The Sports and Pastimes of the People of England*, ed. J. Charles Cox (London: Methuen, 1903; reissued Detroit: Singing Tree, 1968), 83.

42. *An Antidote Against Atheisme* (1653), 95. See Julian Marshall, *The Annals of Tennis* (London: "The Field" Office, 1878; rpt. Baltimore: Racquet Sports Information, 1973), 83.

Fig. 2
A tennis ball as an emblem of life, from Henry Peacham's *Minerva Britanna*, 113. Courtesy of the Rare Book Department, Perkins Library, Duke University.

that now earns them a moment of our attention, however, so much as a feature of their architecture.

The earliest references to tennis—that is, to the indoor game known in England as "real tennis" and in France as "*jeu de paume*" (the play of the palm)—come from France. There, beginning apparently in the twelfth century, they occur in certain ecclesiastical writings that report the popularity of the game among those with a religious vocation, especially in the major training centers toward which youth tended to gravitate. In various monasteries the courtyard within the cloister served sometimes as a playground. Students of the early history of tennis usually write on the subject with seemly scholarly reserve, for the matter is murky, but most are inclined to link tennis with medieval French monasteries and to point out that tennis still comes to us trailing numerous French terms (for instance, *tambour, dedans*, and *bandeau*), the most pertinent of which at the moment is *grille*.[43] According to Randle Cotgrave's *Dictionary* (1611), a grille is simply *"An Iron grate."*

Whether or not the tennis term *grille* may be traced to a grated window overlooking a monastery cloister or simply to any grated window is more than anyone now knows. Beyond doubt, however, it came to be the name for one of the window-sized openings on the hazard side of a Renaissance tennis court. Though individual courts seem always to have differed from one another in variable ways, all have some ingeniously calculated hazards that offer opportunities for a wide variety of strokes. To play the game well, therefore, "experience and subtlety of tactics count for as much as youth and physical fitness."[44] In particular, the back wall on the hazard side (as opposed to the serving side) of the court is known as the grille wall because at this end there is a more or less square opening about three feet by three feet called the grille (see Figs. 3 and 4). Positioned approximately three and a half feet above the floor, this hazard is nowadays framed in wood and backed by wood. The term *grille*, however, is itself sufficient evidence that in early times this hazard was made of iron.

Granted all this, we should know, too, that across the Channel in England *le jeu de paume* entered its "great days" (the phrase is Lord Aberdare's) in the time of Henry VII (who played at Woodstock, Wy-

43. See Clarence Bruce, Lord Aberdare, *The Story of Tennis* (London: Stanley Paul, 1959), 12. One authority on the history of tennis, Albert de Luze, author of *La Magnifique Histoire du Jeu de Paume* (Paris: Bossard, 1933), writes, "La grille, comme son nom l'indique, et comme en font foi les vieilles estampes, était autrefois grillégée" (243). See also Pierre Etchebaster, *Pierre's Book: The Game of Court Tennis*, ed. George Plimpton (Barre, Mass.: Barre Publishers, 1971), xi.

44. John Arlott, ed., *The Oxford Companion to World Sports and Games* (Oxford: Oxford University Press, 1975), 821.

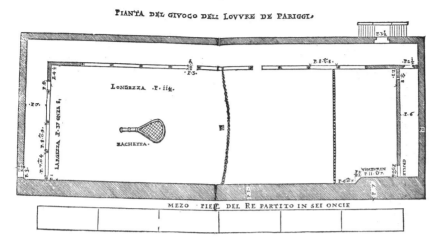

Fig. 3
Floor plan showing placement of grille wall and grille (*lower
right*) in a Renaissance tennis court. From Antonio Scaino,
Trattato del Givoco della Palla di Messer (Venice, 1555), 164–65.
By permission of The Folger Shakespeare Library.

Fig. 4
A tennis grille as depicted in Gatien Courtilz de Sandras,
Memoires de Monsieur de Montbrun (Amsterdam, 1701), facing 149.
By permission of The Folger Shakespeare Library.

combe, Westminster, Sheen, and Windsor).[45] By the time of Elizabeth, one authority observes, "It was . . . the amusement, if not the occupation of all young men of any leisure or wealth."[46] Subsequently, in *Basilikon Doron* (1603), King James commended tennis to Prince Henry, and later he hired a tennis tutor for Prince Charles.[47] Charles seems to have long retained a liking for the game, and was in fact playing tennis at Oxford with Prince Rupert in late December of 1642 when he received Parliament's articles of accommodation. England's next two kings, Charles II and James II, also played the game, Charles II proving a particularly keen sportsman (he kept a spare bed at the tennis court). Nor should one infer from all this that tennis was confined to royalty. John Earle, in his much-read *Micro-cosmographie* (1628), characterizes thus "A young Gentleman of the University": "The two markes of his Seniority, is the bare Veluet of his gowne, and his proficiencie at Tennis."[48] And Mary Palmer, who claimed to be the widow of Andrew Marvell, was actually the widow of a tennis court keeper.[49]

Although it should be plain by now that I wish to invoke multiple possibilities in "To His Coy Mistress" rather than to provide surefire answers, I nevertheless hope that in an age when some readers can associate Marvell's "gates" with an iron river-mouth or with iron labia, others will be willing to consider my next observations. First, that in tennis the phrase "faire un coup de grille" means to strike a ball into the grille. Second, that a ball driven into the grille during play wins the point automatically. And third, that the recurring seventeenth-century image of a bandied tennis ball that is like human life takes on a new quality in connection with Marvell's poem if we can conceive of the lovers as at first playing their long game of courtship mechanically and according to the rules, but at last striking their ball into the grille with such force that it is held fixed, the merely routine game-playing stopped, and the hazardous opportunity for a better game made possible.[50]

45. Aberdare, *Story,* 47. See also Dennis Brailsford, *Sport and Society: Elizabeth to Anne* (London: Routledge and Kegan Paul, 1969).

46. Marshall, *Annals,* 70.

47. James I, *Basilikon Doron* (Edinburgh, 1603), 121; Frederick Devon, *Issues of the Exchequer . . . During the Reign of King James I* (London: John Rodwell, 1836), 116.

48. *Micro-cosmographie,* E5r-v.

49. Fred S. Tupper, "Mary Palmer, Alias Mrs. Andrew Marvell," *PMLA* 53 (1938): 371.

50. If one prefers to think of the lovers as being on opposite sides of the grille (as in the "convent model"), the speaker may be imagined on the outside, asking that the lady turn to more serious play. But if this is the case, with whom is she presently playing? With any simile or metaphor ("O my luve is like a red, red rose"), one needs to know when to stop asking questions.

I am not suggesting that we jettison readings that approach the ball in Marvell's poem as Plato's hermaphroditic spherical union of lovers; or as two lovers' bodies intertwined in the act of love; or as an embodiment of the Renaissance idea that a sphere represents eternity or perfection; or as a sort of explosive, military-amorous cannonball.[51] In fact, pursuing this last possibility in view of my earlier suggestion that grates may be portcullis-like, one well may think of the ball as bursting through seemingly impregnable iron defenses. In "Appleton House," which has other points of contact with "To His Coy Mistress," we certainly find Marvell writing of cannon in terms of love (sighs there are "Loves Cannon charg'd with wind" [716]), and of the nuns' militant resistance to young Fairfax's storming of the Nun Appleton nunnery (the women's "lowd'st Cannon were their Lungs" [255]). In "On the Victory Obtained by Blake," furthermore, the striking verb "tears" is precisely that which Marvell chooses to describe the power of real cannonballs ("Our Cannon now tears every Ship and Sconce" [149]). Viewing the grates in "To His Coy Mistress" as a portcullis, then, or simply as portcullis-like, one may find validity in the cannonball reading.

But if the grates of the poem are also suggestive of the grates of a tennis court, and if a tennis game may be paralleled to life, it becomes possible to think in terms of a tennis ball that in the midst of strenuous play has suddenly encountered the delimiting hazard of iron bars. And it *does* take two to play thus hard. As Thomas Elyot wrote of tennis back in 1531, if "one stryke the balle harde, the other that intendeth to receyue him, is than constrained to vse semblable violence."[52] Furthermore, a "tennis reading" of "Coy Mistress" is the more attractive insofar as it recognizes an everyday seventeenth-century conjunction of a ball with an iron object (as few readings do), and insofar as we find it supported by a feeling of serious play throughout the poem (most clearly in the nicely complex admonition, "Now let us sport us while we may" [37]).

Even though one has at hand various reasonable readings of the

51. Explanations with which I am uncomfortable, however, include interpreting the ball as a pomander, sweetmeat ball, pair of copulating birds, phoenix egg, and egg of Egyptian scarab laid in a ball of dung. R. L. Brett offers one of the most ingenious suggestions: the ball recalls the Yorkshire "custom of tying up the church gates after a wedding and demanding 'ball-money' from the bridal couple before they were allowed through" (8–9). Somewhat dampening is the fact that mere money was thrown through the gates—though it was to be spent on a parish football ("Andrew Marvell: The Voice of His Age," *Critical Quarterly* 20 [1978]: 8–9).

52. Elyot, *The Boke Named the Governour* (1531), 99r. Robert Howlet also writes of the "Violence of its Exercise" (*The School of Recreation* [1696], 96).

"Ball" that is presumed to move through the "grates of Life," one should be cautious about wholehearted acceptance of any one of them alone. The facts are that the ball is an imaginative construct that is unlikely to have any single, concrete referent, and it functions as part of a kaleidoscope of interrelated metaphors. Any effort to reify mechanically what Marvell has created metaphorically is not merely an effort to stabilize what cannot be stabilized, but a threat to destroy the very richness that has drawn readers to the poem. Far from calling in the votes for cannonball or tennis ball, therefore, or for any other sort of ball, I would urge that we simultaneously entertain the possibilities afforded by those various readings to which we may give thoughtful credence.

So it is also with the chief subject of this essay. I have tried to suggest here that the image of iron grates is richly connotative. Moreover, whatever blended hints this image may impart of castle, tomb, prison, cage, trap, convent, or even game court, all will seem the stronger if they illuminate the poem in ways that are consonant both with Marvell's time and the reader's own.

Obviously every life has restricting, nay-saying, pleasure-thwarting iron grates that figuratively parallel those that literally restrict prisoners and nuns. That is to say (with Lovelace), it is not necessarily walls of stone that constitute a prison, "Nor I'ron bars a Cage" (ll. 25–26).[53] In "Daphnis and Chloe," as we have seen, Marvell suggests that nature itself may sometimes be blamed ("Nature, her own Sexes foe, / Long had taught her to be coy" [5–6]). Furthermore, it does my argument no harm that Marvell himself elsewhere chooses to write of thwarted love in connection with iron impediments. The lover-speaker of "The Definition of Love" tells how Fate has driven "Iron wedges" (11) which prevent him from proceeding to that infinitely desirable place where his "extended Soul is fixt" (10). Fate does what it can to prevent the "union" of these "Two perfect Loves" (13–15), in fact issues divisive "Decrees of Steel" (17). In this poem, Marvell writes, because "Fate . . . enviously *debarrs*" (30, emphasis added) the lovers, they will remain separated forever—unless

<hr/>

53. "To Althea, from Prison," *The Poems of Richard Lovelace*, ed. C. H. Wilkinson (1930; rpt. Oxford: Clarendon Press, 1968), 79. Cf. the statement of James Carscallen that "the power of things not physically powerful is one of his favourite themes" ("Marvell's Infinite Parallels," *University of Toronto Quarterly* 39 [1970]: 147). Cf. also the image used by Timothy Perper in writing of the 1980s: "Even in a modern world of seeming promiscuity, it remains easy to speak of the repression of sexuality and to see the iron hand of tradition laying itself on the shoulders of the lovers to remind them that . . . they really shouldn't" (*Sex Signals* [Philadelphia: ISI Press, 1985], 113).

> Earth some new Convulsion tear;
> And, us to joyn, the World should all
> Be cramp'd into a *Planisphere.*
>
> (22–24)

Here is not only the subject of lovers joining and the eye-catching verb "tear" used in conjunction with explosive force, but also the concept of a large world that, far from swelling larger, may be squashed. In "The Definition of Love" as in "To His Coy Mistress," it is only an extraordinary event that will enable the lovers to conquer the iron barriers that separate them.

Whether the iron barriers of life be imposed by victims themselves, by others, by the society of which all are a part, or by fate or nature, we always have them with us. Whether they conquer us or we conquer them is the question. Marvell's speaker in "To His Coy Mistress" is urgently informing his lady that despite what she may think, she has a choice. In a way, he is answering the anguished query of Bianca in John Ford's *Loves Sacrifice* (1632):

> why should the laws
> The Iron lawes of Ceremony, barre
> Mutuall embraces?[54]

Breaking those laws, of course, inevitably has its costs. It is conventional wisdom that "pleasure must bee purchased with the price of paine."[55] As is true, furthermore, of any convent, cage, or prison, there is life of some sort on both sides of the iron barrier. And yet obviously the freer and fuller life lies outside. Passing through the grates, Marvell's speaker implies, will somehow lead to a different and better kind of life, specifically in this case to ecstatic union with a lover. Some readers have thought that to tear one's way through the "g(r)ates of Life" in Marvell's poem is to die. As Lawrence W. Hyman puts it, "The intensity of the physical union . . . leads to death—in both senses of the word."[56] However, the phrase surely draws some of its strength from the very fact of its bracing opposition to the more usual, in fact prover-

---

54. *Loves Sacrifice* (1633), I4r.

55. George Pettie, *A Petite Pallace of Pettie His Pleasure,* ed. Herbert Hartman (London: Oxford University Press, 1938), 107.

56. "Marvell's 'Coy Mistress' and Desperate Lover," *MLN* 75 (1960): 10. The most persuasive statements I have seen of this position are in Alan J. Peacock, "Marvell: *To His Coy Mistress* 41–6," *Hermathena* 114 (1972): 29–30; and Michael Craze, *The Life and Lyrics of Andrew Marvell* (London: Macmillan, 1979), 325–27. Nevertheless, the poem seems to me more life-embracing than death-embracing.

bial, "gates of death." There is always death to come, of course (ahead lie whole "Desarts of vast Eternity" [24]), but the grates of Marvell's poem are best seen as exemplary of such here-and-now life-denying forces that always separate the living from the partly living. The truly living lovers, arriving at intense joy through physical union (the lady's body speaks "At every pore with instant Fires" [36]), may partake of a surpassing state that, for the moment at least, appears to transcend ordinary physical life and yet at the same time to depend upon it.

In other words, the mistress's coyness, which certainly and specifically is a crime ("Had we but World enough, and Time, / This coyness Lady were no crime"), is a self-defeating defense that threatens to lead to her permanent imprisonment (or cloistering or entombment) while yet she lives. And, of course, it threatens also to deny full life to her lover. I find it a major paradox of the poem that the lady will be guilty of some sort of crime whether she continues to waste time and her lover by being coy or, instead, violates those codes that prescribe coyness. More important here, however, is the fact that the lady's coyness may itself be perceived in two distinct yet related ways. If one accept the fact that grates in their many manifestations are generally impediments of some sort; and if one accept the fact that in Marvell's poem the grates are grates (or impediments) "of Life"; and if one accept the fact that the speaker targets the lady's "coyness" as the chief impediment of the moment, then it follows that the coyness is probably not only (1) the crime of the lady, but also (2) the chief present example of life-impedance. That is, coyness and grates are for the moment the same, and the singer's song at its end echoes the elements with which it began—thus making the poem even a little more unified and coherent than we have previously perceived. The "World" that is introduced at the beginning is echoed at the end by a sort of microcosmic lovers' "Ball"; the "Time" which at the beginning is vast but not vast enough is at the end about to be mastered by the cooperatively sporting lovers; and the conventional time-and-world-wasting "coyness" of the lady, which from the outset is recognized by the wittily complaining lover as too restrictive, is figured at the end as "Iron grates" that must be burst through if the lovers are not to continue merely languishing and pining, gradually chewed to death by Time.

Whereas the phrase "Iron *gates* of Life" is always read as referring to an ecstatic way into or out of life, the phrase "Iron *grates* of Life," which conveys the roughness of the passage "Thorough" to the lover's goal, also images forcefully the frustrating obstacles that love is heir to. Like those "Iron lawes of Ceremony" that "barre / Mutuall embraces" in Ford's play, the iron grates of "To His Coy Mistress" must be blasted, destroyed, torn through if the lovers are ever really to love and live fully. Only when such an ecstatic breakthrough is accomplished will both man and woman become masters rather than victims of Time, seizing the day and infusing it with their own creative vitality. Only then will they be able to say—as Jonson says in *Time Vindicated*—

> *Betweene us it shall be no strife:*
> *For now 'tis* Love, *gives* Time *his life.*
>   (ll. 340–41)[57]

Only if and when that much-desired consummation is achieved will the lover-speaker and echoing singer of "To His Coy Mistress" be able at last to exult with Ovid:

> carminibus cessere fores, insertaque posti,
>   quamvis robur erat, carmine victa sera est.
>   (*Amores*, 2.1.27–28)

---

57. *Time Vindicated* in *Ben Jonson*, ed. C. H. Herford and Percy and Evelyn Simpson, 11 vols. (Oxford: Clarendon Press, 1941), 7:666.

Joan Hartwig

Tears as a Way of Seeing

MARVELL ENIGMATICALLY elicits satisfaction with frustration. After the reader struggles with one of his poems and determines upon a reading that seems to make sense, a retrospective glance changes the perspective, and the words take on new meaning. Working with conventional images, emblems, and ideas, Marvell turns them inside out in order to look at the fusedness, the nondualistic nature of things. The limbec of his alchemy is ambiguity, punning, a verging on the literal and metaphysical at the same time. His poetic tone is usually impersonal, distanced by comic perceptions of the incongruency of human nature that wishes to idealize the literal and to literalize the ideal. Although object and subject appear to be different, Marvell's poetic methods present a puzzle that perplexes the rational mind and opens an understanding that object and subject are the same. In addition to "Eyes and Tears," this essay examines parts of other Marvell poems that are related both in content and in method: "The Garden," "On a Drop of Dew," "Mourning," and "The Nymph Complaining for the Death of her *Faun*."

"Eyes and Tears" is a perplexing poem in its metaphors and in their implications. The reader must fight through a thick layer of suggestive playfulness to discover an underlying unity of metaphor as Marvell's poem celebrates tears generically (in its imitation of an established genre) and genetically (in exploring the origin of tears), at the same time it suggests that its hyperbolic extravagances are precisely that.

The liquid drop, both as tear and as dew, has a long and labyrinthine tradition prior to Marvell's use of the image. Louis Martz examines Robert Southwell's introduction of the "literature of tears" into England in "Saint Peter's Complaint" and the prose meditation, *Marie Magdalens Funeral Teares*, and some shorter poems on both subjects. Robert Southwell's prose meditation was first published in 1591 and, despite the author's execution for his activities as a Roman Catholic priest in February 1595, saw seven more editions in London by 1636 and two editions on the Continent. The following passage in praise of the

Magdalen's tears contains much of the imagery that Marvell and other seventeenth-century poets explored later:

> But feare not *B. Mary,* for thy teares will obtaine. They are too mighty oratours, to let any suite fall, and though they pleaded at the most rigorous barre, yet haue they so persuading a silence, and so conquering a complaint that by yeelding they ouercome, and by intreating they com[m]aund. They tie the tongues of all accurses, and soften the rigour of the seuerest Iudge. . . . Repentant eyes are the cellers of Angels, & penitent teares their sweetest wines, which the sauour of life perfumeth, the tast of grace sweetneth, and the purest colours of returning innocency highly beautifieth. This *dew of deuotion neuer fayleth, but the sunne of justice draweth it vp,* and vpon what face soeuer it droppeth, it maketh it amiable in Gods eye. *For this water hath thy hart been long a limbecke, sometimes distilling it* out of the weeds of thy owne offences with the fire of true contrition. . . . the Angels must still bath themselues in *the pure streames of thy eyes,* and thy face shall still be set with *this liquid pearle,* that as out of thy teares, were stroken the first sparkes of thy Lords loue, so thy teares may be the oyle, to nourish and feed his flame.[1]

Richard Crashaw's "Weeper" (drawing upon Southwell and upon Marinistic imagery)[2] is clearly in the background of Marvell's "Eyes and Tears," and it takes the foreground in stanza 8, a stanza which Marvell wrote first in Latin:

> Magdala, *lascivos sic quum dimisit Amantes,*
>   *Fervidaque in castas lumina solvit aquas;*
> *Haesit in irriguo lachrymarum compede* Christus,
>   *Et tenuit sacros uda Catena pedes.*

> So *Magdalen,* in Tears more wise
>   Dissolv'd those captivating Eyes,
> Whose liquid Chaines could flowing meet
>   To fetter her Redeemers feet.

> (29–32)

1. *S. Peters Complaint and Saint Marie Magdalens Funeral Teares 1616,* ed. D. M. Rogers (Menston, Eng.: Scolar Press, 1971), 137–39, italics my emphasis. See Louis L. Martz, *The Poetry of Meditation* (New Haven: Yale University Press, 1962), 12, 119–210.
    2. See Ruth C. Wallerstein, *Richard Crashaw: A Study in Style and Poetic Development* (Madison: University of Wisconsin Press, 1962), 98–109, for a discussion of the resemblances between Crashaw and Marino. Also see Donald M. Friedman, *Marvell's Pastoral Art* (Berkeley and Los Angeles: University of California Press, 1970), 46–47.

Critics have generally recognized the centrality of this stanza in Marvell's poem, but they have not always considered the completeness with which it informs and unites the other stanzas. Lawrence Hyman's comment on the general structure and tone of the poem introduces one of its perceived problems:

> There is . . . a lack of connection in Marvell's "Eyes and Tears" between the separate stanzas. Instead of carrying through the implications of a powerful image, this poem allows each comparison to stand by itself and thus gives us an impression of light, rapid thought instead of strong feeling.[3]

The evaluation that there is a lack of connection between stanzas holds only at the most literal level. At the level of "wit" or intellectual organization several themes join the conceits, and the most consistent of these is the mercantile exchange of values couched in the terminology of the marketplace. Harold Toliver objects that "the early stanzas weigh the price of joys with perhaps too much calculation,"[4] but he fails to notice that the next to last stanza is equally calculating in its precise measuring of the different forms of weeping:

> Now like two Clouds dissolving, drop,
> And at each Tear in distance stop:
> Now like two Fountains trickle down:
> Now like two floods o'return and drown.
>
> (49–52)

To keep each tear "in distance" as it falls and to "stop" each one precisely at specified intervals of space take great control.[5] Although the progressive abundance of tears is clear, the cool precision of marking off the stages from drop, to trickle, to floods suggests also great calculation within the process of weeping itself.

Each stanza carries equal, consistent expression of calculation in mercantile exchange concerning the matters of tears and valuation of the world's objects. Marvell uses images, emblems, and metaphors throughout the poem as subtle connectors to develop a meaning that is larger than a synopsis or a sum of the poem's parts can be. His choice of the Magdalen as a center for this poem of evaluation of what the eye

---

3. *Andrew Marvell* (New York: Twayne, 1964), 47.
4. *Marvell's Ironic Vision* (New Haven: Yale University Press, 1965), 85.
5. See definitions 5 and 9 for "distance," *OED*, 1971: "space between ranks" and "at a specified interval of space *in distance*."

can see through tears is not merely fashionable. Throughout the history of the Magdalen's image in both art and literature, as Marjorie M. Malvern points out, there is a fine balance between seriousness and jest, which allows the *homo ludens* (she adopts this phrase from Johan Huzinga) to perceive the chaste prostitute as reclaimer of a dying world.[6] Marvell's voice in this poem, as in so many of his lyrics, speaks in that delicately balanced tone between jest and seriousness.

The first stanza affirms the wisdom of Nature in decreeing that the same organ should "weep and see," an economic (in the sense that one organ does the work of two) as well as a metaphysically wise decree. When the eye sees the world's objects as vain and so is moved to weep, how frugal it is for the same organ to function as seer and responder to what is seen. Without having to resort to another agent of perception, the eyes are "ready" to weep at the world's vanity because weeping is a function of the eyes. The eyes can fulfill their function immediately—they see vanity, they weep. There is no need to have the mind interfere in the process with thinking such as, "The object is 'vain'; vanity is emptiness; therefore the eye should weep for the object's worthlessness."

The poet sets up a rational hypothesis: the eye sees, the eye weeps; therefore how apt that Nature should have decreed that the eye should see the world's vanity and weep for it, without requiring an intermediary function such as reason to grasp a cause to produce the effect. In other words, intuitive expression supersedes cause-and-effect rationality.

Sight alone, without the tears, is "Self-deluding," as the second stanza states. These lines likewise are concerned with correct evaluation and measurement, although they use an image of surveying[7] to express how tears rectify what is seen:

> And, since the Self-deluding Sight,
> In a false Angle takes each hight;
> These Tears which better measure all,
> Like wat'ry Lines and Plummets fall.
>
> (5–8)

---

6. *Venus in Sackcloth: The Magdalen's Origins and Metamorphoses* (Carbondale and Edwardsville: Southern Illinois University Press, 1975), 180: "For *homo ludens*, seeking to affirm simultaneously the continued blossoming of the 'vines' from generation to generation and the value of human life by preserving in his cosmogony ancient personifications of love and wisdom, works on the borderline between jest and earnest as he creates, with no malicious intent, the Athene-Venus-Magdalen."

7. Friedman, *Marvell's Pastoral Art*, 47, observes: "'Angle' can be simply a line of observation—as in the use of a sextant or astrolabe—or it can refer to the astrological 'house' from which the elevation of a heavenly body, or 'hight', is measured."

Tears have become an instrument to establish accurate measurements. What initially appears to the naked eye as level but is not, when measured by a plumb line can be corrected to its proper line, or angle, for balance.[8] In stanza 3, the words "weigh," "scales," "paid," and "price" are more explicitly of the marketplace than any of the poem's terms to this point. Even though these words are literally of the marketplace, they also connect with the world of emblems (Fig. 1), where such images are commonplace.[9] They prepare us for reading the next stanza's consummation of the drive toward mercantilistic calculation by expanding the literal toward the metaphysical valuation:

> What in the World most fair appears,
> Yea even Laughter, turns to Tears:
> And all the Jewels which we prize,
> Melt in these Pendants of the Eyes.
> (13–16)

True market value "in the World" can be seen only through the literal distortion of the world's objects by tears. With the punctuation after the word "Laughter," the words imply that even laughter causes the eyes to weep. As usual with Marvell, the apparent simplicity of language and syntax dissolves in ambiguity.

In one reading, the pleasure evoked by the fairest objects, which may cause laughter, ultimately produces tears, and these tears are enhancers of the object's fair value. In another, laughter itself "appears fair" in contrast to sorrow, which is usually associated with tears, but even the fair laughter "turns to tears." Yet the proverbial discrepancy between fair appearance and ugly reality implicit in the words turns upon itself because tears are the alembic that makes even the "fair appearing" fair in essence. The tears melt the objects seen as precious into jewels of a greater price, and the literal tears themselves become the pendants, the suspended ornaments imbued with grace.[10] In the melting is not a disappearance of this world's objects, however, but a fusion of this world and one that can be perceived through it. They exist simultaneously and in each other.

As illustration of the emblematic associations suggested by the poem, consider Henry Peacham's "*Hei mihi quod vidi*" with its weeping

8. The modern carpenter's level checks the eye's vision by balancing the bubble, an appropriate analogy to Marvell's plumb line teardrop.

9. See, for example, George Wither, "False Weights," *A Collection of Emblemes, Ancient and Moderne (1635)* (Columbia: University of South Carolina Press, 1975), 100.

10. See definition 2 for "pendant," *OED,* 1971.

100

Falſe Weights, *with* Meaſures *falſe eſchew,*
And, give to ev'ry man, their Due.

88

ILLVSTR. XXXVIII.   Book.2

Orth of a *Cloud* (with *Scale* and *Rule*) extended
An *Arme* (for this next *Embleme*) doth appeare;
Which hath to us in *ſilent-ſhowes,* commended,
A *Virtue,* that is often wanting, here.
The World, is very ſtudious of *Deceipts*;
And, he is judged wiſeſt, who deceives.
Falſe-meaſures, and, *Adulterated-weights,*
Of many dues, the needy-man bereaves.'
Ev'n *Weights* to ſell, and, other *Weights* to buy
(*Two ſorts of weights*) in practice are, with ſome;
And, both of theſe, they often falſifie,
That, they to great, and *ſuddaine-wealth,* may come.
   But, Conſcience make of rayſing your eſtates,
By ſuch a baſe, and ſuch a wicked way:
For, this Injuſtice, *God* expreſſely hates;
And, brings, at laſt, ſuch *thrivers* to decay.
By *Weight* and *meaſure,* He, on all beſtowes
The Portions due; That, *Weight* and *Meaſure,* then,
Which Man to *God,* or to his *Neighbour* owes,
Should, juſtly, be returned backe agen.
Give ev'ry one, in ev'ry thing his owne:
Give *honour,* where an *honour* ſhall be due;
Where you are *loved,* let your *love* be ſhowne;
And, yield them ſuccours, who have ſuccour'd you.
Give to thy *Children,* breeding and *Corrections*;
Thy *Charities,* ev'n to thy *Foes* extend:
Give to thy *wife,* the beſt of thy *Affections*;
To *God,* thy *ſelfe,* and, all thou haſt, commend:
And, leſt thou faile, Remember who hath ſayd,
Such meaſure, *as thou giv'ſt, ſhall be repay'd.*

Fig. 1
George Wither, *A Collection of Emblemes, Ancient and
Moderne (1635).* Courtesy of the Renaissance English
Text Society. Reproduction courtesy of the
University of Kentucky Library.

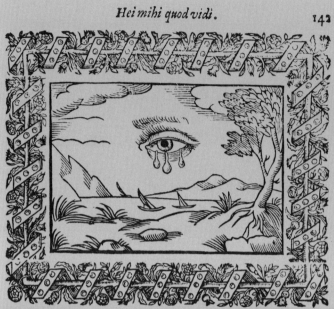

Hei mihi quod vidi.   142

LOOKE how the *Limbeck* gentlie downe diftil's,
    In pearlie drops, his heartes deare quintefcence:
So I, poore Eie, while coldeft forrow fills,
My breft by flames, enforce this moifture thence
    In Chriftall floods, that thus their limits breake,
    Drowning the heart, before the tongue can fpeake.

Great Ladie, Teares haue moou'd the favage feirce,
And wrefted Pittie, from a Tyrants ire:
And drops in time, do hardeft Marble peirce,
But ah I feare me, I too high afpire,
    Then wifh thofe beames, fo bright had never fhin'd,
    Or that thou hadft, beene from thy cradle blind.

Incerti. Exper-
gula Regia:

X I.   *Sic*

Fig. 2
Henry Peacham, *Minerva Britanna* (1612). From the De Capo
Press reprint edition. Reproduction courtesy of the
University of Kentucky Library.

eye set over a lake in which three sailboats appear (Fig. 2).[11] Peacham's emblem voices the conventional Petrarchan complaint, pleading for the Lady to look at the lover and his love with pity, if she be not blind from birth, since tears have moved even the savage beast and the tyrant's anger to pity. Marvell takes the conventional associations and turns them inside out. The tears, at least in stanza 4, are the result of laughter, of feeling pleasure rather than of feeling pain, not from any sense of rejection or deprivation but from a sense of plenitude in this world. Yet the tears turn that fullness into something of greater value, a joy that is unbounded by sorrow because the weeping eye has transformed joy and sorrow into the same feeling.

The "garden" stanza's self-directed irony, "I have through every Garden been," points to an awareness of the pastoral vision in "The Garden," and in contrast to the preceding four stanzas' more generalized observations, it testifies to the speaker's personal experience. The speaker proclaims his experience of the entire world, not only the red and white gardens of sacramental mythology and romance, but also the green garden of the imagination; and the only honey any garden's flower held was drawn off by "these Tears." The syntax of these lines suggests a double meaning: that not only had the tears the power to "draw off" the honey, but also that the only true honey is the tears themselves. Honey, in biblical contexts, suggests both the honeydew of paradise and the manna of sustenance and grace (Exodus 16, John 6), and the colors "red" and "white" reiterate the suggestion of sacramental food.[12] These complex symbolic associations imply that the true and ultimate value, which is heavenly and heaven-sent, can be perceived only through tears, which are typically the sign of humility and repentance. The kind of double meaning contained in the honey attaches itself to almost all of the images of tears in the poem; for example, in stanza 4, the tears transform the world's jewels at the same time they become the true jewels themselves. All of these double values of tears prepare for the final exchange when

> Eyes and Tears be the same things:
> And each the other's difference bears;
> These weeping Eyes, those seeing Tears.
>
> (54–56)

---

11. *Minerva Britanna* (London, 1612), 142. Francis Quarles's more scripturally focused emblem, "O that mine eyes were springs, and could transform / Their drops to seas!", appears in *Francis Quarles: The Complete Prose Works*, ed. Alexander B. Grosart (Hildesheim: Georg Olms, 1971), bk. 3.8.73.

12. George W. Williams, *Image and Symbol in the Sacred Poetry of Richard Crashaw* (Columbia: University of South Carolina Press, 1963), 38–39, 44–45, 101–2.

The "garden" stanza, thus, becomes a fulcrum for the poem's meta-phoric exploration of exchanges that make object and subject the same.

The "all-seeing Sun" of the following stanza makes an exchange with the world each day, distilling "the World with Chymick Ray," and sets up a transformational process by causing the dew to evaporate into a differ-ent form, which then turns into showers. This process Marvell examines more minutely and with different philosophical emphasis in "On a Drop of Dew," but even in that poem the cyclical recurrence of transformations implies a cosmic unity that supports all forms as one despite their appar-ent duality. In distilling the world, the sun finds that its "essence" is only "showers," which "straight in pity back he powers." The rhyme word "powers," spelled as Margoliouth/Legouis spell it, suggests also that a pun on "pours" as an "empowering" agent is at work. (Southwell's spelling of "pours" is "powers" in the second line of "Christ's Bloody Sweat" in the 1595 edition of *Moeoniae*.)[13] The alchemical limbec, the magical process of transubstantiation, the metamorphosis of mundane into heavenly, inform this cyclical process that unites heaven and earth through the emblematic associations of rain (and of dew/manna) with grace. Henry Hawkins's emblem of "The Deaw" in *Partheneia Sacra* (1633) draws these associations together in lines that Marvell probably knew:

> The Deawes are the sugred stillicids of Nature, falling from the Limbeck of the Heauens, as so manie liquid pearls, and euerie pearl as precious as the truest Margarits. . . . They are the verie teares of Nature, dissolued and soft through tendernes, to see the Earth so made a *Libian* Desert, which she supplies of meer compas-sion with the ruine of herself. No teare she sheads, that stands her not in as much, as a drop of her deerest bloud. . . . They are the *Manna* of Nature. . . . And as the showres were wrung and drawne from *Magdalen* through contrition of her sad and clowdie hart: so these *Deawes* are wrung and strained from heauen, through com-pression and mutual collision of the clowds. The Bees are the most laborious and industrious Factours for these Pearls; and they wil venture for them, as farre into the ayre, as any Moor shal diue into the seas for the best pearls. In fine, they are the Milk of Nature, wherewith she is disposed to suckle creatures at her owne breast.[14]

The association of "tears" and "dew" with "grace" is commonplace, as

---

13. This is STC 22954. See *The Poems of Robert Southwell, S.J.*, ed. James H. McDonald and Nancy Pollard Brown (Oxford: Clarendon Press, 1967), 18 n. 2.

14. *Partheneia Sacra (1633)* (Menston, Eng.: Scolar Press, 1971), 59–60. The beautiful eighth stanza of Marvell's "Mourning" echoes the latter lines in Hawkins's emblem. Marvell's last line in this stanza, "And not of one [her tears] the bottom sound," turns the compliment ironically as "sound" opens punningly.

in Shakespeare's familiar lines from Portia's speech in *The Merchant of Venice*, "The quality of mercy . . . droppeth as the gentle rain from heaven" (4.1.182–83) and in some less familiar lines of Richard III's to Queen Elizabeth while wooing her for her daughter—"The liquid drops of tears that you have shed / Shall come again, transformed to orient pearl, / Advantaging their loan with interest / Of ten times double gain of happiness" (4.4.321–24)[15]—as well as in the exchange between Vindice and his mother Gratiana in Cyril Tourneur's *The Revenger's Tragedy*:

> VINDICE.   Pour down, thou blessed dew.—
>   Rise, mother; troth, this shower has made you higher.
> GRATIANA.   O you heavens!
>   Take this infectious spot out of my soul.
>   I'll rinse it in seven waters of mine eyes!
>   Make my tears salt enough to taste of grace:
>   To weep is to our sex naturally given;
>   But to weep truly, that's a gift from heaven.[16]

Marvell's sixth stanza, drawing upon such generally recognized associations, expands upon the poem's opening point that tears are a wise agent for seeing the world.

Playfully expanding upon this notion, stanza 7 generalizes about those grievers who, through weeping, see "less" of the "false angles" of "self-deluding sight":

> Yet happy they whom Grief doth bless,
> That weep the more, and see the less:
> And, to preserve their Sight more true,
> Bath still their Eyes in their own Dew.
>   (25–28)

The tone of this stanza resembles these lines from "The Garden":

> Such was that happy Garden-state,
> While Man there walk'd without a Mate:
> . . . .
> Two Paradises 'twere in one
> To live in Paradise alone.
>   (57–58, 63–64)

15. See Antony Hammond's note, Arden edition, *King Richard III* (London and New York: Methuen, 1981), 289–90, for his use in line 323 of Theobald's emendation "loan" for "love."

16. See notes to lines 48–49, 51–56, 54, on pages 96–97, *The Revenger's Tragedy*, ed. Lawrence J. Ross (Lincoln: University of Nebraska Press, 1966).

Both generalizations paradoxically assert that which is opposed to received valuation: that grief is happiness, that solitude is more blissful than shared love.[17] The outrageousness of the assertion in "Eyes and Tears" is heightened by the fusion of the tears/dew emblematic association into the same eyes. Instead of the tears'/dew's requiring a cyclical process of distillation and shower such as the one that Marvell explores in "On a Drop of Dew," these eyes can produce their own dew without an intermediate step of transformed substance. Or in theological terms, the self is now capable of delivering grace to itself by the process of crying. Their "sight more true" is like the Magdalen's "tears more wise" of the next stanza.

The wisdom of the Magdalen's tears echoes the wisdom of nature from the first stanza, and both wisdoms suggest calculation and manipulation of tears as an instrument of exchange. In order to capture grace for herself, Mary Magdalen wisely "dissolved those captivating eyes" with tears; the eyes are no longer captivating in the "gallant" or "Cavalier" sense, but they are captivating in that they gain the Redeemer's grace and forgiveness. These eyes, which no longer appeal in the visual sense of physical beauty, now show more fair than full sails of a cargo-laden ship hurrying home to unload its riches (a specifically mercantile association); than the chaste lady's pregnant womb (with its suggestion of the Virgin Mary and her womb's inestimable fruit); or than Cynthia's "teeming" full moon. The full sails, full womb, and full moon evoke images appropriate to the concept of fecundity,[18] but the "two Eyes swoln with weeping" to which they are compared and found less "fair" is an impossible image at the literal level, much like Marvell's "vegetable love" in "To His Coy Mistress." The potential puns in these four images further connect what seem to be discrete metaphors. "Sails" were often a euphemism for "harlot" or "whore" in the Renaissance: witness Mercutio's greeting of the Nurse in *Romeo and Juliet* (2.4.96). Mary Magdalen's life before her conversion was that of a prostitute; after she became chaste, her eyes, womblike, issued tears at the

17. See Rosalie L. Colie's discussion of this stanza in "The Garden," *"My Ecchoing Song": Andrew Marvell's Poetry of Criticism* (Princeton: Princeton University Press, 1970), 166–67: "Once more the *faux-naïf* reinterprets a great tradition, this time of Genesis itself, in support of his paradoxical defense of solitude. . . . The Biblical parody, topsy-turviness, and silliness of stanza 8 relies on the knowledge of every civilized man, woman, and child that Adam did not have Eve thrust upon him, but chose to give existence to her."

18. Malvern, *Venus in Sackcloth*, suggests the cultural cross-fertilization between ancient goddesses, like Artemis and Isis, with the Magdalen as Christianity is emerging. Especially interesting regarding Marvell's grouping in this stanza is the association between fertility goddesses of ancient myth and the medieval Magdalen. See 21–22, 31, 169, 170, 177–80.

feet of Christ. The chaste Lady, like Cynthia, the chaste goddess of the moon, teems with fruit as yet unborn. Even without allowing this punning subtext, the Magdalen stanza, so central to "Eyes and Tears" and to the tradition that celebrates weeping, connects all the stanzas of the poem.

"The sparkling Glance that shoots Desire" of stanza 10 may be associated with the Magdalen herself, with those who look upon her, or with anyone who experiences the visual connection between eye and beauty perceived. Petrarchan excesses lurk in the background (tears that cause floods, the fire of desire), and mythological narratives of judgment and punishment through the administering of Zeus's thunderbolt underpin the last two lines. Divine grace "slakes" the destructive lightning bolt in tears that in their abundance have become "waves." Cosmic as well as human fire transforms in this water. The verbal echo connects the Thunderer and the Sun (of stanza 6), as the one "pitty takes" in lessening his wrathful vengeance and as the other "in pity" pours down his graces, and their convergence produces a powerful symbol of universal order: the pagan world (and the wrathful world of the Old Testament), the world of Nature, and the Christian world fuse through the binding power of tears, rain, and dew, which are equivalent products of human and divine sympathy.

The poet's commentary, as he stands back from the poem momentarily to summarize, playfully rewrites assumptions about the workings of the interchange between the mundane and heavenly realms.

> The Incense was to Heaven dear,
> Not as a Perfume, but a Tear.
> And Stars shew lovely in the Night,
> But as they seem the Tears of Light.
> (41–44)

Tears seem to rise to Heaven as easily as the odor of incense. The upward motion, as Donald Friedman points out,[19] is the crucial aspect of the tears' power to please "the gods." Yet this does not explain how the incense became a tear. How does odor become a liquid drop, falling upward?

Crashaw in "The Weeper" describes it this way:

> Upwards thou dost weepe,
> Heavens bosome drinks the gentle streame.
> Where th' milky rivers meet,
> Thine Crawles above and is the Creame.

---

19. *Marvell's Pastoral Art*, 48.

> Heaven, of such faire floods as this,
> Heaven, the Christall Ocean is.[20]

Marvell echoes Crashaw's description in the second stanza of another poem, "Mourning," but he avoids the antigravitational awkwardness:

> Her Eyes confus'd, and doubled ore,
> With Tears suspended ere they flow;
> Seem bending upward, to restore
> To Heaven, whence it came, their Woe.
>
> (5–8)

Marvell resists the literal weeping upward, having Chlora's eyes rather than her tears "bending upward." Nonetheless, in both this stanza from "Mourning" and stanza 11 from "Eyes and Tears" the upward flowing of tears in their "power" seems implicit.

Both couplets in stanza 11 of "Eyes and Tears" use analogy in an unusual way: that is, the unfamiliar term becomes that by which the familiar term is understood. Incense presumably has an odor—a "perfume"—and stars show "lovely in the Night" because they give off light. Yet this incense and these stars are "dear" and "lovely" only insofar as they are, or seem to be, "tears." Tears are the true value that is the referent for what is perceived by analogy. Throughout the poem, Marvell is moving to a physical position that supports his philosophical one—that eyes and tears are the same thing, that heaven and earth are the same thing once seen through the wisdom of tears.

This recognition, however, can be earned only through practice, even as dying well can be achieved only through meditative practice. There is an art of weeping even as there is an art of dying: "ars lachrimandi" and "ars moriendi." Thus, the final stanzas are directives, seemingly to the speaker of the poem.

> Ope then mine Eyes your double Sluice,
> And practise so your noblest Use.

20. This is the first version, 1646, from *The Complete Poetry of Richard Crashaw*, ed. George Walton Williams (Garden City, N.Y.: Anchor Books, 1970), 124. Williams elsewhere, *Image and Symbol*, 100, points out that "the image of the tear falling upward may be a little startling at first, but there are two rich symbolic interpretations to the figure. The first is paradoxical: since Christ's feet actually represent heaven, Mary's tears in falling on them actually are rising. The second interpretation is more meaningful . . . these rising tears [were] a silver stairway to salvation. . . . Like incense of sacrifice or like prayer, these symbols of penance rise heavenward in search of forgiveness."

> For others too can see, or sleep;
> But only humane Eyes can weep.
>   (45–48)

As in other stanzas of the poem, Marvell seems to be serious and yet cannot resist an erudite jest at the expense of the very principle the poem seems to espouse. The Renaissance dictum upon which Marvell draws for the humor of these lines is based on Aristotle's classifications, that man's noblest power, the capacity that distinguishes him from all other living beings, is his ability to reason, to calculate, and to think. Here weeping has been substituted for reason or calculation, but the effect has been prepared for with previous references to the wisdom and calculation of tears. The tone is thus a mingled one that results from the playful touch of inverted traditions combined with a straightforward and serious comment about the validity of distorted vision in a world where appearances seem not to coincide with ultimate values.

Nonetheless, what Marvell seems to be doing with the poem and especially with the final two stanzas is to reassure mankind that weeping is the way to perceive the mysteries, that distortion through tears is a valid way of seeing,[21] and that, if we could but put aside given ways of seeing, of perceiving reality, we might find that all is one—dualities are only apparent. There is no true "this" and "other."

> Thus let your Streams o'reflow your Springs,
> Till Eyes and Tears be the same things:
> And each the other's difference bears;
> These weeping Eyes, those seeing Tears.
>   (53–56)

What Marvell creates in this poem is the possibility of perceiving in a mode that works through and then beyond the rational, cognitive mind toward experience of the thing itself. This mode is, in fact, the calculated process of meditation that leads to awareness beyond the images upon which the mind focuses. Through thought, through the mind's cognitive process, Marvell, like Donne but in a very different way, creates an awareness of objects and subjects as the same, of ourselves as participating in a reality that rips away the limits we set upon it in order to allow us to have direct experience of its meaning.

21. See Thomas Clayton's discussion of the Renaissance interest in the skewed perspective, or "anamorphosis," in " 'It Is Marvell He Outdwells His Hour': Some Perspectives on Marvell's Medium," in *Tercentenary Essays in Honor of Andrew Marvell*, ed. Kenneth Friedenreich (Hamden, Conn.: Archon Books, 1977), 59–73.

Marvell's method of inverting traditional applications of metaphors as he presents them in apparently conventional contexts pervades his poetry. Other poems in which he explores the power of tears and dew as emblematic liquid drops, "Mourning," "On a Drop of Dew," and to some extent "The Nymph Complaining for the Death of Her *Faun*," also set up conventional contexts only to break them into mysterious parts which recombine in transmuted and ambiguous texts.

The nymph, for example, sees, or thinks she sees, her dying fawn weeping (despite the poet's assertion in "Eyes and Tears" that "only humane Eyes can weep"):

> O help! O help! I see it faint:
> And dye as calmely as a Saint.
> See how it weeps. The Tears do come
> Sad, slowly dropping like a Gumme.
> So weeps the wounded Balsome: so
> The holy Frankincense doth flow.
> The brotherless *Heliades*
> Melt in such Amber Tears as these.
>   I in a golden Vial will
> Keep these two crystal Tears; and fill
> It till it do o'reflow with mine;
> Then place it in *Diana's* Shrine.
>   (93–104)

Not only do her tears merge with those precious relics from her dying fawn, but the nymph also anticipates her own swift death following his, as well as the fanciful weeping statue that she will leave to commemorate their fused identity. The funerary stone that shall weep (like Niobe, all tears) will engrave its tears on the nymph's stone breast as her alabaster fawn lies at her lifeless feet. This sad portraiture fits in its excess the sad event of the fawn's slaughter by the "wanton Troopers." The statue, a pietà, will be a miracle wrought in stone to affirm the sainthood of the fawn whom the nymph has canonized by her devotion.

Although he does not point to it directly, Marvell demonstrates his awareness of the "literary cult"[22] that devotes itself to the tears of the Magdalen in "Eyes and Tears." For a similarly aware reader, the weeping nymph parodies the weeping Magdalen and, for her, the fawn is saintlike, if not Christlike, in its martyrdom. The final couplet likewise implies the fawn's "ascension" even while its living whiteness remains in the nymph's memory: "For I would have thine Image be / White as I

22. Martz's phrase, *The Poetry of Meditation*, 199.

can, though not as Thee." With typical ambiguity, these two lines point the reader to three time frames, the future ("would have . . . be"), the present ("as I can"), and the past ("though not as Thee"). The realization that comes to the reader as he or she puzzles through the last four words is very close to what Southwell depicts in *Marie Magdalens Funeral Teares:* through tears she expresses her loss of the physical body of her Lord, and through tears of grief she is able to see clearly that her Lord is risen. The tears are a way of seeing the truth that is able to make joy and sorrow the same thing. The paradox no longer holds but resolves beyond the equally held opposing terms and appropriates both terms through transmutation.

The problems that "The Nymph Complaining" creates for the reader are the same kinds of problems that almost all of Marvell's lyrics create. The surface level seems to resist, and often to deny, that there is any level beneath it. Legouis's reaction to some criticism of this poem illustrates the reader's desire for the surface level to be all there is: "All the allegorical interpretations of the poem, beginning with Bradbrook-Thomas's in 1940, only testify to the recent tendency to scorn the plain meaning of a text."[23] My experience of the poems is that there is rarely a single "plain meaning of a text." The arresting simplicity of the diction and of syntax almost forces us to look again, and that backward glance catches us in a puzzle. Is our first reading the right one? Are Chlora's tears in "Mourning" without bottom or unsound in stanza 8?

> How wide they dream! The *Indian* Slaves
> That sink for Pearl through Seas profound,
> Would find her Tears yet deeper Waves
> And not of one the bottom sound.

Marvell keeps his "silent Judgment" while we try to fathom the depths of his ambiguities in order to secure a reading with which we can rest.

Given Marvell's own caveat in "Mourning"—"How wide they dream!"—the pursuit of Marvell's meaning is nonetheless fruitful, because it is in the process of using our rational powers to penetrate his playful, intellectual, textured levels of ambiguity that our experience of intuitive awareness occurs. Poems like "Eyes and Tears" are themselves meditations—the images which engage the mind displace the rational mind as controller of the experience. Marvell does not, however, exclude the thinking mind; he includes it as a part of the process that is subordinate to the total experience that moves apprehension beyond words and beyond thought.

23. *Poems and Letters* 1:250–51.

Paul R. Sellin

"The Nymph Complaining" as
a Stesichorean Calyca

IF SCHOLARSHIP agrees on anything in our "present uncertainty of interpretation" regarding "The Nymph Complaining for the Death of Her *Faun*," it is the singularity of Marvell's "still vexed poem."[1] "The Nymph Complaining" seems to differ from almost any other lyric in the language. Despite many long and strenuous efforts to locate fellow constructs, no clear analogues in vernacular or extant classical literature have as yet emerged. Ransacking biblical, Hellenic, Latin, English, Italian, or medieval and Huguenot French literature, history, and mythology relating to topics ranging from love, maidens, nymphs, birds, pets, deer, hunting, and metamorphoses to Christ, the church, iconoclasm, royalism, and the great rebellion has yielded surprisingly few passages that can be positively identified as such. Few *loci* apply as well as Catullus's lament on the death of Lesbia's sparrow, Ovid's epitaph on Corinna's parrot, or the "ancestor of Marvell's fawn" residing among the eclogues of Calpurnius.[2] But even of the many poems on the death of pets that have been adduced, "only a few have the remotest resemblance to Marvell's," according to Miner, "and only a few come from sources" that "he would probably have known." Recent emphasis on Marvell's anticipation of modern notions of femininity has only complicated things even further. As Miner has observed, "Original the poem certainly is, to the point of bafflement, but, as discussions of the poem have shown, the whole problem has been precisely one of knowing what tradition, genre, context, or matrix may be presumed relevant."[3] Indeed, the almost absurd amount of disagreement among

1. Margoliouth commentary, "The Nymph Complaining," *Poems and Letters* 1:250–52; Pierre Legouis, "Marvell's 'Nymph Complaining for the Death of her Faun': A *mise au point*," *Modern Language Quarterly* 21 (1960): 30–32.
2. Don Cameron Allen, "Andrew Marvell: 'The Nymph Complaining for the Death of Her Faun'," *Image and Meaning: Metaphoric Traditions in Renaissance Poetry* (Baltimore: Johns Hopkins University Press, 1960), 94–97.
3. Earl Miner, *The Metaphysical Mode from Donne to Cowley* (Princeton: Princeton University Press, 1969), 257, 247.

commentators regarding such elemental matters in "The Nymph Complaining" as the identity and character of the protagonist, the exact activity in which she is engaging, or how we are to relate to either instills little confidence in many critical attempts to untangle the puzzles, and neither biographical nor literary-historical inquiry has proved particularly fruitful, if for no other reason than that we have, in the case of Marvell, so little to go on. The difficulty, in brief, is that traditional attempts to deal with the poem have yielded no clear principles of organization informing it, the nature of the parts and their relationship to the whole remain matters of dispute, and qualitative evaluation of the work—our estimate of Marvell's achievement, if you will—suffers accordingly.

Given the failure to isolate some obvious entelechy driving the poem, perhaps it is best simply to resign ourselves, simply to accept that— since "Marvell's poem on the Nymph is very different in not drawing upon any of several traditions or contexts to the exclusion of others"— his "refusal to sort out in certain ways" implies a wish that "we too would be unable to do so in those ways,"[4] and to prepare to resort to other critical directions because we are at a dead end. Undoubtedly a shift in critical approach—whether analysis as some sort of power game, as a poetic spume playing upon an eternal paradigm of discourse, as a process of cultural evolution, or as a display of epistemological relativity—will yield original, interesting, insightful results. But if assessing Marvell's achievement in assembling this particular artifact is the task before us, then by its very nature the endeavor tends to commit one to some form of essentialist dialectic rather than semiotic, deconstructionist, or postmodernist. Powerful as such critical tools are, they may not necessarily offer the most effective solutions to the problem of casting further light on Marvell as efficient cause or on "The Nymph Complaining" as productive art, whereas direct confrontation of old but unsolved problems involving formal characteristics may provide a more solid base that other interests such as gender criticism, say, may find useful in the future.

In any case, there are some grounds for uneasiness lest improper classification may not be lurking behind a good number of essential difficulties still plaguing critical interpretation of Marvell's haunting poem. Hence I wonder whether some unexplored possibilities of genre criticism might help in approaching certain knotty problems afresh and suggest a few resolutions less complex than we often entertain.

Generally speaking, scholarship has always tended, silently or ex-

4. Ibid., 269.

plicitly, to think of "The Nymph Complaining" in terms of traditional genres, primarily classical Greek and Latin, and I am not sure this virtually universal reaction has been wrong. The impulse is irresistible, largely because of what we know about Marvell himself as well as the imitative habits of his age. As the labors of many others have amply shown, concern with ancient genres is evident everywhere in his work. He teases us constantly with classical paradigms, again and again setting in motion trains of expectation in readers' minds that he can then proceed to confirm, disappoint, or transcend. The technique is considerably more than a simple matter of convention or thematic considerations. Rather it entails such basic critical perceptions as whether a given work is organized as fiction or statement (a moral epigram compared with an Ovidian amor, for instance), as occasional or rhetorical rather than as truly mimetic poetry (a funeral elegy or paean, say, rather than a *skolion* or comedy), as parabolic or self-contained (allegorical pastoral as over against an ode or threnody), or as narrative or dramatic in mode (epic, satire, or pastoral as differing from epicede or anniversary in this respect). Genre may give clues to phenomena like the number of speakers a poem may entail (satiric dialogue as over against monologues customary in elegiac poetry, for example), the scope, setting, and very nature of the activity presented (epicedes or exequies compared with *neniae* or anniversaries), the sense of fictive musical instrumentation (fipple or string as opposed to double reed), and even the kind of *ethos* to look for in speakers (satire compared with Horatian odes). Indeed, such considerations often serve as guides to the most detailed points of stylistics, for genre conventions may be used to suggest what to expect in the way of diction, kinds of meter, and the very sentence structure (the coincidence of sense and closure of couplets customary in epigram as opposed to the enjambment and varying caesura more appropriate to the spontaneous flow of feelings that characterizes certain forms of elegy and ode).[5] None would deny that in this respect Marvell is really a magnificent Neo-Latin poet, albeit largely in the vernacular, so much so that he not only managed to transcend virtually all common restraints of genre but turned ancient inspiration into something that, as J. B. Leishman elegantly said long ago, gives the impression of being "entirely new," something "absolutely Marvellian and absolutely seventeenth-century."[6]

The difficulty in assessing Marvell's artistry in "The Nymph Com-

5. Cf. Julius Caesar Scaliger, *Poetices libri septem*, ed. August Buck (Stuttgart–Bad Cannstatt: Friedrich Frommann Verlag, 1964), 79.
6. *The Art of Marvell's Poetry*, 2d ed. (London: Hutchinson University Library, 1968), 76.

plaining," then, may lie not so much in the method of generic approach per se as our application of it, and if we cannot rightly determine the genre that we think Marvell is using, we are hardly qualified to say how he does so. Now virtually every treatment of the poem starts from the assumption, whether overt or implicit, that "The Nymph Complaining" is unquestionably a "pastoral" lyric. There are at least two reasons for this, presumably. First, many of Marvell's other "early" poems, particularly the dialogues, are overtly "pastorals" (never mind that the "mower" poems too are somewhat peculiar in following an agrarian tradition of husbandry rather than more common herding or even piscatorial variants); second, Marvell's title incorporates the word *nymph*: ergo, this poem must be a pastoral. Such reasoning entails an elementary philological difficulty that is too often overlooked. In its primary meaning, the Greek term νύμφη carries essentially the same sense as Latin *sponsa*. Generally speaking, the noun simply denotes a maiden or young woman of marriageable age.[7] Hence, not all "nymphs"—witness Hamlet's Ophelia or Gloucester's ambling wantons—are or have to be woodland deities in the guise of beautiful young women, for this is but a secondary and extended meaning of the *plural* form of the Latin noun. Unless a poet like Marvell specifically identifies his female characters as rural goddesses or shepherdesses (as he does in the case of Little T. C.), the presence of a figure designated "nymph" does not necessarily make the work a pastoral if the name is our only clue.

Apart from the title, what hard evidence is there that Marvell's protagonist in this poem is in fact a shepherdess or anything like one? The little we know or can infer is that "The Nymph Complaining" seems to entail not so much open fields and countryside as formal gardens. Within this setting, moreover, Marvell's nymph has her own special close, and I doubt that she is the one who tends it. Allen has noted that the "little Wilderness" it features "is not a wilderness at all," not a natural but a cultivated effect.[8] The lilies in the nymph's *hortus*, however neglected they may be (if they are), lie in beds and banks, as presumably the roses do too, and here—still "Ty'd in" the same "silver Chain and Bell" it came with—she has kept a trained fawn given as a

7. Joannis Scapula, *Lexicon Graeco-Latinum* (Amsterdam: J. Blaeuw and L. Elzevir, 1652), s.v. "Nymphe," col. 1058: "sponsa, nova nupta, nupta"; Thomas Cooper, *Thesaurus linguae Romanae et Britannicae* (London: n.p., 1578), s.v. "Nympha." Citing Hesychius and Suidas, Scapula also notes that the *nymphe* is "pars in pudendo muliebri."

8. Allen, "Andrew Marvell," 93, 110; See also, Michael Craze, *The Life and Lyrics of Andrew Marvell* (London: Macmillan, 1979), 74–75. Cf. Donald M. Friedman, *Marvell's Pastoral Art* (Berkeley and Los Angeles: University of California Press, 1970), 103, 175.

pet on the threshold, not so very long before, of "the Spring time of the year" by a self-styled "huntsman" named Sylvio, who presumably obtained it not from the wild but from the park of a civilized estate maintaining a herd of white deer. Indeed, although we do not know her station with certainty, she seems by her own testimony to have more in common with the red-and-white complexioned "Ladies of the Land," with whom she compares herself in line 62, than with sunburnt shepherdesses tending flocks, however fictional, and her hand is soft and white, seemingly uncalloused by teat, staff, trowel, or pruning shears. Finally, the landscape—if that is what it is—seems to include fountains and statuary, not unlike the "Twicknam garden" in which one of Donne's disconsolate lovers also sought cure and comfort, albeit in vain. At least, the nymph anticipates an Ovidian or Petrarchan statue raised in her woeful memory, although she reckons on providing her own waterworks. In itself, this last piece of information can just as readily suggest urban Verona commemorating the sad love of Juliet as the court suffering explicitly sylvan exile in *As You Like It*. If Marvell intended to imply "pastoral" with the details he provides, as Shakespeare certainly did, it is doubtful that the clues he chose afford the best alternatives with which to work. As for political and religious allegory, the possibility of which (witness Virgil and Spenser) one is quite right to suspect among eclogues and their bucolic relatives, it is questionable whether the search for such meaning is as justifiable in other lyric kinds. If "The Nymph Complaining" is not actually a pastoral, the likelihood of an allegorical structure informing it may be less than critics tend to think. Anyone is, of course, free to read a work allegorically if he likes, but we must not think that in so doing one has necessarily laid hold of its essential or even main elements. In short, the welter of sharply divergent parabolic interpretations that "The Nymph Complaining" has provoked through the years may as readily derive from inappropriate assumptions regarding genre as from failure to discover true keys to hidden meaning that rest on sound demonstration.

The other kind of lyric with which scholarship has identified "The Nymph Complaining" is, of course, the funerary elegy, including laments and epitaphs on pets. Obviously the word *complaining* in Marvell's title points directly toward the *planctus* or *querela*, and indeed, a passionate *conquestio* is precisely what the text of the poem offers. Because of presuppositions regarding the pastoral nature of the work, again, critics of more somber mood automatically take it to be a sort of pastoral elegy, as though it were kin to Milton's "monody" on the death of Edward King. However, the work contains little that reminds us of

Theocritus, Bion, or Virgil, nor is there much resemblance to grand and undoubted pastoral elegies by distinguished contemporaries like Milton's *Lycidas* or *Epitaphium Damonis,* Daniel Heinsius's *Thyrsis, Ecloga Bucolica, in obitum* [*Josephi Scaligeri*], Constantine Huygens's *De Uitlandighe Herder,* or for that matter even a "nautical idyll" like Hugo Grotius's *Myrtilus,* if for no other reason than the striking absence of narration, not to speak of metrics. That is, quite unlike such expressly elegiac bucolics, Marvell presents his persona strictly in dramatic monologue; albeit she indulges from time to time in reminiscence, there is no separate narrative voice in the poem.

In terming "The Nymph Complaining" a "pastoral epicedium," however, Don Cameron Allen took a very significant step. As he observed, the word *complaining* in Marvell's title clearly puts the poem "in a recognized poetic tradition," namely that of the "lamenting *Elegiacke,*" with the emphasis on funeral elegy rather than pastoral. However, even this classification is not wholly watertight. That is, thinking of "The Nymph Complaining" not just as an epideictic "pastoral epicedium" but also as one that is "recited while the creature that it celebrates dies," involves contradictory notions that do not fit well together. By definition, the enabling fiction of an epicede is, or should be, a song of mourning chanted over an as yet unburied corpse,[9] whereas reciting "the funeral sermon before the heart stops and the breath is gone" is something else again. In so doing, "The Nymph Complaining" indeed constitutes a "new notion," as Allen himself conceded.[10] But, apparently untroubled by the dubious similarity he implied between "The Nymph Complaining" and a funeral "sermon," he did not stop really to question whether the poem might be something other than a laudatory dirge.

If "The Nymph Complaining" shows little trace of the funeral oration and may not be a true epicede, strictly speaking, then what kind of poem could it be? Have we overlooked other relevant forms of elegiac poetry? Are there any alternative species or subspecies of this genre that might as well or better suit with Marvell's text? More particularly, do we know of any specific patterns of dramatic monologue that portray the lament of a young woman thinking to die of sorrow because something or someone whom she dearly loved was heartlessly taken from or betrayed her?

According to Julius Caesar Scaliger, perhaps the most authoritative of pioneering critics and historians of literature in the early Renaissance to whom students of Latin and Greek literature would be likely to

---

9. Scapula, *Lexicon,* s. v. "Epikedeion," col. 740: "Carmen quod dicitur cadavere nondum sepulto, apud Suid."
10. Allen, "Andrew Marvell," 94.

turn in Marvell's day, there once existed a special group of sad Greek love songs that derived from the funeral lament in an extended sense. Based on received stories and myths, this sort of elegiac poem focused on maidens and youths literally perishing for love. One of the storied representatives of the form was an aulic song known as the *calyca*, composed by the renowned Greek lyricist Stesichorus of Himera (ca. 630–555 B.C.). The original text disappeared in antiquity, but the memory of its remarkable character still survives in virtually all annals of classical literature. As Scaliger describes it:

> Stesichorus's *calyca* too was such [a poem of mourning], so-called after the girl dying of love for a young man named Euathlus. She prays to Venus for marriage with him; spurned notwithstanding, she throws herself headlong from the White Cliff on Leucas. The speech [*oratio*] is a virgin maid's [*virginis*], chaste and shamefast [*pudica*]: She longs to be wed, if possible; if not, she desires death.[11]

Whether Scaliger is Marvell's source is not the issue here, for there is little doubt that a self-respecting seventeenth-century student and practitioner of Greek poetry like Marvell would have turned to and consulted the obvious Alexandrian passage on which Renaissance compilers like Scaliger primarily drew for their accounts: namely, the remarks on aulic poetry in Athenaeus of Naucratis's *Deipnosophistae* (14.616–20). The relevant section translates thus:

> According to Aristoxenus, in the fourth book of his work *On Music*, the women of old sang something called the *kalyke* [καλύκην τινὰ ᾠδήν]. It was composed by Stesichorus, and in it a person named Kalyke [καλύκη τις ὄνομα], in love with Euathlus, a young man, chastely prays to Aphrodite that she may be married to him. But when the young man treated her with despite [ὑπερεῖδεν], she flung herself over a cliff. The sad event [πάθος] took place at Leucas. The poet has represented the maiden's [τῆς παρθένου] character as altogether chaste [σωφρονικὸν δὲ πάνυ], for she is unwilling to consort with the young man at all costs, but prays that she may, if she can, become the lawful wife of Euathlus, or, if that is impossible, be released from life.[12]

11. *Poetices*, 52: "Tale [poema lugubre] & Calyca Stesychori, a puella quae Euathlum deperibat adolescentem: pro cuius coniugio vota facit Veneri. tandem despecta, de Leucadia rupe praecipitem sese dat. Virginis oratio pudica. nuptias optat, si liceat: si non liceat, mortem."
12. Athenaeus of Naucratis, *The Deipnosophists*, trans. C. B. Gulick, 6 (Loeb Clas-

The reason for thinking that Marvell consulted Athenaeus directly is that just a sentence or two earlier in the very same portion of this work (14.618–19), the English poet also would have found a kindred idea that he repeatedly put to creative use in composing several other famous poems. No one, I believe, has pointed out that in the course of exploiting this very passage, Renaissance Hellenists necessarily also encountered a remarkable description of songs of "reapers" and "hired men who work regularly in the fields." Particularly in light of Scaliger's reliance on this section of Athenaeus, it seems to me extremely doubtful that either the idea or the practice of populating aulic songs in the Renaissance with mowers or husbandmen is as likely to have originated with Marvell as some suggest.[13] In all likelihood, the inspiration for employing an agrarian tradition of husbandry rather than the more common herding or even piscatorial variants in pastorals sprang directly from Athenaeus. And inasmuch as in the process of digesting this very account touching *messes* and *messores* in ancient poetry, Marvell could hardly have avoided Athenaeus's description of the Stesichorean *calyca* either, it is meet to believe that, just as he seems to have capitalized on Athenaeus in composing the "mower" poems, so he put Athenaeus's words regarding the *calyca* likewise to work in "The Nymph Complaining."

In any event, Athenaeus's perception of Stesichorus comes rather close to specifying much of the snug pattern that inhabits Marvell's lines. Consider, first, the mode and scope of action that Stesichorus's song seems to share with "The Nymph Complaining." Both Scaliger and Athenaeus appear to distinguish between received story and what the ancient bard did with it. That Kalyke loved a young man who jilted her and committed suicide when she could not marry him constitutes the bare, unvarnished bones of the mythical narrative on which both accounts agree the poet drew. But what the two commentators evi-

---

sical Library; Cambridge, Mass.: Harvard University Press, 1980): 336–39:

Ἀριστόξενος δὲ ἐν τετάρτῳ περὶ Μουσικῆς " ᾖδον, φησίν, αἱ ἀρχαῖαι γυναῖκες Καλύκην τινὰ ᾠδήν. Στησιχόρου δ᾽ ἦν ποίημα, ἐν ᾧ Καλύκη τις ὄνομα ἐρῶσα Εὐάθλου νεανίσκου σωφρόνως᾽ εὔχεται τῇ Ἀφροδίτῃ γαμηθῆναι αὐτῷ ἐπεὶ δὲ ὑπερεῖδεν ὁ νεανίσκος, κατεκρήμνισεν ἑαυτήν. ἐγένετο δὲ τὸ πάθος περὶ Λευκάδα. σωφρονικὸν δὲ πάνυ κατεσκεύασεν ὁ ποιητὴς τὸ τῆς παρθένου ἦθος, οὐκ ἐκ παντὸς τρόπου θελούσης συγγενέσθαι τῷ νεανίσκῳ, ἀλλ᾽ εὐχομένης εἰ δύναιτο γυνὴ τοῦ Εὐάθλου γενέσθαι κουριδία ἢ εἰ τοῦτο μὴ δυνατόν, ἀπαλλαγῆναι τοῦ βίου."

13. Pierre Legouis, *Andrew Marvell: Poet, Puritan, Patriot*, 2d ed. (Oxford: Oxford University Press, 1968), 49–50, 90 (first additional note); Victoria Sackville-West, *Andrew Marvell* (London: Faber and Faber, Ltd., 1929), 41–42; Friedman, *Marvell's Pastoral Art*, 120–21.

dently thought Stesichorus made of the tale was a monologue, a dramatic lamentation uttered by a chaste maiden evidently represented not in an act based on past or future incidents, such as her first falling in love, vainly praying to Venus, suffering rejection, or throwing herself off the cliff—though the poet might have had her refer to any or all of these events in the course of her soliloquy—but in one of simply pouring forth in first person the touching thoughts of a broken heart choosing to die because there is no hope of honorable union with the object of her desires. In terms of structure, at least, it looks as though in composing "The Nymph Complaining," Marvell was striving for poetic object and effects much resembling those informing Stesichorus's lost poem as Athenaeus and Scaliger saw it. In other words, "The Nymph Complaining" may very well be the product of a special endeavor at experimental *imitatio* in which any conscientious student of classical literature even today might still indulge.

Secondly, the creature that Marvell portrays is remarkably similar to Athenaeus's description of Stesichorus's Kalyke, both in character and what befalls her. There is no doubt that, much as her Greek forebear longed for Euathlos, Marvell's nymph loved her Sylvio deeply; that like Kalyke, she feels she has suffered cruel, arbitrary rejection by a deceitful beguiler from whom her innocent, nurturing love deserved better; and that her sorrow is so great she longs to die. While there is no overt reference to suicide or prayers to Venus in Marvell's plotting of the poem, some do find the nymph's words "but bespeak thy Grave, and dye" suicidal. As Shakespeare well knew, whiteness (λευκός) suggests the sepulcher as well as purity, and the fates of Ophelia and Juliet should ever remind us of the possibility. As for the pious nature and bootless supplication to the gods that both Athenaeus and Scaliger stress, the very first paragraph of Marvell's poem has long troubled critics on this very score, for it seems oddly to go out of its way to have the nymph evince her religious propensities, turning her other cheek to what ought to be hated enemies (7–8) and fervently praying that the life of her fawn be spared; to manifest her innocent sense of right and wrong, her abhorrence of gratuitous ill-doing; and amply to display her moral, if naive, concern with such issues (Christian rather than Pagan) as "Sin," guilt, atonement, redemption, mercy, and forgiveness.[14] Above all, the purpose of Marvell's adducing at this point in the work her faith that surely "Heavens King / Keeps register of every thing"

14. Cf. Matt. 18:1–10; John Klause, *The Unfortunate Fall: Theodicy and the Moral Imagination of Andrew Marvell* (Hamden: Archon Books, 1983), 85–88, suggests that Marvell may have been attempting to portray a pagan from antiquity.

(13-14)—a childlike belief that contrasts grimly with the fawn's actual expiration later in the poem (93-105) *despite* the "simple Pray'rs" she hoped would "Prevail with Heaven" (9, 10)—seems clearer in light of Kalyke's experience. Seeking to move deep pathos at the nymph's plight by augmenting its sadness, the poet is careful to remind us that, just as in Stesichorus's arrangement of the story, providence remains strangely indifferent, inexplicably suffering evil repeatedly to injure goodness and innocence, and failing to answer such deserving prayers, although, even with respect to beasts, heaven promises a world in which justice will be done ("Else Men are made their *Deo-dands*," [17]).

As for hopes of marriage, which brought Kalyke to the edge of despair, and her concomitant refusal to associate with the youth she loves except under honorable circumstances, Marvell seems to eschew any direct reference to such issues. Or does he? If, as we recall, the basic meaning of the word νόμυη in Greek is "betrothed woman" or "bride," perhaps we have all missed a salient point. Marvell's designating his speaker as a "nymph" may be intended first and foremost to imply not necessarily a woodland deity but a vulnerable, surely as yet unmarried *sponsa* who has suffered some sort of breach of promise ("beguil'd" [33])[15] at the unclean, "guilty hands" (18) of what turned out to be a "wild" (34), "false" (50), "counterfeit" (26), "cruel" (55), and "unconstant" (25) man with whom she perhaps too quickly ("soon" [33]) fell desperately in love: a haughty, mocking, pushy "huntsman" (31) of a youth,[16] quite unlike Cyparissus of old, who, in pursuit of his "*Dear*" (32), proved no more heedful of her "Smart" (35) than did the "Ungentle" (3) troopers of her and her fawn's pain when they wantonly shot it in her garden—one so "Unkind" (46) that, evidently untouched by an affection that had once probably "seem'd to bless / Its self" (43-44) in him as the fawn in her, he dealt with her as innocent she could scarcely conceive treating even a loving beast, and lightly took back his "Heart" (36) with hardly a qualm.

But the element that perhaps most inclines one to try viewing "The Nymph Complaining" as an elegy along the lines of a *calyca* is Scaliger's description of the diction that he thought Stesichorus had employed. In characterizing it as the *pudica* ("chaste," "shamefast") speech of a "virgin" or virtuous "maiden" (Scaliger: *virginis*; Athenaeus: παρθένου), his words read almost like a formula that Marvell might well have tried

15. Note the obsolete sense of the verb according to the *OED*: "To cheat (hopes, expectations, aims, or a person in them); to disappoint, to foil."
16. The name *Euathlos* means "strenue certans" (Scapula, *Lexicon*, s. v. "euathlos," col. 49).

to follow. With stunning success, one might add, if we are to judge by the virtually universal subscription for better or worse by nearly all critics to the illusion of the indeed pure, childlike innocence, perhaps even naivete that her words project. Suppose for a moment that Scaliger's formula for diction in the *calyca* were read prescriptively. Could it possibly have obtained any better realization than in the unpretentious, sensitive, touching, finely polished, yet vividly natural language that Marvell put in the mouth of the nymph?[17] While some think her expression too simple, too childish, too credulously pious, too naive, too concerned with "slight" things, too self-indulgent, even almost too "inhuman" for a young woman undergoing the experiences she has been,[18] such judgments regarding character depend largely on how readers perceive her age. In such a situation, classical nouns and names like "nymph," "Kalyke," and "*calyca*" are fraught with powers of intertextuality that can help guide our perceptions. For, right in tune with the wonderfully delicate speech Marvell assigns her, the Greek form κάλυξ, which literally denotes an "unopened rose," and the form νύμφαι, which also carries the peculiarly apt—if secondary—sense of "caelices rosarum, paullulum se aperientes,"[19] both point squarely to a tender "budlet" of a Renaissance maiden, Poe's "little damsel" or "bereaved child" perhaps,[20] scarcely much more than halfway between Shakespeare's Juliet and Little T. C. In light of the explicit meanings overtly inherent in Marvell's title, may a critic not simply ask whether, when all is said and done, the younger we think his "nymph" is, the greater the verisimilitude of speech and character, the deeper the power of her innocence to affect us?

If the Stesichorean *calyca* provides a useful touchstone by which to reassess some essential aspects of "The Nymph Complaining" like these, what happens when we try to apply the idea of this type of elegy to some of the many corollary issues that sharply divide present interpreters? In the war between allegorists and literalists, the character of Stesichorus's poem as sketched by Scaliger and Athenaeus clearly

17. Cf. Scaliger's character of the *materia* of the elegy, *Poetices*, 169: "Candidam oportet esse [elegiam], mollem, tersam, perspicuam, atque ut ita dicam, ingenuam. Affectibus anxiam, non sententiis exquisitis. Non conquisitis fabulis offuscatam. Cultus nitidus potius quam pexus."

18. T. S. Eliot, "Andrew Marvell," *Selected Essays*, new ed. (New York: Harcourt, Brace, and Co., 1950), 257; Peter Berek, "The Voices of Marvell's Lyrics," *Modern Language Quarterly* 32 (1971): 153.

19. Scapula, *Lexicon*, s. v. "Kalupto," col. 696: "flos rosae non expansa"; s. v. "Nymphai," col. 1058.

20. *Andrew Marvell: The Critical Heritage*, ed. Elizabeth Story Donno (London: Routledge and Kegan Paul, 1978), 164–65.

comes down on the side of proponents of the latter party like Pierre
Legouis, E. S. Le Comte, Don Cameron Allen, J. B. Leishman, Robert
Ellrodt, or Leo Spitzer; and it weighs against critics like Muriel Brad-
brook, Everett Emerson, Earl Miner, Harold Toliver, Donald Friedman,
Michael Craze, Geoffrey Hartman, Annabel M. Patterson, or Yvonne
Sandstroem. Viewed as a descendant of the ancient *calyca*, "The
Nymph Complaining" should consist of basically straightforward,
affecting mimesis depicting a piteous maid in throes of sorrow, though
executed with utmost skill and beauty, as nearly everyone acknowledges. There is not the slightest suggestion in Athenaeus or Scaliger
that either antiquity or the early Renaissance ever conceived of aulic
elegies like this as symbolic or tropological vehicles for conveying
ideas, and hence there is no particular reason to think "The Nymph
Complaining" does either. The "meaning" or "identity" of any given
item or action in a poem of this nature such as the fawn bleeding or
eating roses, the troopers, or the garden gone wild may not be so very
important in and of itself that one must turn everything upside down
to find analogues external to the poem in order to account for it. This is
not to say, of course, that what these things signify or symbolize *to the
nymph* is unimportant, for in a *calyca*-like poem such detail may serve
primarily as a technique of characterization, something altogether different from allegory or pure symbol, though no less rich for all that.

    There is also considerable disagreement as to exactly what Marvell's
nymph is lamenting. T. S. Eliot thought that the "theme" of *The Nymph
and the Fawn* (as he called it) was "a slight affair, the feeling of a girl for
her pet"; he also believed it to be "a very slight foundation" upon
which to build a great poem.[21] Taking the title very strictly indeed,
many do follow Eliot closely and hold that she is essentially lamenting a
dead and dying pet. According to others, though, Marvell's "subject"
is the nymph's psychological development from false love to true grief
via true love; some think it entails the destruction of innocence, failure
in understanding, or the loss of poetic possibilities; and some have
even gone so far as to conceive the action as that of a bereaved mother
weeping over "the arbitrary murder of her illegitimate but beloved
infant."[22] Although, oddly enough, many critics note the several parallels between the story of Sylvio and the story of the fawn he gave the
"nymph," few treat her soliloquy as a straightforward "love complaint"
or spend much time expounding why, in mourning over her dying fawn,

---

21. "Andrew Marvell," 257–50.
22. Evan Jones, "Marvell's 'The Nymph Complaining for the Death of Her Faun,' "
Explicator 26 (1967–1968): item 73.

she simultaneously laments the hurt she received from Sylvio, or just how the loss of her fawn compounds the suffering she has already been undergoing because of him. Yet if we take the ancient Greek story that Stesichorus followed as a paradigm, we should expect the emotional weight informing the poem to center not so much in the death of the fawn as in the given of Sylvio's "wanton" rejection from which there seems to be no recovery. Whereas the pointless killing of the little animal undeniably serves as the proximate cause of her grief, comparison with Kalyke's suffering suggests that for the taproots of the nymph's sorrow, we should look to the anterior hurt done by Sylvio, which, springing from the same mean urge to hunt and kill for the sake of hunting and killing, is still as pointless and mortal to her as the troopers's shots were to the fawn. If Stesichorus had composed "The Nymph Complaining," we would doubtless have to interpret both of the leucous statues she envisions, the marble and the alabaster, as monuments in her heart to senseless cruelty, the arrogant and aggressive behavior of the strong toward the weak and innocent, the despicable violation of plighted troth, and the hard deafness of the gods. In such light, the nymph's resolve to die, as well as the tears that she envisions her "unhappy" statue shedding for very woe of loss, would not in the first place be for the dead beast, however inimitably pure and lovely she thought it was.

Closely related to this issue is the question of the nymph's honor. Has she been seduced, did she lose her virginity to Sylvio? For many critics, she is a young, simple, pure, chaste, unsullied virgin, just about the person that Stesichorus dramatized, if we are to believe Scaliger and Athenaeus. As Phoebe S. Spinrad trenchantly put it, women do not necessarily have to lose the maidenhead in order to have their hearts broken.[23] To others the question is too "ungentle" to be asked, much less answered, and we have to live with the uncertainty.[24] According to adherents of this line of thought, the nymph has undoubtedly suffered a loss of innocence, though not necessarily a physical one; whereas to still others, her change constitutes psychological growth. The range of opinion is wide enough to include the nymph as a seventeen-year-old unmarried mother, and even rape has been suggested, if not absolutely insisted upon.[25] But if one thinks of the tale of Kalyke the "budlet"— that "flos rosae non expansus," that "Rosalind" *folia non habens expansa et dilatata*—then the answer is as obvious as the ethos that many have taken as implicit in the nymph's sweet speech, and the persistent allusions to

23. "Death, Loss, and Marvell's Nymph," *PMLA* 97 (1982): 52.
24. Miner, *The Metaphysical Mode*, 253–55.
25. Jack E. Reese, "Marvell's 'Nymph' in a New Light," *Etudes Anglaises* 18 (1965): 399–400.

whiteness and roses in the poem are perhaps not nearly so mysterious or psychologically complex as some make out. After all, the ancient poet was right. Vulnerability does augment pathos, if that is the *desideratum*.

Finally, views radically differ regarding even so basic a question as how readers should respond to the nymph. Are we to admire her goodness, sympathize with her plight, pity her? Or is she myopic, self-indulgent, naive, escapist, an ironic expression of femininity that Marvell disapproves of, even the butt of the poem? Again, if we refer "The Nymph Complaining" to Scaliger and Athenaeus, the answer seems clear: she should generate in us the same sense of affection, love, respect, and rue that we entertain for such sister victims as Juliet, Ophelia, and Desdemona. Indeed, are not Ophelia's mad and Desdemona's willow songs willy-nilly abbreviated cater-cousins of the same type of *carmina* as the *calyca*? Albeit as overt *melopoeia* they capitalize more explicitly on the fiction of a common aulic heritage to which Renaissance lyrics constantly appeal.[26]

In this context something should perhaps be said about J. B. Leishman's disapproval of Marvell's handling of couplets in "The Nymph Complaining," for the rhythms of the girl's speech profoundly affect our opinion of her. Specifically, he thought octosyllabic verse more successful when "comparatively closed," and he judged Marvell's use of consecutive run-on lines in this work as uncharacteristically clumsy and "profoundly unsatisfying." Inasmuch as he conceived the poem as a combination of "Elizabethan pastorales and picturesqueness with something of the seventeenth-century epigram," maybe his taste too was grounded in the wrong genres. Evidently Leishman was expecting conformity to conventions closer to the epigrammatic,[27] whereas surely the elegist's attempt deliberately to suppress end-stopped rhymes and prevent the sense from always closing with the couplet is one of the chief reasons why the sorrow of the nymph seems so spontaneous, so winningly genuine and credible.[28]

In a particularly memorable anatomy of Marvell's artistry some years

---

26. The former is particularly suggestive of the *erigone* also mentioned by Scaliger, *Poetices*, 52, a song named after another story of a virgin who committed suicide for love, though by hanging rather than drowning. In referring to it (and others—but they appear to involve men rather than women), Scaliger is again following Athenaeus, and he thinks of this *carmen* as quite different from the *calyca*. That is, the object the erigone represented seems to have been the actual activity of resolving on suicide, since "quo in poemate restis frequens mentio."

27. *Art*, 163–65.

28. Cf. Scaliger's discussion of elegiac meter, *Poetices*, 70, in which he observes that "nec . . . verum est quo aiebant: Elego semper finiri sententiam. nanque ab Elegiacorum nullo id servatum invenias."

ago, Rosalie Colie took special note of his deft "examination of the implications of theme and genre" and how he made "different kinds of tacit comment on them." Sometimes he observed how conventional genres failed in various ways; sometimes he would expand, exhaust, transform, or transcend them completely; and although he made endless capital of their conventions, he was always on the attack, striving constantly to "see what alternatives he could offer" and to come up with "new alternatives to a failed type." One of his finest solutions, Colie thought, was to mix genres, "fusing them with the themes, conventions, and implications of other generic forms" because the "technical elements" in them "point to other associations, other feelings and considerations."[29] Undeniably, this is true. But in the case of "The Nymph Complaining"—precisely the poem, ironically, that she sees as a failed exercise in "mixed forms"—there seems to be something else at work too. Perhaps dissatisfied with constrictions that limited his originality in plotting lyrics, he turned as was his wont to lore of the ancients for license to do something unusual, and there, among the very pages of our main source of information about Hellenic poetry and drama, he encountered a description of an elegiac model that appealed to him. Conceived as a Stesichorean *calyca*, "The Nymph Complaining" does not necessarily remain the noble yet botched attempt at *genus mixtum* that Colie suggested. Instead, it metamorphoses into a superbly successful attempt to revive in modern vernacular an ancient Greek form of which all had vanished except curt but telling sketches.

29. *"My Ecchoing Song": Andrew Marvell's Poetry of Criticism* (Princeton: Princeton University Press, 1970), 57, 71.

Barbara L. Estrin

The Nymph and the Revenge of Silence

> THE TIME IS out of joint. O cursed spite,
> That ever I was born to set it right.
> *Hamlet* 1.5.187–89

> Go, intercept some Fountain in the Vein,
> Whose Virgin-Source yet never steept the Plain.
> *Hastings* is dead, and we must finde a Store
> Of Tears untoucht, and never wept before,
> Go, stand betwixt the *Morning* and the *Flowers*;
> And, ere they fall arrest the early *Showers*.
> *Hastings* is dead; and we, disconsolate,
> With early *Tears* must mourn his early *Fate*.
> Andrew Marvell,
> "Upon the Death of Lord Hastings" (1–8)

I

Like Atlas shouldering his burden, Hamlet responds to his father's murder sociologically, registering a filial obligation to return the world to its correct and previously held position. Describing the vision at the end of revenge tragedies, Wendy Griswold writes, "A ritual feast is often undone in blood. In its place what is celebrated is the return of order following the period of disorder represented by all those dead bodies lying about."[1] The purging returns the world to health. But in an early poem, "Upon the Death of Lord Hastings," Andrew Marvell illustrates yet another motive for revenge: that of depriving, not reviving, the world. The "deflowering" the speaker envisions responds in kind to what the gods did to Hastings. Avenging that violation, the speaker attempts rape by defoliation. Seeking to reverse the flow of nature even as he appropriates the best of nature to represent his desolation, the disconsolate narrator enjoins his fellow mourners to intercept the early

---

1. *Renaissance Revivals: City Comedy and Revenge Tragedy* (Chicago: University of Chicago Press, 1986), 65.

101

showers and so prevent a normal spring. Similarly, in "To His Coy Mistress," the lovers "break thorough the iron grates of life," smashing restraints, as their fantasy disrupts the orderly process of the heavens. The revengers of both poems project cosmic changes. Hastings enlists already sympathetic others to effect the blockage he envisions. The "Coy Mistress" narrator persuades the woman to join him as, together, they outwit time. Destructive impulses spur many of Marvell's narrators on to visionary heights from which they later voluntarily descend. The social disengagement of "The Garden" is cancelled by the orderly acceptance of time in the last stanza, that of "Appleton House" by the complacent return of the concluding "let's in." In "Hastings" and "Coy Mistress," the cosmic subversion results in a similar social impasse, acknowledged as the impotence of poetic vision ("Art . . . is Long but Life is Short" [60]) in the early poem, the oblivion of sexual rapture (act *now* and forget time) in the later one.

In "The Nymph Complaining," Marvell invents a narrator who remains steadfast where the others fail to follow through. Refusing to come back to an orderly fold, the nymph retreats entirely and single-handedly enacts the deprivational revenge the bereaved speaker of "Hastings" and the argumentative lover of "Coy Mistress" only propose. She *does* deny her enemies a richness defined in the course of her poem. The most interesting fact about her success is that Marvell chooses a female speaker to achieve it. In her denial she answers those who wronged her, taking on the unfaithful Sylvio and then the murderous soldiers. Her answer to Sylvio opens up a mythical world based on the fact of her loss. Her rebuttal to the soldiers, corroborated by her silence, consists of a refusal to share the world she initially created. Hamlet may face an "unweeded garden / That grows to seed" (1.2.135), but the nymph invents a new one. The play ends with a reaffirmation of the social order, the world resting on Fortinbras, whose ("strong-armed") name itself carries the burden of Hamlet's initial shouldering. Wholly otherworldly, the nymph is utterly indifferent to setting anything in the earthly realm right.

While taking into account the nymph's vindictiveness, recent critics have failed to emphasize the relationship of gender to the revenge genre. In so doing they make less of the initial libertine violation in Sylvio's abandonment, eliding it too easily with the soldiers' callous indifference. Such readings imply one revenge and one story, whereas the poem has two: the story of the nymph's triumph over Sylvio's dismissal (her re-creation of his gift) and the story of the nymph's triumph over the soldiers (her de-creation of the world she made). The first story describes her artistic success in the form that celebrates male failure; the second reveals her dismissal of the form that consoles men who fail. In the first story, the nymph inverts the conventions of the Petrarchan situation, expanding the *Rime sparse* conversions and making herself a Petrarch who succeeds and the deer a Laura who listens and responds. In the second story, the nymph turns from tale to tableau, referring to a statue (Diana's shrine) and commissioning one (the marble memorial she envisions). The first revenge answers one unfaithful man; the second denies all men. Jonathan Goldberg alludes to the retaliative impulse in his seminal essay on "The Nymph Complaining" when he calls it "a poem whose plot entirely comprises the moment of creative annihilation," and when he refers to the nymph's statue at the end as "created in dissolution, made by erosion . . . a self consuming artifact."[2]

But Goldberg's claim that the poem offers "Marvell's most elaborated version of the meaning of the [annihilating] moment for his poetry and for himself as poet" does not go far enough in categorizing the poem as a peculiarly female vision. Goldberg begins by accepting Geoffrey Hartman's conclusion that "we must assume a . . . unity between the poet and his persona. Once we do this, the nymph begins to appear as a Muse in little, a figure created by the poet to mourn his own loss of power or perhaps that of poetry."[3] I will argue that, in "The Nymph Complaining," Marvell fabricated another poet, one who goes beyond lamentation. Her initial poetic triumph and her final artistic destruction redefine the poetics of failure. "The Nymph Complaining" does not mourn losses; it creates loss. Its revenge is double: first, as Goldberg and Hartman imply, it portrays an artist who invents a figure for her expressiveness and a receptacle for her inventiveness. In the garden, the nymph creates artist, art, and audience—a representation in miniature of the poetic process. She has one lover and one reader, the deer's incorporation of her message eliminating any need to record it. When he eats the roses of her words, the fawn imbibes the text that names love. When the nymph commissions a statue that will eventually corrode, she destroys the text that commemorates love. Harry Berger, Jr., calls the nymph a "refin[er] of the escape artistry of the ovidian sculptor, Pygmalion as well as her statue."[4] But he is talking about the nymph at the end and failing to recognize (as Goldberg does) that her art there is intended to be annihilating. The revenge within the

2. *Voice Terminal Echo* (New York and London: Methuen, 1986), 14.
3. "'The Nymph Complaining for the Death of her Fawn': A Brief Allegory," *Essays in Criticism* 18 (1968): 115.
4. "Andrew Marvell: The Poem as Green World," *Forum for Modern Language Studies* 3 (1967): 297.

garden is an artistic retaliation: new life substitutes for loss. The second revenge, after the garden, represents the destruction of that art.

With the nymph, Marvell creates not, as Goldberg and Hartman imply, someone who might have been himself but a projection as different from him as Damon the mower or the "I" of "The Gallery," "To His Coy Mistress," or "The Unfortunate Lover." That difference is measured by the nymph's femaleness. Her experience is not Marvell personalized but Marvell personified. Metamorphosed by loss, the nymph becomes a metamorphoser, aligning herself with a creative impulse and then with a de-creative one. The counterself Marvell invents for "The Nymph Complaining" is a countergender, and that contrariety is itself significant. Through it Marvell formulates a separate category of revenge which places "The Nymph Complaining" in a genre that relates to (but is ultimately at variance with) *The Duchess of Malfi* and *The Winter's Tale*, works in which women answer the men who deny them by creating enclaves of self-enabling silence. If, in *The Winter's Tale* and *The Duchess of Malfi*, male writers project women who rewrite their lives by living a secret experience, in "The Nymph Complaining," Marvell centralizes the female writer by making the experience she lives a public elaboration of the writing process. Each of the nymph's stories enacts a separate aspect of the Petrarchan process. Her strategy in, what will be called, the interior story of lines 25–92 reverses Petrarch's. If he seeks to displace the always psychologically and sometimes physically absent Laura with the permanence of his poetic laurel, the nymph, working through the same desire for sympathetic "pity" (*Rime sparse* 1), generates the understanding presence Petrarch never achieved. For a Laura who refuses to listen and, therefore, who refuses to react, the nymph creates an audience who acts out her fantasy. She rears the sympathetic reader Petrarch lacked, retaining all the qualities of the idealized Laura—the purity, the pastoralized loveliness—and dismissing all the traits—the denial, the hardness—of the vindictive and canonized Laura. The nymph is not just a woman who realizes and then loses her mixture of amorous and maternal desire. She nurtures a situation in which her desires can be understood, finding a vehicle of expression that transmits the feelings Sylvio dismissed. The nymph's motherly fostering of her audience earns her the responsive lover she wants. Restoring to a woman the creative wellspring of language Petrarch appropriated from Laura, Marvell regenders identification, the nymph first mothering the fawn as child-object and then naming him as love-object. Her exploitation of the Petrarchan model reifies its transactions, the fleshly deer responding to her expressiveness in the interior story. But her Petrarchan subversions extend one step further, as (in the framing story of lines 1–24 and 93–122) she converts the public homage of Petrarchan fame into the private victory of original vision. When she withdraws at the end, she takes her laurel with her, leaving only a fading sign of what she realized in the garden, tantalizing us with her achievement only to pull it away. Since she finds the solace of Petrarchan sympathy in the interior story, the nymph has no need for the comfort of Petrarchan fame in the framing story. Petrarch wooed his readers, accepting their laurels instead of Laura. Having persuaded her Laura inside the garden, the nymph has no interest in the future laurels that lie beyond.

Marvell's female voice of revenge is the absence of voice—and it is that absence that enables the nymph to evade the usual accusations against women's anger. Carolyn Heilbrun summarizes the history of literary misogyny by quoting Mary Ellmann who argues: "The most consistent critical standard applied to women is *shrillness:* blame something written by a woman as shrill, praise something as not shrill." Then Heilbrun adds, "The other favorite term, of course, is *strident.*"[5] Shrillness and stridency are tones that wanton soldiers and lovers—who expect women to react hysterically or violently to their betrayals—might anticipate. The nymph's silence is strident in a way that neither Sylvio nor the soldiers imagine. As the Duchess of Malfi creates a life for herself by not answering her brothers, as Hermione creates a death for herself by withdrawing from Leontes, the nymph shapes both her life and death, revenging first Sylvio, then the soldiers. The Duchess of Malfi and Hermione react by not reacting directly. They succeed by refusing to allow the men who victimize them the customary dismissals of women. Retreating, they dismiss the world. The nymph's ploy is different. While the Duchess and Hermione bury their resourcefulness only to disclose it later, the nymph confides in us, persuades us of her accomplishment, and then stops telling. Her silence is unexpected. She tricks us by revealing what she later retracts. Beginning by opening up—before the poem to Sylvio—in the poem to us, she concludes by retreating, her closure cutting off the disclosure that constitutes the Petrarchan legacy.

Unlike the conventionally Petrarchan heroines of so many other Marvell poems, from the coy mistress to Damon's Juliana, who refuse to say "yes" to their beseeching lovers, the nymph has acquiesced before her poem even begins. When she says "no"-thing at the end, that refusal punishes not just the lover but the world. Her silence, too, is qualitatively different from the vengeance at the end of Donne's "The Funerall" or "The Dreame" where the male speaker threatens to stop

5. *Writing a Woman's Life* (New York: Norton, 1988), 15.

praising the woman he had previously deified. Donne's promised
silence takes away nothing but his earlier, conventional platitudes. The
nymph withdraws the substance of a shared, and original, vision.
Having penetrated the "mystery of things," Marvell's nymph becomes
mysterious herself. In *The Duchess of Malfi*, Ferdinand and Bosola are
punished by the demons they unleash. In *The Winter's Tale*, Apollo
helps Hermione achieve her retribution. But Marvell's nymph designs
and executes her punishment on her own.

The double invention enables her to wreak a revenge that lasts. The
nymph remains firm in her withdrawal, achieving in fact what the
"Hastings" narrator only wished to do. However, that double power
distinguishes her from those Renaissance women to whom she is most
closely aligned. Their classical model is Demeter, the goddess who
withdraws and then forgives by taking the future into account. Similarly abused by men, the Duchess of Malfi, for example, still plans for
the normal lives of her children:

> I pray thee, look thou giv'st my little boy
> Some syrup for his cold, and let the girl
> Say her prayers ere she sleep.[6]

In *The Winter's Tale*, Hermione, who retreated into silence for sixteen
years, nevertheless comes back to see the daughter she lost. Hermione
and the Duchess share a tender concern for what comes after. Initially
hardened, they soften in the end. Marvell's seemingly tender nymph
calcifies, damning the future in her silence. She suffers on a smaller
scale than the Duchess or Hermione. In fact, the crisis in "The Nymph
Complaining" borders on the absurd.[7] Modern instances of the revenge
plot as Marvell uses it are indeed parodic: Poe's raven, or Irving's Ellen
Jamesians, or Beckett's endlessly spinning silence at the end of *Krapp's
Last Tape*. What saves Marvell's nymph from the ludicrous is the psychic
and spiritual breadth of her vision. She dares to go beyond the limitations thrust on her because she moves into a self-created mythical
sphere. In the process, she challenges men who marginalize women,
escaping their confines altogether.

In "The Nymph Complaining," Marvell's classical model is neither

6. *The Duchess of Malfi*, ed. Fred Millet (Northbrook, Illinois: AHM, 1953), 75.
7. Asking "what, in short, separates the Nymph from Emmeline Grangerford,"
John J. Teunissen and Evelyn J. Hinz conclude that "the secrets of its foundations lie
in the fact that the Nymph is complaining not of . . . the death of her pet but the
death of her offspring." See "What is the Nymph Complaining for?" *ELH* 45 (1978):
412–13.

the passive Philomela whose nightingale beautifies the bloody land-scape that shaped her nor the forgiving Demeter who restores the landscape she temporarily withdrew. In her activism, the nymph resembles the Diana of two different stories: Actaeon and Agamem-non.[8] Departing from Ovid and Petrarch, most late Renaissance writers follow Giordano Bruno in the idealization of Actaeon's Diana. In *The Heroic Frenzies,* Actaeon uses his victimization to "turn the appre-hended object into himself" and so absorbs her powers. As Leonard Barkan observes, "A story which could be (and had been) seen as a tissue of blasphemy, personal and social victimization, thwarted love and pagan frivolity, has become in this very High Renaissance version, a universal affirmation and testimony to the divinity of man and nature." When he turns Diana into a *herself,* Marvell invents a fictional parallel for such Renaissance women writers as Louise Labé and Veronica Fran-co who, Ann Rosalind Jones maintains, "take possession of masculine discourses even as they desublimate amorous conventions."[9] With a fe-male Petrarch, Marvell explores the limits of poetic consolation,[10] even as—with two Dianas—he returns linguistic primacy to the woman Petrarch marginalizes.

The second Diana allusion is based in part on conventional Renais-sance depictions of Diana as avenging goddess. Richard Linche sum-marizes the mythographers' reading of Greek and Roman sources:

> It is read likewise with Pausanias, that in Arcadia was a statue made of Diana, all covered over with the skin of a Hind, and from her shoulders there hung a quiver of arrowes: in one hand shee held a burning lampe, and in the other shee leaned upon the heads of two gentle serpents and before her feete there stood a hound, cout out and proportioned with wondrous great art and indus-trious labour of the workeman. The auncients first began to conse-

8. Most critics ignore the Diana–Agamemnon reference. Carolyn Asp, "Marvell's Nymph: Unravished Bride of Quietness," *PLL* 14 (1978): 402, speaks of two Dianas but not by linking either of them with specific mortals.

9. Giordano Bruno, *The Heroic Frenzies,* trans. Paul Eugene Memmo (Chapel Hill: University of North Carolina Press, 1965), 125; Leonard Barkan, "Diana and Actaeon, the Myth as Synthesis," *ELR* 10 (1980): 344–45; Ann Rosalind Jones, *The Currency of Eros: Women's Love Lyric in Europe, 1540–1620* (Bloomington: Indiana Uni-versity Press, 1990), 9.

10. Taking a completely opposite approach to "The Nymph Complaining," Elaine Hoffman Baruch, "Marvell's 'Nymph': a Study of Feminine Consciousness," *Etudes Anglaises* 31 (1978): 152–60, argues that Marvell offers "a study of a feminine sen-sibility that sums up a host of Western stereotypes from the point of view of some-one who believes them" (159). Baruch maintains that any hint of aggression in the poem is the "voice of the poet . . . coming through and overpowering the Nymph's" (159).

crate Hinds unto Diana. Since that time that shee sent such infec-
tious plagues among the Grecians, in token of her displeasure that
shee conceived against Agamemnon for killing a Hind.[11]

Linche's Diana doesn't just work out her anger on Agamemnon; she
spreads it, with plagues, generally among all the Greeks. Marvell's
nymph is more subtle, her affliction psychological not physical. Hinting at riches the world might garner or wonders it might see had it
chosen to forget and forgive, she nevertheless causes blights. Her
statue at the end—with the deer at her feet—mirrors Pausanius's
description and renders her Agamemnon's Diana, wreaking her displeasure by depriving the world. Hamlet tries to cure the world; the
nymph takes her cure with her into the death she carefully stages.

Appearing in sequence as the Actaeon and (then) the Agamemnon
Diana, the nymph projects a twofold revenge. In the interior story, she
creates a revenge of mirrors, living well by living doubly, inverting the
Diana–Actaeon myth and answering Sylvio by taking seriously the
token he offered in the fawn as a sign of his indifference; her second
revenge, the revenge of silence, emerges in the framing story where
she evokes the Diana–Agamemnon myth, responding to the murder by
taking the deer out of the human realm as Diana took Iphigenia and
made her a priest in Tauris. With the second revenge, she dies well,
privileging what she earlier shared. In *Romeo and Juliet,* Shakespeare
undoes the damage of Petrarchan self-cancellation, curing Romeo by
having Juliet participate in the sonnet of 1.2.92–105. The lovers' first
meeting is celebrated in the very form whose content signalled Romeo's
damaged psyche in the opening scene. Here Marvell goes beyond
Shakespeare in granting a woman power. The nymph succeeds at Petrarch's quest. She finds a way to convey her inner life by transmitting it
safely to an audience she creates. When the sympathetic other is taken
away, she annihilates all others.

II

When she alludes to the Diana–Actaeon myth, the nymph incorporates the god assimilating possibilities assumed by Bruno. Only she
retains them, granting herself the power Venus gave Pygmalion. If that
empowerment rendered art into life for Pygmalion, the nymph uses it
to humanize nature, to cross gender and *genus,* cultivating first child,

11. *The Fountaine of Ancient Fiction* (London: Adam Islip, 1599), Hiii.

then lover, then audience. And that communion converts the nymph into a poet, not Marvell himself as Hartman and Goldberg claim, but a representation of the female creative sensibility. With the deer-man of the interior story, Marvell explores Bruno's appropriations as the nymph offers her being to the deer. Marvell suggests how the idealized communication in the garden (the nymph using her body as her text, the deer receiving her text as child and responding to it as lover) figures the poetic process as an absorbative cycle. The deer may be the inspiration of the nymph's creativity, but he is also its audience that she molds by sensitizing him to her. The deer is her creation, a male aware of female needs, one who reads her body because he understands her text. As crucial first reader, he paves the way for us. His response encourages the nymph to share her feelings. When he is no longer there to respond, the text emerges pointless. With the second revenge, all correspondences are effaced, and Marvell reverts to the Diana of Ovid and Petrarch, as the nymph denies us the Brunonian understanding she shared with the fawn. Hermione takes away and then gives. The nymph gives and then takes away, the corroding statue replacing the perfected poem and offering instead a statute of limitations on how long her story can be retold.

In the complex mirrorings of the Diana–Actaeon myth, the nymph weaves a foundling plot, complete with abandoned child and pastoral retreat. That life answers Sylvio's trivialization of her love and inverts the myth. In Ovid, a man becomes a deer; in the nymph's versions, the deer becomes a man. In Ovid, the "bare" Diana withholds her secrets, underscoring Actaeon's impotence to tell by urging him to "tell if he can." In this version, the nymph encourages the fawn, allowing him to absorb her and, finally, to print that knowledge in the kisses he returns to her. He knows and tells. These inversions are part of the process of substitution constituting the retribution of the interior story. As Petrarch drifts into Laura in the *Rime sparse,* calling himself the laurel tree her name initially signifies or converting Laura into the deer he becomes in his numerous allusions to Actaeon, so the nymph mirrors and plays with the mythic possibilities of transformation, using the myth and the Petrarchan poetic situation to demonstrate the shifting possibilities for success. She succeeds by creating the sympathetic audience Petrarch lacked. Her dismissal in one story (Sylvio's suggestion with the gift that she busy herself with the fawn so he can be free to busy himself with others) prods the invention of a new one where the fawn becomes literally what Sylvio casually suggested: his replacement.

The substitution initiates a reversal of narrative sequence and allows the traditional ending of the family plot (culminating in the birth of a child) to serve as the opening event in the courtship story (usually initiated by the discovery of a desirable other). Condensing the fawn's life, the nymph becomes first the mother in the family plot and then the lover in the courtship plot, as the fawn waxes from infant to man. Pairing a familiar plot line with a familiar myth and giving both the originality of her vision, the nymph makes herself the fawn's savior. Her version of the family plot is further complicated by its conversion into a foundling story. For the literal birth, the nymph stages an adoption. Her foundling story is based on substitution, on crossing over social, generic, and gender barriers. In most foundling plots, a royal scion is adopted and raised by peasants in pastoral surroundings, acquiring for a time at least a hardiness and innocence he could not have had at court. In the nymph's telling, the adoption works two ways—lending her an animal resilience and allowing the deer a human sensitivity. Her pastoral retreat gives him a privileged status; his acquired sensitivity galvanizes her inventive powers.

Isolated from man, the nymph becomes one of a kind with the beast. The movement downwards through solitude, which is a movement inward toward her animal nature, reduces her to the fawn's level even as it raises him above the humans he replaces:

> But I am sure, for ought that I
> Could in so short a time espie,
> Thy love was far more better then
> The love of false and cruel men.
>   (51–54)

The fawn is doubly better than "false and cruel men." As prelapsarian animal, it is superior in *genus* to mankind; as spawn of woman, it is superior (in loving) to the *gender* of men. His adoption by a woman renders him closer to a woman; her adoption of an animal arouses her promiscuity. He imbibes her femininity as she acquires his robustness. The conversion of kinds occurs by a progression of similarities. The nymph merges the separated parts of her body and world as the first stage in crossing over into the fawn's being. Her extension turns her into the fawn's wet nurse, facilitating the adoption of the foundling plot:

> With sweetest milk, and sugar, first
> I it at mine own fingers nurst.
> And as it grew, so every day

It wax'd more white and sweet than they.
It had so sweet a Breath! And oft
I blusht to see its foot more soft,
And white, (shall I say than my hand?)
NAY any Ladies of the Land.

  It is a wond'rous thing, how fleet
'Twas on those little silver feet.
With what a pretty skipping grace,
It oft would challenge me the Race:
And when 'thad left me far away,
'Twould stay, and run again, and stay.
For it was nimbler much than Hindes;
And trod, as on the four Winds.

(55–70)

The process of extension begins as the nymph replaces breasts with fingers and as she stretches "sweetest milk" into sugar. The redundancy—the overflowing sweetness (like the superfluity of world enough *and* time)—is almost immediately received and given back as the nymph realizes the first return ("it had so sweet a breath"). With the second elongation from her hand to his foot, the nymph transfers the whiteness of the milk and sugar to the fawn's body, rendering it still another part of the lengthening process. Nursing replaces *in utero* feeding, fingers substitute for breasts, feet link up to hands. In Golding's Ovid, Actaeon's *endeerment* begins similarly with an elongation:

She sharpes his eares, she makes his necke
    both slender, long and lanke.
She turnes his fingers into feete, his armes
    to spindle shanke.
She wrappes him in a hairie hyde beset
    with speckled spottes,
And planteth in him fearefulness.[12]

The deer's softening and whitening in the nymph's story is a reverse mirror of Ovid's descriptive roughening and darkening, the fawn's feet whiter than any lady's hand, the whiteness excelling in refinement, the foot exceeding in dexterity, the ordinary human dimension: "NAY any Ladies of the Land."

The extension of mother into child fosters another attachment as the

---

12. *Shakespeare's Ovid: The Metamorphoses,* trans. Arthur Golding, ed. W. H. D. Rouse (New York: Norton, 1961), 67.

deer returns the maternal love she gave with the sexual love she wants. In Ovid, fingers turn to feet. In the nymph's story, feet are "softer" than "hand[s]." Yet their softness makes the nymph blush, presumably because they suggest other organs she manipulates. The extension of her hand in the script she writes is corroborated by the distension in the body she covets. Softness waxes into form as the nymph shapes the fawn's desire. The feet then become "fleet" (63), retreating as they disappear, boldly tripping as they reappear (84), phallic in their nimble goings and comings. The fawn emerges from her—an extension she creates, and returns to her—the lover she needs. As child, the fawn reflects her; as man, he corroborates their similarities by recompensing her support with his understanding. The sexual-procreative process resolves itself into a vegetative organic cycle, the feeding and bleeding (82–83), a result of the nymph's breeding. With the story her writing hand records and with the child her breast hand nurtures, the nymph brings female reproductivity into the Petrarchan complex, her sexual remembering of the deer repairing Actaeon's specular dismemberment.

When she refers to the garden where he becomes most like her, she switches stories. Now adopted by her, the deer-child emerges a deer-man. And the emergence is complicated because the mirrorings are doubled. Earlier, as child of woman, the fawn is softened and feminized; later, as man and lover, the fawn is sensitized and responsive. Similarly, the feminizing nymph is masculinized by the fawn, gaining from him a confidence in herself. But as a woman, she awaits the response she taught him to give. The earthly bower signals the nymph's entrance into the mythical realm where sexual thoughts sexualize the landscape. The conversion from boy to man through the perception of the woman is very much like the shift in Joannes Secundus's "The First Kiss":

> When Venus carried the sleeping Ascanius off
> to her mountain of love, she laid him on soft violets
> in a white thunder of roses she drenched him, and left
> Her liquid fragrance everywhere like dew.
> And then she remembered Adonis; and the old
> insinuating fire burned
> in her marrow bones.
>
> How often she longed to embrace him, flesh of her own
> flesh, exclaiming, "Adonis has risen again!"
> but afraid to arouse the boy in his innocent dreams
> she kissed a thousand nearby roses instead—
> and suddenly they flush crimson, a low

> passionate moan parts her astonished lips:
> on every rose she touches a fresh kiss blooms,
> and in the goddess herself shivers
> of multiple joy.[13]

The nymph's Diana parallels Secundus's Venus. Like the nymph, Venus has a garden. As the nymph adopts the fawn and makes him her lover, so Venus kidnaps her grandson and turns him into Adonis. Both Venus and the nymph raise their boy-children into men-lovers: "Adonis has risen again." And, as the nymph moves from child to man, so the thought of Ascanius revives in Venus a longing for her earlier love. That longing is transferred to the reddened blooms, which record her self-induced orgasmic pleasure. If the nymph blushes, admitting her physical excitement, Venus flushes the world, expressing her sexual release in a roseate shiver. The protective Venus emerges as the emblazoned lover, extending her body into the landscape, the red roses signifying her union with the gored Adonis, her love linked to death. Both the nymph and Venus create the enclaves where their fantasies are fleshed out, but while Venus's pleasure is self-contained, the nymph rears a substitute who is awake to and aware of her needs. Extending her being into the fawn, she initiates the sexual cycle predicated by his responsiveness. The circle of love the nymph describes is incestuous. She mothers the fawn's love as he arouses her sexuality; she fosters the fawn's manliness as he corroborates her womanliness. Where Venus reddens the landscape, transferring her displaced feeling to it, the nymph whitens it: "lillies without, roses within" (92). The ingested red roses suggest that the nymph's sexuality is absorbed and requited. The remaining white lilies bear witness to the divine innocence she confers on her love.

Unlike Ascanius, who cannot know his relationship to Venus and cannot resolve his destiny through her, the nurtured fawn recognizes his maternal origin in the nymph and publishes his erotic future with the kiss. His is a knowledge that registers in acknowledgment; hers is a desire that can be realized. Within the circle of the garden, the deer is a Laura who says "yes," the nymph a Petrarch who shapes her audience. His rosy kiss not only corresponds in kind to the nymph's rosy blush on discovering his white foot, but it satisfies her being, appeasing in kindness a longing that led to the initial prolongation. With the returned kiss, the nymph explores one more version of the Diana–

---

13. "The First Kiss," *Poems,* trans. F. X. Mathews (Kingston, R.I.: Winecellar Press, 1984).

Actaeon myth, turning what Actaeon lost into what the deer discovered: the woman's desire. The deer does know the nymph, and he
responds to that knowledge the way Petrarch wishes Laura had: with a
kiss. With the Diana of the interior story, Marvell identifies a form of
communication that builds on the cycles of the love poetry convention.
It begins with the nymph's "blush" and its initial discovery of longing
and progresses through the transference of desire into an object of
desire (the fawn-child). In the foundling experience, the nymph raises a
child who embodies and extends her love. In the garden experience,
the deer emerges a reader of her love, ingesting the roses and returning
them to her with the blushy-red kiss. The rapid transfers in the garden
reflect the ideal relationship between author and reader because the
reader responds with an act that demonstrates an understanding of
what lies behind the text.

And the multiple transformations of the garden—the deer's conversion from animal to child, from child to man, from offspring to love; the
nymph's reversion from victim to creator to expressor to recipient—
suggest a circle of connection (mirrored in the multifoliate rose, the
understanding readers, the embracing lovers) that at once underlines
the object of poetry and eliminates the need for it. Petrarchan poetics
are based on absence. As Kenneth Cool observes: "Every object in the
landscape has the metonymic power to evoke the beloved's total presence. And to this end, the entire natural scene becomes a vast sign
system jogging the lover's memory of its absent referent."[14] The
nymph's garden contains all the conventionalized *flora* and *fauna* of the
Petrarchan landscape, but the objects fade into abstraction (the roses
are eaten, the deer hides) as the thoughts are materialized in the realized kiss. The text is immediately read and the response is a gift that
corroborates presence. As she condenses the fawn's life, raising him
from child to lover, so she enacts the Petrarchan process, turning its
desired end for a sympathetic other into her conversional premise. If,
as Gordon Braden suggests, Petrarchan poetics are based on the equation between romantic "frustration and poetic success,"[15] the nymph
changes the dynamics of the equation. The Laura-fawn satisfies her,
reading her desire and fulfilling it. By making Petrarch an unfrustrated
woman, Marvell subtracts the usual Petrarchan repertoire of loss. Once
the nymph gets what she wants, she no longer needs to sublimate her
desire in its replacement (the poem) or to sublimate her presence in its

14. "The Petrarchan Landscape as Palimpset," *The Journal of Medieval and Renaissance Studies* 11 (1981): 94.
15. "Beyond Frustration: Petrarchan Laurels in the Seventeenth Century," *SEL* 26
(1986): 8.

denial (the self-canceling metaphor). With a woman who realizes femaleness through an art usually privileged to males, Marvell can expend with the text; the nymph is Petrarch (a man) and the deer is Laura (a woman) in the poetics of the garden. Her feminization of the deer in terms of sensitivity and his empowerment of her in terms of initiative suggest how the poetics of failure can be reversed. At the same time, the nymph and fawn reverse the reversals. He is both male lover responding (with the roseate kiss) to her female desire and a female reader who understands—and hence obviates the need for—the poem. The deprived Petrarch of the *Rime sparse* is immortalized in the laurel of his poetic remains. A satisfied nymph can expend with the remains. Inside the garden, the nymph and the fawn successfully annul the text.

III

Outside the garden, the text seems much more important, its context visual rather than auditory, statue rather than poem. Inside the garden the nymph suggests ideas that are then enacted. Outside, the nymph "bespeaks" images that she then withdraws. There's the rub. The statues are necessary reminders that the nymph dangles and then, retaliatively, renders fragile. The statues become "the absent referent" of the naturalized landscape, recalling both garden and beloved. But if Petrarchan poetry replaces the missing beloved with a verbal image that lasts, the nymph's retaliation elaborates a concrete image that will eventually dissolve. In the bower, the fawn is an Actaeon invited to join and read Diana. Outside the garden, the Diana of the Iphigenia myth takes over and subtracts what was engendered, pulling fawn, child, and lover into a privileged country. In the framing story, the nymph withdraws the idealized text she created in the bower, presenting instead two tableaux: one that hardens gradually as she speaks, the other that softens gradually as she invents. In the first she reflects her situation, the nymph and fawn in a last moment of impassioned communication; in the second she deflects her vision, ostensibly preserving the first tableau but actually effacing the eternalizing possibility. The first image turns backwards toward the lost garden:

> The Tears do come
> Sad, slowing dropping like a Gumme.
> So weeps the wounded Balsome: so
> The holy Frankincense doth flow.

The brotherless *Heliades*
Melt in such Amber Tears as these.
(95–100)

The scene (he weeping her tears/she weeping his) is first crystallized in
a kind of *mise-en-abyme*—eternally self-referential and then (the shining
crystal, the sparkling gold) eternally blocked by Diana's shrine:

I in a golden Vial will
Keep these two crystal Tears; and fill
It till it do o'reflow with mine;
Then place it in *Diana's* shrine.
(101–4)

Sequestering the vial from the marble statue she commissions, the
nymph closes off from posterity the "whiteness" she experienced with
the fawn and the *Elizium* she projects for him. When the nymph places
the "crystal" tears with her overflowing ones inside the golden vial, she
hides (in the darkness) what she now sees. Depriving the world of the
sight of saint and hagiographer, her "keeping" becomes a guarding of
the secret, the golden vial, a grail reserved only for the initiate. The
nymph preserves the first tableau but reserves it for Diana.

In sonnet 65, Shakespeare similarly plays with hidden and exposed
jewels. Seeking to immortalize his beloved, the speaker states the
problem and finds a solution:

where, alack,
Shall Time's best jewel from Time's chest lie hid?
Or what strong hand can hold his swift foot back,
Or who his spoil of beauty can forbid?
O none, unless this miracle have might,
That in black ink my love may still shine bright.[16]

The nymph hides the crystal jewel of the fawn in the golden "chest" of
Diana's shrine; Shakespeare locks his love in "black ink," imprisoning
him in his arsenal against time, even as he exposes him to future
observers. While Diana's shrine succeeds in hiding the nymph's
beloved, Shakespeare's shrine is designed to let his lover "shine
bright." His blackness preserves the light. Promising exposure, Shakespeare negotiates with Time; promising secrecy, the nymph transcends

16. *The Sonnets*, ed. Douglas Bush and Alfred Harbage (Baltimore: Penguin, 1961),
87.

Time. Her shining shrine blackens the memory of the fawn simultaneously as it releases him to romp in *Elizium*. He is protected from earthly exposure in the silence of the nymph's now secretive self. Her foundling-life with the fawn gave her the metamorphic power of Diana-like substitution. Her afterlife with the fawn leaves her the triumph of Diana-like revenge. Shakespeare's black words allow the beloved's image to outlive gilded monuments. The nymph chooses instead the art that Shakespeare's sonnet 55 argues will be "besmear'd with sluttish time."

The second image—the ostensibly public tableau of the marble statue—self destructs. The nymph uses her grief to create a deliberately immolative form. Her tribute will gradually rob the world of its memory. Undoing what she did, the nymph withdraws into silence, breaking the bond of author-audience confidence, as Laura-Mercury undercut the to-be-stoned Petrarch: "I am not perhaps who you think I am" (*Rime sparse* 23). In the carefully designed double tableaux, she seems doubly victimized. But is she what *we* think she is: the weeping victim of the world's brutality? Or does she turn what seems to be the source of her misery (the tears reflecting what is lost) into the arsenal of her defense (the tears obliterating the little that is left)? The statue brings up the question of posterity and underlines our exclusion from the vision, nullifying Bruno's absorption, and leaving only a Petrarchan and Ovidian separation. By the time she gets round to the second tableau, the nymph has aligned herself with a separatist vision. When she runs away, she suggests a finality that Petrarchan memory overcomes. Her monument corrodes the form that consoles Petrarch. Like the decimated Actaeon, the statue falls apart. Like that of Agamemnon's dynasty, the future seems endangered. If Petrarchan remembering reconstitutes the male inscriptions lost in the Actaeon disintegration, the nymph's incipherability emasculates and erases. Petrarch's Diana withdraws from the deer and dismembers the man: "I felt myself drawn from my own image."[17] She is unknowable, he unknown, emerging, like Ovid's Actaeon, a hunted-object. Like Actaeon's dogs, the wanton soldiers see only the deer-as-hunted object. Because they cannot possibly understand it, the nymph hides the text, shrinking the vision, pulling it out of sight (inside the inside, tears enclosed in vial, vial hidden in shrine) and so guards its secrets. To the many Sylvios she leaves a fractured world, her statue one of many adornments Marvell's mower cited "against gardens." She bequeaths only a decaying reminder, taking with her into *Elizium* the reflective crystal of her exclusive vision.

---

17. *Petrarch's Lyric Poems,* trans. Robert Durling (Cambridge: Harvard University Press, 1976), 64, 66.

For a brief time simultaneous to the interior story, we saw what the
fawn read. Now we stand outside the discourse. Without the deer as
first reader, the nymph loses her desire to tell, to play with the inversions of love poetry. Marvell's nymph plans her silence, substituting
deprivation for violation and rendering herself fundamentally inviola-
ble. The revenge of silence makes the world seem "wronger" than it
ever was initially. Though Hamlet rambles and Lear rages, their worlds
are purged by their violence. The quiet withdrawal in this poem leaves
us feeling deprived of a richness the nymph takes with her into *Elizium*.
As she tracks the fawn into the heaven she projects for him, so she
tempts her audience—through the story she tells and the statue she
designs—to follow her sightings. But when she arrives at *Elizium*, her
story will end; when future generations arrive at the statue, it will be
corroded. She enlists no Horatios to tell and retell. The transforming
power of her imagination—the elisions of gender and *genus* she made
possible—constitutes the private genius she withdraws. If Petrarch
reverts to the eternalizing conceit, finding solace in the poetic rather
than fleshly laurel, the nymph leaves no artistic comfort. Petrarch violates Diana/Laura's command. He makes "word,"[18] recording what she
forbad him in *Rime sparse* 23, of his heart/change and ends hart/changed.
In the interior story, the nymph begins with the hart/change and ends
with an exchanged heart, sharing all her secrets with the fawn. She
extends her vision and fosters in the deer a sympathetic subjectivity,
one which we see through her telling. But in the revenge of silence, she
privatizes that mutuality, taking the deer out of range. There can be no
earthly reprintings of the responsiveness (the blush of desire/the rush
to requital) imprinted by the kiss. The kiss is an immediately sympathetic reading of the love text she creates. When she effaces the
vision, the nymph destroys our relationship to it, leaving us nothing to
read and inadequate to respond. Geoffrey Hartman is right when he
says that the subject of "The Nymph Complaining" may be "musings
generally,"[19] both as poetic kindling and reflective afterthought.
Inspired by the deer, the nymph reared him to be the ideal reader. Each
sustained the circle of mutual support essential to the creative act.
Deprived of that responsiveness, the nymph by her silence deprives
the world, keeping from it what she gave.

While Hartman, Berger, and Goldberg see the nymph as a figure for
Marvell, their elisions fail to take her success fully into account. With
the nymph's realized love, Marvell questions the Petrarchan poetic of

18. Ibid., 62.
19. " 'The Nymph Complaining for the Death of her Fawn': A Brief Allegory," 125.

loss even as he uses its dynamics of desire to flesh out a female voice and to imagine a female inventiveness. The nymph's procreative powers (her motherly instincts toward the fawn) energize her creative powers (her poetic wooing of the fawn). The fostering of the deer guarantees her what Petrarch lacked: the sympathetic other. As her child, the fawn imitates the nymph even as he instills in her the need to draw him back, to get him to respond at the end with the reddened kiss that matches the initial reddening blush of her desire. That he does respond is a tribute to the nymph's power to direct his response. As her reflection, he is a Narcissus whose object of desire is still an other, she an Echo whose voice is her own. Even in the oblique mythic allusions, the nymph remembers Petrarch's dismemberment. In the garden, the nymph and fawn form an enclosed pair, organically self-referential.

The nymph avenges Sylvio (the lover who, like the lady in Donne's "Jeat Ring Sent," gives a gift as a way of writing the beloved off) by creating a lover who writes her in. With the deer responding fully to what she feels, the nymph exploits the Petrarchan poetic situation to eliminate the need for the Petrarchan text. She avenges the soldiers by creating an art that fades, her garden paling as the red roses are ingested. In the second story, where the tableau becomes the presence that evokes the absent referent, she mocks the eternalizing conceit in the Petrarchan convention by annihilating its sign. With a female Petrarch, Marvell reempowers the source and returns poetic privileging to its original wellspring, the appropriations of Petrarchism restored. Petrarch wrote for two audiences—the unyielding Laura who rejected him and the pliant readers who would give him, beyond his life and hers, the sympathy he couldn't immediately win. The nymph writes for one audience who returns, with the response she shapes, the spirit of her letter. When she takes the spirit with her, she eschews the form and the eternalizing baggage of sublimation, her secrecy constituting a critique of the Petrarchism that initially energized her. In letting go of sublimation, the nymph dissolves Petrarch's sympathetic others. The little story of the nymph's triumph has a larger critical context when seen in the light of what the nymph takes away. This wallflower's revenge constructs a wall between her private visions and the world's image of her. Her form prefigures formlessness, her formulations privileged only—as with Iphigenia at Tauris—to the initiates now sequestered in Diana's shrine, now hurrying to *Elizium*.[20] Like the dissolving

20. Hartman comments, referring also to "The Nymph Complaining" and "Coy Mistress," on Marvell's *hastening* lovers. " 'The Nymph Complaining for the Death of her Fawn': A Brief Allegory," 123.

Manna in "On a Drop of Dew," (40), like the sun in "To His Coy Mistress" (46), the nymph and fawn *run* (119), finding a resolution in dissolution and evaporating into the heavens from which future readers, reduced to wanton soldiers, are excluded.

With the nymph's triumph—her dying into an Elizium she envisions and her escape from the engravement she commissions—Marvell gives formlessness wings of thought. The whitened fawn follows the pure "swans and turtles," the redness of the digested roses now totally within, the unrealized passion they symbolize already experienced. Diffusing her redness with his whiteness, the deer passes it back to her, as she absorbs inwardly with the kiss what in her blush she showed outwardly. Coursing through her veins, the nymph's passion is lived rather than symbolized. Understood by the fawn and returned, her feelings become acts rather than thoughts, expressed energy rather than repressed libido. Inside the garden, the deer reads her heart and returns with artlessness the roses of her blush. When the roses are ingested, the bower itself is whitened, and its purity becomes the earthly footing for what will become the heavenly wings. The rose of idealized love is replaced by the lily of transposed divinity. The nymph's garden is a rehearsal stage for the grand theater in Elizium, its processes, the whitened statues worn down, the running deer headed up, preparations for the longer flight, anticipations that, like the dew's self-enclosing roundness, already enact their expectations. If statues are visual representations of the sublimations engendered by Petrarchan fame—words solidified as things—the nymph's corroding monument demonstrates how little she relies on substitution. Her things fade into words. Her words fade into silence. Petrarch marbleized Laura, calcifying her hardness and eternalizing his tears in distilling and stilling words. The nymph softened the fawn and preserved him for herself, her privacy effacing and rendering unnecessary the consolations of public fame. In the nymph's revenge, Petrarchism first finds a material expression for, then a sublime transcendance of, the feelings it consolidates.

Eugene R. Cunnar

Names on Trees, the Hermaphrodite, and "The Garden"

FOR ALL THE COGENT explications of "The Garden," that poem remains elusive in its powerful allusiveness. As a pastoral poem on the contemplative life it takes on added dimensions when one considers the numerous philosophical (Cartesian dualism, Stoicism, Hermeticism, neoplatonism), theological (Augustinian, Pauline, Song of Songs, biblical, Christological, apocalyptic), and aesthetic (pastoral, typological, allegorical, classical, metaesthetic) themes perceived as operating within it.[1] Like Virgil, one of his pastoral predecessors, Marvell has the ability to incorporate into one symbol or a phrase disparate elements from philosophy, theology, and literature. Through this technique of incorporation, as numerous critics have pointed out, Marvell modifies, extends, and subverts the pastoral as a genre even as he uses its conventions for his ultimate thematic purposes.[2] Although the poem treats seriously problems of theology, epistemology, and ontology, Marvell also provides a clear statement of his anti-Petrarchan attitudes as well as a contrasting statement about the ideals of prelapsarian love and poetry. When the speaker in "The Garden" states,

> No white nor red was ever seen
> So am'rous as this lovely green.
> Fond Lovers, cruel as their Flame,
> Cut in these Trees their Mistress name.
> Little, Alas, they know, or heed,
> How far these Beauties Hers exceed!

I want to thank the Huntington Library and the American Council of Learned Societies for grants enabling me to complete research for this paper.

1. For a brief overview of critical approaches to the poem see Christine Rees, *The Judgment of Marvell* (London: Pinter, 1989), 179–97.

2. See Marion Meilaender, "Marvell's Pastoral Poetry: Fulfillment of a Tradition," *Genre* 12 (1979): 181–201, for a concise summary of this position; Donald M. Friedman, *Marvell's Pastoral Art* (Berkeley and Los Angeles: University of California Press, 1970), 1–92; and Rosalie L. Colie, *"My Ecchoing Song": Andrew Marvell's Poetry of Criticism* (Princeton: Princeton University Press, 1970), 30–42.

Fair Trees! where s'eer your barkes I wound,
No Name shall but your own be found,
(17–24)

he initiates a movement in the poem that replicates, or echoes, the
standard *topos* of carving one's mistress's name in the bark of a tree,
which, in turn, begins a critique of Petrarchism that will be resolved in
his interpretation of the Hermaphroditus myth. As the speaker contemplates his retreat from a corrupt world, in which sexual and political relationships have become destructive, into the garden of the mind,
he condemns the unrequited and destructive love inherent in Petrarchism along with its enslaving representations of the feminine as disturbing and disruptive forces in life and art that his retreat is meant to allay.
Marvell's anti-Petrarchan stance emerges in stanza 3 in the image, considered ludicrous, parodic, or typical by many, of carving trees' names
on trees.[3] Conventionally understood as a comment on the divisive
nature of love as opposed to the "lovely green" of nature, this stanza
embodies Marvell's witty ability—"betwixt jest and earnest"—to sub-
sume and modify generic conventions in order to develop his own
concept of representation antithetical to that of Petrarchism. When one
understands the background of this *topos*, then one can begin to understand better how Marvell's art works so well and why elements of his
poem have remained so elusive.

I

Numerous critics have stated that the *topos* of cutting one's mistress's
name into a tree is a pastoral convention but without explaining the
sources, history, or significance of the convention for Marvell's poem.
A brief overview of the convention will help us understand better
Marvell's use of the *topos* in the poem. The *topos* finds its origins in
classical literature beginning with Aristophanes, Callimachus, and
Theocritus and continues through Virgil, Propertius, and Ovid, who

3. See, for example, John Carey, "Reversals transposed: An aspect of Marvell's
imagination," in *Approaches to Marvell*, ed. C. A. Patrides (London: Routledge &
Kegan Paul, 1978), 136–67; Colie, "*My Ecchoing Song,*" 24, 159–60; Friedman, *Marvell's
Pastoral Art*, 156–57; and Robert Wilcher, *Andrew Marvell* (Cambridge: Cambridge
University Press, 1985), 133. Critics who mention this *topos* do not point out its ante-
cedents or what they might imply for Marvell's poem. On Marvell's use of
Petrarchism see Pauline Palmer, "Marvell, Petrarchism and 'De gli eroici furori,'"
English Miscellany 24 (1973-1974): 19–57. Palmer does not treat "The Garden."

provided it with a pastoral and amatory context that would be carried into the Renaissance.[4]

The *topos* appears in Virgil's *Eclogues* as a central image for the failure of pastoral poetry to achieve the order and harmony that the poet seeks. In the search for the ability to order human experience, the poet realizes that unrequited love, excess passion, death, and political upheaval can destroy that order. In *Eclogue 5*, a traditional dialogue and singing contest, Mopsus proposes to sing new and experimental verses in his lament for Daphnis, who represents Julius Caesar as a civilizing power: "Nay, rather I will try these songs which I recently wrote down on green beech-bark and noted the melody line by line."[5] Here the poet attempts to impose order and restore the presence of Daphnis as a model through his carving of the poems and melodies on nature as a metaphor for the power of his song.

In Virgil's tenth *Eclogue*, Gallus, suffering from unrequited love and hoping to escape the corruption of civilized experience, escapes into the pastoral world where as a stranger he hopes to replace artificiality with nature.[6] Gallus's love, Lycoris, has been unfaithful to him by running off with a soldier. Lamenting Lycoris's absence, he says,

> I will go revise all those poems I wrote in Chalcidicean verse, recasting them to the rhythms of a Sicilian shepherd's oaten straw. I am certain I would prefer to endure the life of the forest, among the caves of the wild beasts, and would prefer to cut my love songs into the bark of tender trees. The trees will grow, and you too, my passions, will increase.

In abandoning the sophisticated elegiac poetry of court and unrequited love for nature, Gallus hopes that his *amores* as both love and poems will grow with the trees and transcend the uncertainties of human emotion and corrupt civilization. However, Gallus's attempt to find relief in the pastoral world fails as he must again return to the elegiac

---

4. For a thorough survey of the classical background of the *topos* see Callimachus, *Opera I: Fragmenta*, ed. Rudolf Pfeiffer (Oxford: Oxford University Press, 1949), frag. 73; R. J. Enk, ed., *Propertius, Elegiarum Liber I: Monobiblos* (Leiden: E. J. Brill, 1946), 165–66; and Thomas G. Rosenmeyer, *The Green Cabinet: Theocritus and the European Pastoral Lyric* (Berkeley and Los Angeles: University of California Press, 1978), 202–3.

5. See Michael C. J. Putnam, *Virgil's Pastoral Art* (Princeton: Princeton University Press, 1970), 3–19, 166–94; and Paul Alpers, *The Singer of the Eclogues* (Berkeley and Los Angeles: University of California Press, 1979), 190–200, 212–22. Virgil, *Eclogues*, trans. H. Rushton Fairclough (Cambridge: Harvard University Press, 1917), 2–77.

6. See Eleanor Winsor Leach, *Vergil's Eclogues: Landscapes of Experience* (Ithaca: Cornell University Press, 1974), 157–70; Putnam, *Virgil's Pastoral Art*, 342–94; and Alpers, *Singer*, 222–40. I quote Leach's translation.

mode. Subsequently, the *topos* functions as more than a pastoral lament by providing Gallus with poetic compensation for his unrequited and faithless love.

Embedded within the *topos* is the problem of language's ability or inability to represent the object it signifies; that is, the *topos* functions as a metaphor for writing or poetic creation. In this instance, the *topos* also suggestively anticipates the patriarchal metaphor of what Susan Gubar describes as the pen-penis inscribing the feminine as blank page in order for the male writer to subordinate and control the feminine.[7] The patriarchal implication that woman and nature are a blank page, a lack, or absence to be created by the male poet also aptly describes Petrarch's sublimation of the feminine into the poetic word.

Ovid, in the fifth epistle of the *Heroides,* has Oenone, who has been deserted by Paris for Helen, lament that "beeches still conserve my name carved on them by you, and I am read there Oenone, charactered by your blade; and the more the trunks, the greater grows my name."[8] Because Paris had also written his pledge of undying and faithful love for Oenone on a tree, his carving ironically comes to represent masculine betrayal of the feminine. Oenone's name carved in the bark represents the failure of words to preserve love. Propertius expresses his grief over unrequited love for Cynthia by wondering if trees understand love: "How often do my words echo beneath your tender shades, how often is Cynthia's name written upon your bark?"[9] Although the grief of unrequited love exceeds the limits of art, the male poet strives to exert his will over nature and the feminine.

The mistress's name carved into the bark as compensation for her absence and unreciprocated love appears in Petrarch's important *Canzoniere* 30 where, standing in the shade of a laurel tree, the speaker worships "my idol carved in living laurel."[10] Petrarch's numerous puns upon Laura/laurel become analogous to carving the mistress's name upon the tree. In doing so, Petrarch substitutes a private and idolatrous liturgy of love for the liturgy of the cross in this sonnet. His destruction of the poetic sign's sacred referentiality replaces God's creative signs

7. " 'The Blank Page' and the Issues of Female Creativity," *Critical Inquiry* 8 (1981): 243–73.

8. *Heroides,* trans. Grant Showerman (Cambridge: Harvard University Press, 1914), 58–59. Paris's pledge of love reads as follows: "If Paris' breath shall fail not, once Oenone he doth spurn, / The waters of the Xanthus to their fount shall backward turn."

9. *Elegies I-IV,* ed. L. Richards, Jr. (Norman: University of Oklahoma Press, 1977), 51–52.

10. Robert M. Durling, trans., *Petrarch's Lyric Poems* (Cambridge: Harvard University Press, 1976), 87–89. See also numbers 127, 129, 160.

and creation with the poetic autonomy of the poet. By equating language with desire, Petrarch compensates his unrequited love with poetic creation that fragments the woman's body as he idolatrously worships his own creation. In effect, Petrarch abandons the linguistic theory of correspondence assumed by Dante in which the word by virtue of the Logos both signifies and participates in its referent.[11] In privileging *verba* over *res*, or the poetic image of the beloved over the actual woman by insisting on the self-referentiality of language, Petrarch commits the sin of pride and introduces ontological equivocation and epistemological uncertainty into love's discourse, which now celebrates the male poet's creation and control of the feminine other.

Following Petrarch, other Renaissance writers, such as Jacopo Sannazaro in the *Arcadia* and Boiardo in the *Amori*, employ the *topos* in various ways.[12] In the prologue to the *Arcadia*, Sannazaro, echoing Virgil, argues for the pleasures of nature over those of court, stating that "woodland songs carved on the rugged barks of beeches no less delight the one who reads them than do learned verses written on the smooth pages of gilded books."

The most popular and unusual use of the *topos* appears in Ludovic Ariosto's *Orlando Furioso*, when Angelica carves Medoro's name on trees and rocks, "Among so many pleasures, whenever a straight tree was seen shading a fountain or clear stream, she had a pin or knife ready at once; likewise if there was any rock not too hard; and outdoors in a thousand places and likewise as many times on a wall in the house, ANGELICA AND MEDORO was written, bound together with various knots in different ways."[13] Ariosto inverts the *topos* so that now it celebrates the happiness of love in the pastoral paradise instead of recording the poet's frustration and grief and the inability of art to represent that grief.

Following Ariosto, painters and poets quickly adapted this new motif and began to innovate upon it. The theme appeared in woodcuts illustrating the *Heroides* and *Orlando Furioso* and was depicted by paint-

11. For these aspects of Petrarchism see John Freccero, "The Fig Tree and the Laurel: Petrarch's Poetics," *Diacritics* 5 (1975): 34–40; Robert M. Durling, "Petrarch's 'Giovene Donna Sotto Un Verde Lauro,'" *Modern Language Notes* 86 (1976): 1–20; Giuseppe Mazzotta, "The *Canzoniere* and the Language of the Self," *Studies in Philology* 75 (1978): 271–96; and Thomas M. Greene, *The Light in Troy: Imitation and Discovery in Renaissance Poetry* (New Haven: Yale University Press, 1982).

12. Sannazaro, *Arcadia and Piscatorial Eclogues*, trans. R. Nash (Detroit: Wayne State University Press, 1966), 22; Boiardo, *Opere Volgari, Amorum Libri*, ed. P. V. Mengaldo (Bari, 1962), 64–76.

13. Ariosto, *Orlando Furioso*, trans. Guido Waldman (London: Oxford University Press, 1974), 220.

ers from Spranger through Liberi and Blanchard.[14] Jacob Cats included it as one of his emblems of the folly of love. Tasso employed it in both the *Aminta* and his *Gerusalemme Liberata*, where Erminia carves Tancred's name on a tree.[15] In *Colin Clouts Come Home Again*, Edmund Spenser utilizes it as a means of representing his praise of Elizabeth I:

> Her name recorded I will leave for ever,
> Her name in every tree I will endosse,
> That, as the trees do grow, her name may grow;
> And in the ground each where will it engrosse,
> And fill with stones, that all men may it know.[16]

Spenser suggests that it is his art that has not only the power to praise Cynthia's (i.e., Elizabeth I's) realm, but also the power to shape and control it because, as Colin says, "her upraising, doest thy selfe upraise" (355).

In *As You Like It*, Shakespeare mocks the ubiquity of the *topos* by having Orlando vow that he will carve in Herculean fashion Rosalind's name on every tree but also explaining, "O Rosalind, these trees shall be my books, / And in their barks my thoughts I'll character."[17] Thomas Carew turns it to erotic purposes in "The Rapture," where Lucrece,

> To quench the burning Ravisher, she hurles
> Her limbs into a thousand winding curles,
> And studies artfull postures, such as be
> Caru'd on the barke of every neighbouring tree
> By learned hands, that so adorn'd the rinde
> Of those faire Plants, which, as they lay entwinde,
> Have fann'd their glowing fires.[18]

---

14. On the *topos* in art, see Rennselaer W. Lee, *Names on Trees: Ariosto into Art* (Princeton: Princeton University Press, 1977); Colie, "*My Ecchoing Song,*" 159, points to the emblem in Jacob Cats, *Silenus Alcibiadis* (Amsterdam, 1622), 11. For other examples, see Arthur Henkel and Albrecht Schone, *Emblemata* (Stuttgart: Metzlersche, 1976), cols. 181–83.

15. Torquato Tasso, *Jerusalem Delivered*, trans. Edward Fairfax (New York: Capricorn, 1963), 135. See also *Aminta*, 1.1.318ff.

16. *Poetical Works*, ed. J. C. Smith and E. De Selincourt (London: Oxford University Press, 1969), 542. See also *The Faerie Queene*, 5.7.46, where Timias, the enslaved Petrarchan squire, carves Belphobe's name on every tree in a gesture of unrequited love.

17. *Riverside Shakespeare*, ed. G. Blakemore Evans (Boston: Houghton Mifflin, 1974), 383. Cf. l. 127: "Tongues I'll hang on every tree."

18. *The Poems*, ed. Rhodes Dunlap (Oxford: Clarendon Press, 1970), 52.

For Carew, the images of Aretino's sexual postures carved on the trees promote sexual congress instead of just lamenting unrequited love.

The problem of representation now apparent in the *topos* is exploited by Fulke Greville, who uses it cynically to punish his mistress after his language fails to move her:

> My songs they be of Cynthia's praise,
> I wear her rings on holy-days,
> On every tree I write her name,
> And every day I read the same.
>   Where Honor, Cupid's rival, is
>   There miracles are seen of his.
>   If Cynthia crave her ring of me,
> I blot her name out of the tree.[19]

If art can create, it can also uncreate the reluctant mistress.

The *topos* reveals the split between *res* and *verba,* subject and object, body and soul as those problems emerge as central to the Renaissance concern for the relationship between word and thought.[20] In this context, Francis de Sales redefines the *topos* in his *Introduction to the Devout Life* as a powerful metaphor for the contrast between earthly and heavenly love:

> In fine, those who love with a human and natural love have their thoughts incessantly engaged by the thing they love, their hearts filled with affection for it, and their mouths ever employed in its praise. When absent, they lose no opportunity of testifying to their affection by letters. They do not come upon a tree without inscribing the name of their beloved on its bark. Thus, those who truly love God can never cease to think of Him, to sigh for Him, to aspire to Him, and to speak of Him. Were it possible, they would engrave the Holy and Sacred Name of Jesus on the breasts of all mankind.[21]

De Sales internalizes the *topos* as an appropriate representation of Christian love.

---

19. *Poems and Dramas,* ed. G. Bullough, 5 vols. (Edinburgh: Oliver and Boyd, 1939), 1:104.

20. For this tradition see A. C. Howell, "*Res et Verba:* Words and Things," *ELH* 13 (1946): 131–42; more recently, Margreta De Grazia, "Shakespeare's View of Language: An Historical Perspective," *Shakespeare Quarterly* 29 (1978): 374–88, and "The Secularization of Language in the Seventeenth Century," *Journal of the History of Ideas* 41 (1980): 319–29; and Martin Elsky, "Bacon's Hieroglyphics and the Separation of Words and Things," *Philological Quarterly* 63 (1984): 449–60.

21. *Introduction to the Devout Life,* trans. John R. Ryan (Garden City: Doubleday, 1955), 95.

In "To Groves," Robert Herrick echoes Donne's "The Canonization"
as he wittily employs the *topos* to reveal the folly of courtly love:

> Yee silent shades, whose each tree here
> Some Relique of a Saint doth weare:
> Who, for some sweet-hearts sake, did prove
> The fire, and martyrdome of love.
> Here is the legend of those Saints
> That di'd for love; and their complaints:
> Their wounded hearts, and names we find
> Encarv'd upon the Leaves and Rind.[22]

These lovers are remembered "By all those True-love-knots, that be /
With Motto's carv'd on every tree." Herrick wittily calls attention to the
problematical relationship between nature and art that manifests itself
in his poetry. Abraham Cowley, subscribing to an aesthetics that priv-
ileges nature over art in that art should imitate the order of nature, uses
the *topos* to show both the damage and disorder that false art and
passion create. In "The Tree," he says,

> I chose the flouri'shingest *Tree* in all the Park,
> With freshest Boughs, and fairest head;
> I cut my Love into his gentle Bark,
> And in three days, behold, 'tis *dead*;
> My very *written flames* so vi'olent be
> They'have burnt and wither'd up the Tree.[23]

In this instance, words are more than symbols, having an ontological
or phenomenal connection to the things they represent. His carving his
love into the bark with "written flames" burns and withers up both
nature and the woman and reasserts the power of the masculine pen-
penis to create and control the feminine.

   Along very different lines and preparing the way for Marvell, Kath-
erine Philips uses the *topos* in "Upon the engraving of her Name upon a
Tree in Barnelmes Walks":

> Alas how barbarous are we.
> Thus to reward the courteous Tree,
> Who its broad shade affording us,

22. *The Complete Poetry*, ed. J. Max Patrick (New York: Norton, 1968), 277.
23. *Poems*, ed. A. R. Waller (Cambridge: Cambridge University Press, 1905),
140–41.

> Deserves not to be wounded thus;
> See how the Yielding Bark complies
> With our ungrateful injuries.
> And seeing this, say how much then
> Trees are more generous then Men,
> Who by a Nobleness so pure
> Can first oblige and then endure.[24]

Philips uses the *topos* to underscore the paradox of the superiority of natural beauty and love to fickle masculine love, which wounds both nature and the feminine in its false declarations.

II

Marvell's use of the *topos* in "The Garden" reveals his ingenuity in being able to critique the underlying generic assumptions of the forms he employs while he revitalizes and redefines those inherited traditions in what Rosalie Colie calls his "ecchoing song," and what Thomas Greene calls a subtext engaged through dialectical imitation.[25] But more importantly, it is his innovation upon the echoes that reveals his serious use of the *topos* in a dialogic encounter with the traditions of pastoral, Petrarchan love, and their representations of the feminine. Marvell can be both Petrarchan and anti-Petrarchan as he engages the texts that compose the traditions he critiques. In "Upon the Hill and Grove at Bill-borow," Marvell employs the *topos* to celebrate the love between Fairfax and his wife:

> Fear of the *Master*, and respect
> Of the great *Nymph*, did it protect,
> *Vera* the *Nymph* that him inspir'd,
> To whom he often here retir'd,
> And on these Okes ingrav'd her Name;
> Such Wounds alone these Woods became:
> But ere he well the Barks could part
> 'Twas writ already in their Heart.
>
> (41–48)

The symbiotic relationship between Fairfax and his trees posits nature as the model for human love and its representations. Here Fairfax's

---

24. *Poems* (1678), in *Minor Poets of the Caroline Period*, ed. George Saintsbury, 3 vols. (Oxford: Clarendon Press, 1905), 1:583.
25. Colie, *"My Ecchoing Song,"* 13–39; Greene, *Light in Troy*, 43–48.

writing his wife's name on the trees suggests not the violation of nature, but instead a correction to his Petrarchan idolatries in that the trees have already written Vera's name in their cores: " 'Twas writ already in their Heart."

Marvell's use of the *topos* in the Latin poem "Hortus" and again in "The Garden" reveals a similar redeeming approach to the tradition:

> Whom does the grace of maidenly beauty not arrest?
> Which, although it excels snows in whiteness and purple in
>   redness,
> Yet your green force (in my opinion) surpasses.
> Hair cannot compete with leaves, nor arms with branches,
> Nor are tremulous voices able to equal your whisperings.
> Ah, how often have I seen (Who would believe it?) cruel lovers
> Carving the name of their mistress on bark, which is more
>   worthy of love.
> Nor was there a sense of shame for inscribing wounds on sacred
>   trunks.
> But I, if ever I shall have profaned your stocks,
> No *Neaera, Chloe, Faustina, Corynna* shall be read:
> But the name of each tree shall be written on its own bark.
> O dear *plane tree, cypress, poplar, elm!* [26]

As in the "The Garden," Marvell not only rejects courtly or Petrarchan love by privileging nature over art, but he also repudiates the *topos* as a love complaint and as a celebration of pastoral love by having art inscribe the tree's name on its own bark. As in his other pastoral poems, Marvell explores the idyllic correspondence between man and nature, word and thing ("My Mind was once the true survey / Of all these Medows fresh and gay") that was lost with the Fall.

As a Puritan, Marvell was aware of the dichotomy between nature and grace created by the Protestant Reformation and of the split between matter and mind fostered by Descartes and Bacon. In the new desacralized universe Marvell seeks an appropriate Protestant landscape of the mind in which he can internally re-create that lost world.[27] Marvell's use of the *topos* within a pastoral poem on the pleasures of contemplative retirement reflects on the major cultural shift in attitudes

26. *The Latin Poetry of Andrew Marvell,* trans. William A. McQueen and Kiffin A. Rockwell (Chapel Hill: University of North Carolina Press, 1964), 25–27.

27. See Barbara Kiefer Lewalski, "Marvell as a religious poet," in *Approaches to Marvell,* 251–79; and Pierre Legouis, *Andrew Marvell: Poet, Puritan, Patriot* (London: Oxford University Press, 1965).

toward nature that Keith Thomas has analyzed. Under the impetus of the new, empirical science the old, analogous and anthropocentric view of nature was attacked as "vulgar errors."[28] Within this shifting paradigm trees and gardens planted with trees took on a revered status, becoming metaphors for man's relationship to society, nature, and eternity. As Thomas points out, tree-filled gardens became favored retreats for contemplation. Just as significantly, gardens were perceived as attempts to recapture the purity of Paradise. John Beale wrote in 1657: "We do commonly devise a shadowy walk from our gardens through our orchards (which is the richest, sweetest and most embellished grove) into our coppice-woods or timber woods. Thus we approach the resemblance of Paradise." A similar sentiment was echoed by James Shirley who thought that gardens "shew how art of men / Can purchase Nature at a price, / Would stock old Paradise again."[29]

Marvell's entry into his garden and his veneration of the trees is a clear attempt to reinstate an older attitude toward nature where trees and flowers were spiritual emblems. Joseph Summers and others have pointed out that nature provides the basis of Marvell's central vision in numerous poems.[30] This attitude is clearly reflected in "Upon the Hill and Grove at Bill-borrow," where Marvell says the following of trees:

> For they ('tis credible) have sense,
> As We, of Love and Reverence,
> And underneath the Courser Rind,
> The Genius of the house do bind.
> Hence they successes seem to know,
> And in their Lord's Advancement grow.
>
> (49–54)

A similar reverence for trees occurs in "Upon Appleton House" where

28. *Man and the Natural World: A History of Sensibility* (New York: Pantheon, 1983), 17–87, 192–241. Marvell may also be addressing the antifeminine bias of the new science that is succinctly expressed by Joseph Glanvill, *The Vanity of Dogmatizing* (1661; rpt. New York: Columbia University Press, 1931), 117–18: "The *Woman* in us, still prosecutes a deceit, like that begun in the *Garden;* and our *Understandings* are wedded to an *Eve,* as fatal as the *Mother* of our *miseries.*"

29. Beale and Shirley as quoted in Thomas, *Man and the Natural World,* 216, 236. For other accounts of seventeenth-century gardens as re-creations of Paradise, see John Priest, *The Garden of Eden: The Botanic Garden and the Re-Creation of Paradise* (New Haven: Yale University Press, 1981).

30. "Marvell's Nature," *ELH* 20 (1953): 123.

in *"Natures mystic Book"* tree leaves become prophets and Marvell can
state:

> How safe, methinks, and strong, behind
> These Trees have I incamp'd my Mind;
> Where Beauty, aiming at the Heart,
> Bends in some Tree its useless Dart.
>
> (601-4)

Here trees become a sacred refuge protecting the speaker from the
slings and arrows of Petrarchan love. Subsequently, nature emblem-
atized in the tree provides the paradigm for regeneration and serves as
the ordering principle for man, who imitates the principles in art in an
attempt to recapture prelapsarian life.

   According to Marvell, "Passions heat" enters "The Garden" after the
Fall and becomes one of the elements that destroys the prelapsarian
harmony that existed between mind and nature, male and female. The
traditional "white" and "red" of Petrarchan or courtly love and stereotypical feminine beauty is not "So am'rous as this lovely green."
Petrarchan or "Fond Lovers" become "cruel as their Flame" of unrequited desire when they "Cut in these Trees their Mistress name" as a
displaced representation of that unfulfilled love. Marvell is mockingly
aware of the delusions inherent in such literary love as he is of the fact
that Petrarchan representation is cruel to both nature and the woman in
that it wounds both in the very act of writing on the tree.[31] When
Marvell rejects "the Palm, the Oke, or Bayes," he is rejecting not only
martial, civic, and poetic laurels but also Petrarch's idolatrous elevation
of masculine desire's sign over God's sign.[32] The act of carving one's
mistress's name in the tree's bark represents masculine desire's deluded
imprisonment and wounding of the feminine as well as the violent and
cruel destruction of God's chain of verbal referentiality that previously
unified body and soul, flesh and spirit, male and female. For Marvell,
the Petrarchan act of naming feminine beauty in order to capture,
control, or preserve it becomes an act dividing and destroying the

   31. On this aspect of Petrarchism see especially Nancy J. Vickers, "Diana
Described: Scatterd Woman and Scattered Rhyme," *CI* 8 (1981): 265–79; and Freccero,
"The Fig Tree and the Laurel," 34–40. Colie, *"My Ecchoing Song,"* 154, suggests
Petrarch's sonnet 10 as one source for "The Garden."
   32. See Elaine Hoffman Baruch, "Marvell's 'Nymph': A Study of Feminine Consciousness," *Etudes Anglaises* 31 (1978): 152–60, on Marvell's attack on Petrarchan and
patriarchal notions of the feminine.

previously united dualities and preventing the possibility of realized mutual love.[33]

The attempt to make the absent mistress present through language inscribed by the phallic knife can only fail and profane nature whose "Beauties Hers exceed." Accordingly, Marvell says in parodic fashion that it is better to inscribe or reinscribe God's sign: "Faire Trees! where s'eer your barkes I wound, / No Name shall but your own be found" (23–24). Rather than play the forever pining and unfulfilled Petrarchan lover/poet, Marvell prefers the tree's own name to that of the Petrarchan mistress, who is, after all, only a literary creation. Marvell's witty modification of the *topos* clearly denotes his attempt to distance himself from its associations with unfulfilled love. For Marvell, the tree's own name is more like God's sign—the Book of Nature inscribed by God's own hand—and becomes his model for attempting to reunite *res* and *verba*, nature and art, male and female. Like others in the seventeenth century, Marvell seeks an Adamic language of nature in which the things of nature should be intrinsically related to their very existence as signs. Paradoxically, Marvell acknowledges that mutability and death are part of love and life. Love, like the tree inscribed with its own name, will grow, change, and eventually die. However, it is this very process that embodies the regenerative power of nature and the potential for the regeneration of mutual human love.

Marvell's replication—his "ecchoing song"—and repudiation of Petrarch's quest for the poetic laurel as substitute for the real Laura is clarified in the fourth stanza where the poet rewrites the myths of Apollo and Daphne and Pan and Syrinx, both central to Petrarch's vision of frustrated love. These myths form one of the central defining images of Petrarchan love, that of the man forever chasing but never capturing the woman and instead receiving the poetic laurel as compensation. Through these myths, Gordon Braden argues that Marvell converts Petrarch's twin sins of lust and pride into the means of achieving a higher, neoplatonic reality.[34] In this context, the poet's words are

33. On this aspect of naming in Marvell see Phoebe S. Spinrad, "Death, Loss, and Marvell's Nymph," *PMLA* 97 (1982): 54–55. For a discussion of male dominance over language and the woman's loss of the power of naming see Adrienne Munich, "Notorius Signs, Feminist Criticism and Literary Tradition," in *Making a Difference: Feminist Literary Criticism,* ed. Gayle Greene and Coppelia Kahn (London: Methuen, 1985), 238–59.

34. "Beyond Frustration: Petrarchan Laurels in the Seventeenth Century," *Studies in English Literature* 26 (1986): 5–23. For the Apollo–Daphne myth as a defining feature of Petrarchism see Leonard Barkan, *The Gods Made Flesh: Metamorphosis & the Pursuit of Paganism* (New Haven: Yale University Press, 1986), 209–12; Mary E. Bar-

only signs pointing to their referent, which is unobtainable. Marvell
mocks the Petrarchan notion that loving the woman's image is better
than loving the woman herself by preferring the trees to the woman.
Subsequently, he repudiates the self-destructive narcissism inherent in
the sustaining myths of Petrarchism when he explains that

> The *Gods,* that mortal Beauty chase,
> Still in a Tree did end their race.
> *Apollo* hunted *Daphne* so,
> Only that She might Laurel grow.
> And *Pan* did after *Syrinx* speed,
> Not as a Nymph, but for a Reed.
>
> (27–32)

Marvell's qualifications—"Still," "Only," and "but"—show that he is
not endorsing Petrarchism's substitution of poetic fame for unrequited
love; instead he is pointing out explicitly its folly of ending without
fruition as well as destroying a more unified relationship between sign
and signified, as in the mower's complaint: "For She my Mind hath so
displac'd / That I shall never find my home."

Ovid's account of Daphne's metamorphosis into the laurel was subjected to various interpretations in the Middle Ages and the Renaissance,
ranging from Christian allegories to comic explanations. Frequently,
her metamorphosis was interpreted as a punishment for frustrating
Apollo, the god of poetry. In medieval allegorical interpretations Apollo
was understood as Satan pursuing the chaste soul, whose chastity is
saved by the metamorphosis, that is, the return to nature and God's
art.[35] Embedded in numerous accounts of the myth were clear anti-
feminist sentiments implying the subjection and sublimation of the
feminine as the material for masculine art. Representative of this attitude is Bernini's *Apollo and Daphne* in which the Ovidian myth receives
a patriarchal interpretation from Cardinal Borghese (later Urban VIII),
for whom it was sculpted, when he has carved on its base the following:
"Whoever, loving, pursues the joys of fleeting forms fills his hands

---

nard, *The Myth of Apollo and Daphne from Ovid to Quevedo* (Durham: Duke University Press, 1987), 82–109. For the chase motif, see Michael J. B. Allen, "The Chase: The
Development of a Renaissance Theme," *CL* 20 (1968): 301–12.

35. For the multiple interpretations of the Apollo–Daphne myth see Christine
Rees, "The Metamorphosis of Daphne in Sixteenth and Seventeenth-Century En-
glish Poetry," *Modern Language Review* 66 (1971): 251–63; Barkan, *The Gods Made Flesh,*
85–86, 209–11, 225–26; Barnard, *The Myth of Apollo and Daphne;* and Wolfgang
Stechow, *Apollo und Daphne: Mit einem Nachwort und Nachtragen zum Neudruck*
(Darmstadt: Wissenschaftliche Buchgesellschaft, 1965).

with sprays of leaves and seizes bitter fruits."[36] One implication of this statement is that Daphne's primitive but feminine forces need to be captured, controlled, and converted by masculine rational or religious precepts. This masculine subjection and remastery of the feminine is echoed in the myth of Pan and Syrinx when Syrinx is metamorphosed into reeds and Pan transforms the reeds into the enabling instrument of pastoral song.[37] Along similar lines, Nancy Vickers sees Petrarch's fragmentation and scattering of the mistress's body across his *Rime sparse* as a means of defeating the threat the feminine poses for the masculine poet.[38] Marvell uses the myth as criticism of Petrarchism while suggesting the purity or chastity of his own poetic vision by indicating that the metamorphosis instead implies the end of masculine desire and the return to nature where the human and the divine may meet. From this perspective, the nymph escapes male desire by returning to nature as an emblem of prelapsarian harmony.

Marvell's vision of poetry is one in which the poet imitates the prelapsarian poet who collapses word and thing by carving the tree's name on the tree in an attempt to reinvest his *verba* with the substance and stature of *res* as it was in Paradise. It is this poetic mind that

> Does streight its own resemblance find;
> Yet it creates, transcending these,
> Far other Worlds, and other Seas;
> Annihilating all that's made
> To a green Thought in a green Shade.
> (44–48)

For Marvell, poetry subsumes and annihilates Virgil's pastoral shade and the poetic shade of Petrarch under the laurel tree, replacing it with the "green Shade" of hope for the return to Paradise where signifier and signified are joined, where type and antitype are one.

This vision of poetry that imitates God's creative process is echoed in Marvell's ideal of prelapsarian love represented by the hermaphrodite. Although some have argued that the hermaphrodite and the idea that

36. Howard Hibbard, *Bernini* (Baltimore: Penguin, 1965), 236. On Bernini's work see S. Howard, "Identity Formation and Image Reference in the Narrative Sculpture of Bernini's Early Maturity," *Art Quarterly* 2 (1979): 140–71.
37. Louis Adrian Montrose, "The Elizabethan Subject and the Spenserian Text," in *Literary Theory/Renaissance Texts*, ed. Patricia Parker and David Quint (Baltimore: Johns Hopkins University Press, 1986), 317–27; Louis Adrian Montrose, "'The perfecte paterne of a Poete': The Poetics of Courtship in *The Shepheardes Calender*," *Texas Studies in Language and Literature* 21 (1979): 37–39.
38. "Diana Described," 265–79.

"Two Paradises 'twere in one / To live in Paradise alone" suggests
Marvell's misogyny, I would argue that the image is in accord with his
vision of poetry and a more positive view of the feminine.[39] The concept of the hermaphrodite was subject to *in malo* and *in bono* interpretations.[40] In the *in malo* interpretations of the Ovidian myth, Hermaphroditus represented the curse of emasculation or castration brought
about when one misnames one's own desire, that is, attributes one's
own sexual desires to the female. In the *in bono* tradition, the hermaphrodite was a popular image for the ideal union of male and female
before the separation into genders and the subsequent Fall, becoming
in the Renaissance an emblem of Christian love and marriage. Varia-
tions of this interpretation were found in Plato and Philo Judaeus, with
neoplatonic versions by Ficino, Pico della Mirandola, and Leone Ebreo.
Typically, an initial creature or Adam was understood as being created
asexual or androgynous and then separated into male and female
before the Fall. For some, the separation was equated with sin and the
subsequent gender divisiveness caused by the Fall. In turn, the desire
for an androgynous state was perceived as an ideal obtainable through
coition and marriage. In this tradition, the hermaphrodite represents
the attempt to regain the wholeness of the sexually undifferentiated
creature or androgyne that existed before the separation into genders
and serves as an apt metaphor for ideal human love that imitates God's
androgynous creation.[41]

39. See, for example, Renate Poggioli, "The Pastoral of the Self," *Daedalus* 88 (1959):
694–99; Harry Levin, *The Myth of the Golden Age in the Renaissance* (Bloomington:
University of Indiana Press, 1969), 176; Friedman, *Marvell's Pastoral Art*, 72; Margarita Stocker, *Apocalyptic Marvell* (Athens: Ohio University Press, 1986), 251.

40. For the varying interpretations of the hermaphrodite in the Renaissance see
A. R. Cirillo, "The Fair Hermaphrodite: Love-Union in the Poetry of Donne and
Spenser," *Studies in English Literature* 9 (1969): 81–95; Jerome Schwartz, "Scatology
and Eschatology in Gargantua's Androgyne Desire," *Etudes Rabelaisiennes* 14 (1977):
265–75; Julie Ann Lepick, "The Castrated Text: The Hermaphrodite as Model of Par-
ody in Ovid and Beaumont," *Helios* 8 (1981): 71–85; Marilyn R. Farwell, "Eve, the
Separation Scene, and the Renaissance Idea of Androgyny," *Milton Studies* 16 (1982):
3–20; Carla Freccero, "The Other and the Same: The Image of the Hermaphrodite in
Rabelais," in *Rewriting the Renaissance*, eds. Margaret W. Ferguson, Maureen
Quilligan, and Nancy J. Vickers (Chicago: University of Chicago Press, 1986), 145–58;
Marie Delcourt, *Hermaphrodite: Myths and Rites of the Bisexual Figure in Classical
Antiquity* (London: Studio Books, 1961).

41. For discussion of this tradition in patristic writers and in Marvell's time see
Mieke Bal, "Sexuality, Sin and Sorrow: The Emergence of the Female Character (A
Reading of *Genesis* 1–3)," *Poetics Today* 6 (1985): 21–42; Mary Nyquist, "Gynesis, Gen-
esis, Exegesis, and the Formation of Milton's Eve," in *Cannibals, Witches, and
Divorce: Estranging the Renaissance*, ed. Marjorie Garber (Baltimore: Johns Hopkins
University Press, 1987), 147–208; George Boas, *Essays on Primitivism and Related Ideas
in the Middle Ages* (Baltimore: Johns Hopkins University Press, 1948), 15–86; and

Marvell's assertion, "Two Paradises 'twere in one / To live in Paradise alone," looks both at the *in malo* and *in bono* interpretations by acknowledging the Ovidian tradition and its Petrarchan manifestations while also looking toward the ideal. The Petrarchan poet embodies the emasculating myth of Hermaphroditus in his substitution of words for substantial love of the woman.[42] In the *in bono* concept of the hermaphrodite, male and female are united equally in harmony so that procreation takes place internally much as the Renaissance thought some trees to be asexual or androgynous in their production of fruit.[43] An emblem of ideal human marriage by Barptolemaeus Anulus depicts a male and female figure as Hermaphroditus entwined around a tree producing the fruit of harmony. The figure is flanked by Moses and a satyr, representing respectively spiritual union and its dissolution with the Fall.[44] The congruence between male and female, word and thing, echoes the congruence between the Books of Nature and of God that the sin of "Passions heat" or Petrarchan idolatrous love of one's creation has severed. Marvell's image emphasizes linguistic and sexual similarity, not difference. The hermaphrodite reinternalizes masculine and feminine and becomes Marvell's figure for his own poem, which carves the tree's own name on the bark.

Priest, *Garden of Eden*, 78–82. Joshua Sylvester, *The Divine Weeks of Du Bartas*, ed. Susan Snyder (Oxford: Clarendon Press, 1979), 291, summarizes much of this tradition: "Source of all joyes! sweet *Hee-Shee*-Coupled One / Thy sacred Birth I never thinke upon, / But (ravisht) I admire how God did then / Make Two of One, and One of Two againe."

42. See Lauren Silberman, "The Hermaphrodite and the Metamorphosis of Spenserian Allegory," *ELR* 17 (1087): 207–23.

43. Priest, *Garden of Eden*, 78–82; Maren-Sofie Røstvig, *The Happy Man: Studies in the Metamorphosis of a Classical Ideal* (New York: Humanities Press, 1962), 1:270–73; Sir Thomas Browne, *The Major Works*, ed. C. A. Patrides (Baltimore: Penguin, 1977), 148, says that "I could be content that we might procreate like trees, without conjunction, or that there were any way to perpetuate the world without this triviall and vulgar way of coition."

44. *Picta Poesis* (Gottingen, 1552), fols. 14ff. A similar emblem of "amor coniugalis" appears in Mathia Holtzwart, *Emblematum Tyrocinici* (1581), emblem 35. Marvell's interpretation also echoes Paracelsus, *Paracelsus: Selected Writings*, ed. Jolandt Jacobi (Princeton: Princeton University Press, 1951), 73: "A man without a woman is not whole, only with a woman is he whole"; and Thomas Vaughan, *Anthroposophia Theomagica, or A discourse of the nature of man and his state after death*, ed. Arthur E. Waite (London: Theosophical Publishing House, 1919), 34: "As . . . the conjunction of male and female tends toward a fruit and propagation becoming the nature of each, so in man himself that interior and secret association of male and female, to wit the copulation of male and female soul, is appointed for the production of fitting fruit of Divine Life. . . . For life is nothing else but an union of male and female principles, and he that perfectly knows this secret knows the mysteries of marriage—both spiritual and natural. . . . Marriage is no ordinary trivial business, but in a moderate sense sacramental. It is a visible sign of our invisible union to Christ."

In Marvell's myth of human love in "The Garden," before the Fall, when there is infinite time and "coyness" is no crime, there is no need to carve a mistress's name on the tree. However, after the Fall, lovers, with "Time's winged Charriot hurrying near," become "am'rous birds of prey" who "tear [their] Pleasure with rough strife" ("To His Coy Mistress," 22, 38, 43). It is precisely this strife between male and female, art and nature, that is encoded within and represented by Petrarchism and the *topos* of carving the mistress's name on trees. In "The Garden," Marvell wittily dismantles the *topos* by preferring to carve only the tree's own name on the bark, reflecting his desire for a return to an Edenic time when signifier and signified, male and female, were united without division or tension. The self-deluding sustaining myths of Petrarchan unrequited love are replaced by Marvell's ironic image of the hermaphrodite in whom there is ideal and real union without strife. In these terms, Marvell seeks a time that is "sweet and wholesome" and is "reckon'd but with herbs and flow'rs"—a return to nature as the model for human love. In Marvell's garden love reaches fruition just as words become things, with both replicating God's love and creation so that the poet's moral vision echoes his aesthetic vision.

Douglas D. C. Chambers

"To the Abbyss"
Gothic as a Metaphor for the Argument about Art and Nature in "Upon Appleton House"

THE OPENING LINES of "Upon Appleton House" place architecture at the center of the poem's debate about nature and art: "Within this sober Frame expect / Work of no Forrain *Architect*." Marvell's "this" is teasingly ambiguous. It refers both to the house and to the poem that, for the reader, is the "sober frame" in which we see the house. His identification of the frame of the poem with the frame of the house is also in the context of a rebuke to foreign architecture. What is "foreign" to both house and poem is not simply a borrowed style but a structure that is not natural or organic. The italicizing of the word *Architect,* moreover, introduces the theme of false architecture in order to contrast this with both poem and house, which are organic creations "composed here / Like Nature." Marvell is, of course, somewhat disingenuous in this contrast. Both poem and house are the works of men and, thus, of artifice. Even his comparison of Appleton House to "*Romulus* his Bee-like Cell" suggests how man is *not* like the bees. And the attention that he draws to the artifice of his comparison is underlined by a simile that employs both "like" and "as."

What the poem suggests, indeed insists upon, right from the outset is that the reader make the sort of discriminations in the poem about nature and art that the poet's persona comes to make in the course of the poem's narrative. And central to those discriminations is Marvell's metaphor underlining the relation between poetic and architectural structures: *ut architectura poesis,* so to say. As the poem assumes the "sober frame" of its subject (the house), so the house has a life in the poem that is reflected in such borrowed bibliographic phrases as "*Frontispiece of Poor.*"

The poem's initial attention to the difference between natural and artificial structures in architecture draws our attention to its own structure, an oratorical structure in which the long history of the convent serves as a *narratio.* Coming as it does so early in the poem (after the *exordium* and *propositio*), this *narratio* foregrounds the gothic past and its "wasting Cloister" as an architectural symbol of moral artifice set over against the true nature of Lord Fairfax's house and estate. Against the "unnatural" life of the convent is set true nature, "Nature, orderly and near," that the house represents. Against the dissembling piety of the nuns is ranged the true virtue of Sir William and Lord Fairfax, just as against the falsity of the nuns' liturgical needlework is ranged the *"antick Cope"* of the poet-prelate of *"Natures mystic book."*

In this discrimination architecture is important, not only that of Appleton House but its antecedent (and "quarry") the convent. Architecture becomes a metaphor for the argument between art and nature, passive and active virtue.[1] To admire the building only (whether house or convent) is to neglect the inward and spiritual for the outward and visible. The abbess is guilty of just this in her counsel to Isabella Thwaites, a speech in which she compares the Virgin Mary to the novice instead of the other way round.

> 'But much it to our work would add
> 'If here your hand, your Face we had:
> 'By it we should *our Lady* touch;
> 'Yet thus She you resembles much.'
>   (129–32)

Marvell's treatment of the history of the convent, then, mocks a superficial religiosity that confuses aesthetics with ethics.

In this argument true architecture has its place: the "green, yet growing Ark" of the wood is compared to Noah's *navis*, the nave of the true church, and contrasted to the abbey's enchanted castle and its "wasting Cloister." But as always in Marvell, these oppositions are not mere antinomies. In the midst of a poem of confusing appearances they too remind us of the necessity of attentive reading and discrimination. What is being rejected here is not building but a literally deracinated and artificial architecture, an architecture at the furthest remove either from Fairfax's house or the *"Fairfacian Oak[s]"* of his woods.

The abyss to which Marvell's persona passes in stanza 47 is an abbey of another kind. The word *abbyss* is itself an interesting clue to Marvell's dialectic here, suggesting as it does in its original spelling a lexical

---

1. Marvell's poem, taking its cue from Lord Fairfax's poem on the house, even seems to suggest that the house may be a sort of "incarnation" of Lord Fairfax. See Fairfax's "Upon the new-built House at Appleton." The metaphor picks up Augustinian commentary on the Greek verb "dwelt" (ἐσκήνωτε)—that Christ's was a temporary dwelling, a dwelling in a tent (σκηνὴ).

connection with the ruined abbey and its history in the preceding stanzas.[2] Against that artificial architecture is deployed a natural one whose "green spir's" are a sort of redeemed gothic in which nature is not hedged out but embraced. In stepping into it the poet passes not only through a redemptive baptism (as the Red Sea analogy suggests) but also into a new sense of nature in which "Sanctuary in the Wood" replaces the false sanctuary of the cloister.

Much of this has been noticed by previous critics. What has not been noticed is that Marvell's espousal of nature and his rejection of the gothic antiquarianism represented by the cloister is also political and occasional. In a recent article, Richard Helgerson has noted that by the first decade of the seventeenth century, a preference for native gothic culture had become a term in a "specifically nationalist discourse" that was increasingly anticourt and antimonarchical.[3] By midcentury this discourse was well developed and thoroughly associated not with architectural antiquarianism but with parliamentary opposition to royalist imperial usurpation.

In the apparently digressive history of the convent, Marvell takes on an argument about the nature of the gothic past that was not only central to mid-seventeenth-century polity but very much an issue in the Fairfax household at the time of the poem's composition. His affirmation of the natural model and his rejection of the antiquarian is political;[4] it rebukes the whole carapace of ersatz mediaevalism that had become associated with Stuart claims to ancestral privilege. This natural model is consonant with the republican principles expressed by Marvell's friend, James Harrington, in his political treatise, *Oceana*, published in 1656. Like Harrington, who saw that there was an "irreversible drift towards republican forms in England,"[5] Marvell observed that "men may spare their pains when Nature is at work."[6]

2. In her recent article, "'Twas no *Religious House* till now': Marvell's 'Upon Appleton House,'" Patsy Griffin has noted that "Marvell's naming of the meadow 'the Abbyss' invites its comparison to the cloister of the abbess" (*Studies in English Literature* 28 [1988]: 69). It seems to me just as likely that "abbyss" is a visual pun on the plural of "abbey."
3. "Barbarous Tongues: The Ideology of Poetic Form in Renaissance England," *The Historical Renaissance: New Essays on Tudor and Stuart Literature and Culture*, ed. Heather Dubrow and Richard Strier (Chicago: University of Chicago Press, 1988), 289–90.
4. Cf. Marvell's argument from nature to justify Charles I's execution in l. 41 of "An Horatian Ode."
5. Christopher Hill, *Puritanism and Revolution* (Harmondsworth: Penguin, 1986), 290.
6. *The Rehearsal Transpros'd*, ed. D. I. B. Smith (Oxford: Clarendon Press, 1971), 135. Whether Marvell was or was not a thorough republican, his argument from nature was a republican argument.

In this republican position, as Christopher Hill has pointed out, Marvell's principles are consistent not only with subsequent Whig theory but with earlier "Whig" arguments about the nature of the English constitution, arguments usually traced to the writings of Sir Edward Coke.[7] Marvell's position is also consistent with the interest of many early seventeenth-century historians in another aspect of the term *Gothic:* its identification with the political freedom of pre-Norman English history. Indeed, the works of Camden and Speed, associated with the first foundation of the Society of Antiquaries, were so closely identified with claims for Gothic "freedom," as enshrined in early English constitutions, that James I came to disapprove of their historical labors.

By the early eighteenth century all this was very familiar.[8] To the Enlightenment, Lionel Gossman has observed, "history was above all a means of freeing men (not necessarily all men, but at least those who had sufficient intelligence) from superstition, from routine and, as far as possible, from the brute force of circumstance by revealing them to themselves as responsible agents, creators of themselves, of their institutions, of their societies, and of all existing or possible explanations of the universe."[9] The early eighteenth-century English espousal of a Gothic enlightenment and an Anglo-Saxon constitution, however, rested upon seventeenth-century claims not only for true Gothic liberty but for a native language and constitution. Throughout the first four decades of the seventeenth-century, but especially in the 1640s, the arguments that had been used in the sixteenth century against the claims of the Church of Rome came to be used against arbitrary monarchical power. Citing Tacitus's *Germania,* Bede's *Ecclesiastical History,* Ralph Higden's *Polychronicon* and, more recently, Sir Thomas Smith's *De Republica Anglorum* (1583), a host of writers, literary and historical, sought to establish that "Gothic" precedent limited the king's powers under the rule of law.[10]

Opposition to what came to be called "the Norman Yoke" of royal supremacy took as its chief argument that even William the Conqueror,

---

7. *Puritanism and Revolution,* chaps. 3, 13.
8. Lord Cobham, the opposition Whig and supporter of "Wilkes and Liberty," built himself a Gothic temple at Stowe and wrote over the door, "I thank God I am no Roman." In this he was doing no more than Lord Bathurst at Cirencester or Henry Hoare at Stourhead, both of whom built Gothic memorials to King Alfred as symbols of opposition to Walpole's tyranny.
9. *Mediaevalism and the Ideologies of the Enlightenment* (Baltimore: Johns Hopkins University Press, 1968), 154.
10. For this survey I am indebted to Samuel Kliger, *The Goths in England* (Cambridge: Harvard University Press, 1952), chap. 2.

in asserting a *legal* claim to the throne of England, bound himself to the ancient Saxon and "Gothic" customs affirmed by his predecessor Edward the Confessor. Nathaniel Bacon's *Historical and Political Discourse of the Laws and Government of England* (1647) observed that the ancient Saxons were happier in their liberties and laid his claim to the restoration of that liberty in "the ancient Gothique law as this Island hath."[11] Even Milton, who was not unaware of the vices of the Saxons, upheld the same doctrine of Gothic freedom in his *Defense of the English People*, published early in 1651.

Marvell, whose "Horatian Ode" (written in 1650) deals with just these questions of royal power and prerogative, can hardly have been unaware of the place of the Gothic metaphor in this debate. That poem, written in the year of Marvell's taking up residence at Appleton House, seems also to include Lord Fairfax in its account of the king's execution.

> So when they did design
> The *Capitols* first Line,
> A bleeding Head where they begun,
> Did fright the Architects to run.
> (67–70)

The "Architects" who run from the "bleeding Head" discovered in the construction of the Capitol must surely, by analogy, include men like Fairfax who deserted the republican cause because of the king's execution.[12] And Marvell's sense of the loss to the state by such desertions is no less evident in "Upon Appleton House" than in the "Horatian Ode."

Fairfax's withdrawal from public affairs, moreover, was a withdrawal from the debate about Gothic liberty to an interest in antiquarian Gothicism. At the same time (c. 1650) that Marvell was composing "Upon Appleton House," the antiquary Roger Dodsworth was also living at Appleton under the patronage of Lord Fairfax and compiling what was to become the greatest of English monastic histories, the *Monasticon Anglicanum.*[13] In the compilation of that work Dodsworth was assisted by most of the antiquaries in England, among them John Aubrey and Sir William Dugdale, both of whom had occasion to lament

11. Cited in Kliger, *Goths*, 141.
12. Claude J. Summers, "The Frightened Architects of Marvell's 'Horatian Ode,'" *Seventeenth-Century News* 28 (1970): 5.
13. In her *History of the Society of Antiquaries* (Oxford: Oxford University Press, 1956), Joan Evans gives an account of Dodsworth's employment by Lord Fairfax and of how Dugdale came to take over Dodsworth's work and publish it as his own.

the destruction of these monuments of antiquity. In the year after the
publication of the first volume of the *Monasticon,* Dugdale wrote: "Of
the *Religious Houses, Hospitalls* and *Chantries* (those signall Monuments
of our Forefathers Pietie) I have shewed their Foundations, endow-
ments, and continuance, with their dissolution and ruine, which gave
the greatest blow to Antiquities that ever *England* had, by the destruction of so many rare Manuscripts, and no small number of famous
Monuments."[14] Dugdale here strikes a note that had been heard in
England almost since the dissolution of the monasteries in the sixteenth century. As early as 1549, John Bale, in his "Preface" to John
Leyland's *The Laboryouse Journey & Serche . . . for Englandes Antiquities,*
observed: "But alas our owne noble monumentes and precyouse Antiquities, whych are the great bewtie of our lande, we as lyttle regarde
them as the parynges of our nales."[15]

By the early seventeenth century, this criticism had become widespread. Writing in 1631, John Weever deplored the greed of Henry VIII
in destroying these "conspicuous and certaine Monuments of zealous
devotion towards God."[16] And indeed partly out of this spirit of reaction arose the Laudian repair and reconstitution of (largely gothic)
church buildings, represented by George Herbert's restoration of the
church at Leighton Bromswold, the repair of the chapel at nearby Little
Gidding by Nicholas Ferrar, and Sir James Shirley's famous gothic
rebuilding of the church at Staunton Harold. This reactionary and
antiquarian gothicism was largely Anglican and Royalist. In preempt-
ing gothicism for the side of tradition and establishment, it threatened
one of the most potent republican metaphors: gothic as representative
of the liberty of the people before Norman royalist impositions.

The antiquarian reaction against the destruction of the monastic past
had three themes that were relevant to the situation at Appleton House
and, therefore, to Marvell's poem. The first was a lament for the
destruction of manuscripts. The second was a belief that the sacrilege of
destruction would bring a curse on families taking possession of conse-
crated property. And the third was a regret that the disappearance of
monastic institutions left no place for spiritual retreat.

The lament for the destruction of manuscripts (the first theme) is

14. Preface, *Antiquities of Warwickshire* (London: by Thomas Warren, 1656), sig. b3v.
15. London: for S. Mierdman, 1549, sig. [E7v].
16. *Ancient Funerall Monuments within the united Monarchie of Great Britaine,
Ireland, and the Ilands adiacent, with the dissolved Monasteries therein contained; their
Founders, and what eminent Persons have been in the same interred* (London, 1631), 322. I
am indebted for this survey of antiquarian responses to Gothic buildings to Margaret Aston's "English Ruins and English History: The Dissolution and the Sense of
the Past," *Journal of the Warburg and Courtauld Institutes* 36 (1973): 231–55.

much canvassed by Bale in his preface to *The Laboryouse Journey & Serche . . . for Englandes Antiquities*. Indeed he quotes a letter of Charlemagne to Alcuin of York asking that the library at York be copied and sent to Turin: "Let not the wele kepte garden be so reserved in Yorke, but that we maye also taste in Turon the fruytes of that swete paradyse."[17] Although the garden metaphor might be Marvell's, literary scholarship is not dealt with directly in his poem. This concern with ancient manuscripts is germane, however, to the literary antiquarianism that characterized both the work of Dodsworth and his patron Lord Fairfax, and that is seminal to the family's history as treated in the poem.

Before the Siege of York by the Parliamentary forces in 1644, Fairfax had employed Dodsworth to copy the huge store of old manuscripts in St. Mary's Tower (part of the former abbey) there, and after the destruction of the tower in the siege Dodsworth was again employed to collect what manuscripts remained intact. Fairfax himself owned many mediaeval manuscripts, among them a copy of Gower's *Confessio Amantis* that had belonged to "the blooming Virgin *Thwates*."[18]

Indeed the history of the Thwaites family occurs several times in the "one hundred and twenty-two volumes of his own writing" that Dodsworth compiled and subsequently left to Fairfax.[19] So too, in several places, there are references to the foundation and charters of the Nunappleton convent. Indeed, it was probably from Dodsworth's researches that Marvell gleaned that convent's "history."[20] It is to this history that he offers a corrective reading (and a rebuke to sentimental antiquarianism) at the end of his long *narratio* of the convent.

"Upon Appleton House," however, is less concerned with the destruction of historic manuscripts than with the second of these themes, the theme of sacrilege. In stanza 27, Sir William Fairfax's rebuke to the nuns employs a forceful retributive image:

17. Leyland, sig. [F2v].

18. Clements R. Markham, *A Life of the Great Lord Fairfax* (London: Macmillan, 1870), 148–49, 369. Fairfax is also commonly credited in York with having saved the medieval glass of the Minster by refusing to allow his troops to smash it.

19. Richard Gough, *British Topography* (London, 1780), 2:305, cited in Joseph Hunter, *Three Catalogues describing . . . the Dodsworth Manuscripts in the Bodleian Library* (London, 1838), 60. There are in fact 160 manuscript notebooks by Dodsworth in the Bodleian, see Joan Evans, *Society of Antiquaries*, 24.

20. This material is largely collected in the entry on Nun Appleton on page 107 of volume three of the *Monasticon* (1603), but some of it also appears variously in Dodsworth's manuscript collections. Joseph Hunter's *Three Catalogues* lists no. 121 as containing the foundation charter of the convent. The *Index to the first seven volumes of the Dodsworth Manuscripts* (Oxford, 1879) has several entries on the Thwaites family, and volume five gives their descent at 34b. The Thwaites material is also dealt with in the edition of Dodsworth's *Yorkshire Church Notes*, ed. J. W. Clay, *Yorkshire Archaeological Society Record Series* 34 (1904): 55, 101, 153.

'Were there but, when this House was made,
'One Stone that a just Hand had laid,
'It must have fall'n upon her Head
'Who first Thee from thy Faith misled.'

                                              (209–12)

Marvell seems there to be replying to the prophecies of disaster cata-
logued in Henry Spelman's *History and Fate of Sacrilege*. Although his
book was not published until 1698, Spelman spent twenty years collect-
ing this material before his death in 1648, and his work was certainly
known by Dodsworth with whom he corresponded. In it he catalogues
many instances of disasters befalling those who despoiled monastic
buildings, among them cases of stones falling from despoiled buildings
and killing the new owners or their workmen. Indeed these observations continued to be repeated throughout the seventeenth century. In
the "Preface" to the 1717/18 edition of the *Monasticon* the antiquary
Thomas Hearne noted that the "visible Effects of God's *Vengeance* and
Displeasure" for seizures of monastic lands were evident "in the strange
and *unaccountable* Decay of some Gentlemen in [his] own time."[21]
    Certainly the tone of these recriminations is reflected in the frontis-
piece of the *Monasticon* itself, a plate engraved by Wenceslas Hollar (Fig. 1).
If Marvell's "*Frontispiece of Poor*" alerts us to his poem's interchange
between architecture and literature, Hollar's engraved frontispiece to the
Monasticon demands a "reading" of its allusive historical and emblematic
meanings. At the top of the page a depiction of the granting of Magna
Carta includes an assembly of lords spiritual and temporal. Among the
spiritual lords, to whom in fact the charter is being given, must be
included the abbots of the great medieval monasteries. This in itself
constitutes a rebuke to the usual post-Reformation identification of monastic orders with tyrannical authority and corruption.[22]
    This central incident is flanked by smaller depictions of pre-Reforma-
tion piety and faith (on the left) whose learning is passed on (apparently in the form of Anglo-Saxon manuscripts) to a melancholy antiquity (on the right), darkened by the destruction of the monasteries.[23]

---

21. Hearne's remarks appeared first as "Preliminary Observations" on Browne
Willis's *An History of the Mitred Parliamentary Abbies* (1718).
    22. Hollar's depiction of King John, for example, may be a refutation of the plate in
Foxe's *Book of Martyrs* in which the king is forced to relinquish his crown to an
assembly of clerics including a cardinal, bishops, abbots, and priests.
    23. John Bale complained about the loss of these ancient manuscripts as early as 1549:
"Neyther the Britaynes under the Romanes & Saxons, nore yet the Englyshe people under the Danes and Normanes, had ever such dammage of their lerned monuments, as
we have seane in our time." ("Preface" to John Leyland, *Englandes Antiquities*, sig. B2).

Fig. 1
Frontispiece by Wenceslas Hollar for William Dugdale,
Monasticon Anglicanum (London, 1718).

As if that weren't enough, the plate includes, at the bottom of the page, the conventional antiquarian image of Henry VIII as a despoiler uttering the words of the Renaissance tyrant "*Sic volo*" (i.e. "*Sic volo, sic iubeo*") in contrast to the saintly Edward the Confessor, the endower of the church.

King Edward's portrait in this engraving is obviously taken from William Marshall's famous portrait of Charles I (Fig. 2) in the *Eikon Basilike* (1649), an engraving that Hollar was to use again in the plate for Lancelot Andrewes's *The Form of Consecration of a Church* (1659). In the plate in the *Monasticon*, Hollar, in other words, makes overt what lies covert in Dodsworth's work: the identification of antiquarian interest with the royalist cause and traditional Anglican sanctity. In other words, as Annabel M. Patterson has pointed out, the royalist cause was given "the unambiguous status of a religious emblem."[24]

Indignation against the sacrilege of monastic spoliation was not confined to historians and antiquaries. John Denham's *Coopers Hill*, one of the classics of seventeenth-century topographical poetry, was written in 1640 and went through five unauthorized impressions before its publication in 1655. In it the poet turns from his survey of the landscape between Windsor and London to a historical *narratio* curiously similar to Marvell's written a decade later. Denham, however, deplores Henry VIII's destruction of the monasteries and ascribes it to the king's intemperate, unchaste injustice.

> Who sees these dismal heaps, but would demand
> What barbarous Invader sackt the land?
> But when he hears, no Goth, no Turk did bring
> This desolation, but a Christian King;
> When nothing, but the Name of Zeal, appears
> 'Twixt our best actions and the worst of theirs,
> What does he think our Sacriledge would spare,
> When such th'effects of our devotion are?[25]

24. *Marvell and the Civic Crown* (Princeton: Princeton University Press, 1978), 20. Compare Patterson's treatment of the Stuart tradition of apotheosized power represented by the image of Charles I/Caesar in Francis Cleyn's plate for *Eclogue* V in John Ogilby's 1654 edition of Virgil. Annabel Patterson, *Pastoral and Ideology* (Oxford: Clarendon Press, 1988), 175.

25. *Poems and Translations* (London, 1668), ll. 149–56. Denham's obvious linking of the Henrician spoliation with the destruction of the civil wars is a telescoping of time morally that is like Marvell's linking of the dissolution of the cloister with Lord Fairfax's assumption of its ownership. Cf. Rosalie Colie's useful phrase, "radically pleated" (*"My Ecchoing Song": Andrew Marvell's Poetry of Criticism*, [Princeton: Princeton University Press, 1970], 254). Denham's "Instructions to a Painter" (1667) were later to be answered by Marvell's "Last Instructions to a Painter."

Fig. 2
Portrait of Charles I by William Marshall for Charles I,
Eikon Basilike (London, 1649). Courtesy of Thomas Fisher Rare
Book Library, University of Toronto.

In this *narratio* Denham (an ardent Royalist though a convinced Protestant) is plainly addressing not only the spoliation of the Henrician reformation but the destruction of ecclesiastical fabric in the civil wars as well.[26] This gives added point to Marvell's rebuke to antiquarian outrage about the destruction of ecclesiastical buildings, a rebuke delivered by Sir William Fairfax to the nuns: "Vice infects the very Wall. / But sure those Buildings last not long, / Founded by Folly, kept by Wrong" (216–18).

In *Coopers Hill*, Denham also takes up the theme of "sweet retir'd

---

26. Annabel Patterson, in *Pastoral and Ideology*, 162, similarly notes how the language of Virgilian pastoral was appropriated by royalists to express an encoded loyalty.

content," a theme that is central to the passage (stanzas 35–46) that immediately follows the *narratio* of the convent in "Upon Appleton House."
Solitary retirement is not, of course, a theme confined to monastic withdrawal, though Robert Leighton the seventeenth-century Archbishop of
Glasgow struck a common note when he complained that the abolition of
monasteries left no "retreat for men of mortified tempers."[27]

Fairfax's withdrawal from the world, however, is a central subject in
Marvell's poem, not least in the poet's own serio-comic reenactment of
that withdrawal in the latter part of the work.[28] Solitude, moreover, was
a theme very dear to Fairfax's heart. His collection of prose writing he
called *The Recreations of my Solitude* and his poetry collection, *The Im-
ployment of my Solitude*. In the latter, Fairfax's poem "The Solitude" (a
translation of Saint-Amant's earlier seventeenth-century poem) expresses a pleasure in ruins. Saint-Amant's "ancient Ruinated Towers,"
"Marble Stones here strew'd about," and "lowest Valts" may not (in
Fairfax's translation) have been monastic, but the appeal of such a
subject to the owner of the ruined convent is clear.[29] Marvell's *narratio*
on the convent ruins, moreover, goes beyond a mere rebuke to antiquarianism. It also invokes the identification of ruins with collapsed
royalist hopes that Annabel M. Patterson notes in connection with the
plate for *Georgics* 2:530 in John Ogilby's edition of Virgil.[30]

What is clear as well, as Rosalie Colie points out, is that at the center
of "Upon Appleton House" is a debate about "the retired and active
life," and that the terms of this debate are set out in the "long historical
nunnery episode" that she describes as "weighing heavily on the
poem." She also notes that the poem contains "the contrary moods of
l'allegro and *il penseroso*" in an equivocal dialectic: a dialectic that is
obvious as early as the tension between "Forrain" and "*Architect*" in the
first stanza.[31] Of course, the poem contains the monastic metaphors of

27. See Margaret Aston, "English Ruins and English History," 237.

28. In *Marvell and the Civic Crown*, Patterson notes how Fairfax, even in retirement,
could not avoid having to deal with the biblical and "georgic" claims of the Diggers,
claims that press upon the haymaking passage in "Upon Appleton House" (156). She
also remarks that Ogilby's royalist edition of Virgil in 1649 speaks "to the circumstances
of engagement politics, circumstances unique to the years 1649 to 1655" (*Pastoral and
Ideology*, 173). This is no less true of the hermeneutic of "Upon Appleton House."

29. Markham, *A Life*, 421–22. Fairfax's poems have been edited by Edward Bliss
Reed in *Transactions of the Connecticut Academy of Arts and Sciences* 14 (1909). The
quotations from "The Solitude" appear on 265–67.

30. *Pastoral and Ideology*, 180. Although these plates did not appear until the 1654
edition, their emblematic currency was part of earlier royalist imagery, and Marvell's
poem may in part be a response to the royalist tone of Ogilby's 1649 edition.

31. "*My Ecchoing Song*," 264, 281. See also Warren Chernaik on the poem's unre-
solved polarities in *The Poet's Time: Politics and Religion in the Work of Andrew Marvell*
(Cambridge: Cambridge University Press, 1983), 28.

Milton's earlier poems, too. Indeed, Milton, who was no advocate of "a fugitive and cloistered virtue," is instructive in the use of monastic metaphors as well as in the tension between passive and active, subjective and objective, involved and withdrawn, art and nature that Marvell also takes up.

Perhaps as interesting in the English history of the *beatus ille* theme is its treatment in that most popular of seventeenth-century romances, Sidney's *Arcadia*. There, too, the themes both of solitude and retirement are treated at best ambiguously. The Dorus who sings "O sweet woods . . . how much I do like your solitarines!" is nonetheless rebuked for his false love of withdrawal from a life of active virtue. And Basilius, the central figure of the romance who withdraws from an apprehension of dangerous insurrection into a fortified garden very like Fairfax's, is also the subject of a moral humbling.[32] As late as 1718, in Stephen Switzer's *Ichnographia Rustica* and in his designs for Grimsthorpe (Fig. 3), we can see the survival of bastions within a landscape: safe vantages from which to view rude nature.[33] They are in part a testimony to the continuing popularity of Sidney's *Arcadia* where Basilius's garden is similarly described as a pentagon against the world's dangers. But Basilius's withdrawal is an erroneous escapism; moral dangers will not stay beyond his fortified defenses.

By the time that Marvell wrote "Upon Appleton House," it must also have been obvious that the boundary between tamed and untamed nature could no longer be enforced by a gate, a wall, or a moat. In 1645 for example, the destruction of Campden House, Gloucestershire, by the royalist forces that had been occupying it with the consent of its royalist owner, was evidence that the rude world of Parliamentarianism could not be kept out by a meager wall or gate.[34] Fairfax himself, as Parliamentary general, was responsible for the execution of Baron Capel of Hadham, a Royalist who attempted to begin the civil war again

32. Dorus, who becomes Musidorus in the 1590 Arcadia, sings this song at the end of the second eclogues in the *Old Arcadia*; quoted from *The Poems of Sir Philip Sidney*, ed. W. A. Ringler, Jr. (Oxford: Clarendon Press, 1962), 68. The ironic distancing of pastoral escapism is, of course, present in the *locus classicus* of the *beatus ille* theme, Horace's *Epode* 2.

33. See William Stukeley's drawing of this design from Bodleian MS. Top. Gen. d. 14, fol. 36v, reproduced in *Journal of Garden History* 8.2–3 (1988), 52.

34. Inigo Jones's many designs for gates, indeed van Somers's portrait of Anne of Denmark standing at the gate of Oatlands, are evidence of the potency of this metaphor of containment to royalists. See Paul Everson, "The Gardens of Campden House, Chipping Campden, Gloucestershire," *Garden History* 17:2 (Autumn, 1989), 116.

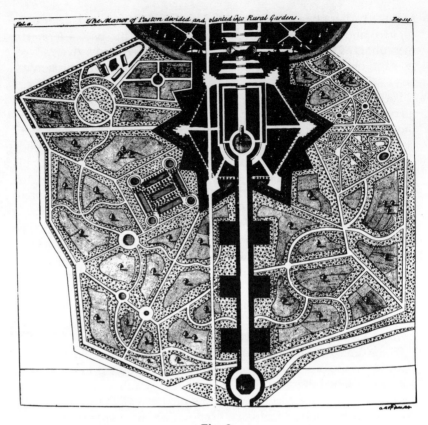

Fig. 3
Stephen Switzer, *Ichnographia Rustica* (London, 1742).
Courtesy of Trinity College Library, University of Toronto.

in 1648. In the famous portrait of Capel's family by Cornelius Johnson, for example, one can see clearly the sort of elaborate Italianate enclosed garden that the civil wars swept away. Fairfax was also involved in the strategy of "slighting" castles—of destroying their military advantage by blowing up one wall of the fortifications. Is not this point underlined by the very vulnerability of "proud *Cawood Castle*" to the mental and visual "*Battery*" of the "*Bastions*" of Appleton House?

"Upon Appleton House" espouses a right kind of retirement as against its monastic perversion. Similarly, its argument is not against Gothicism per se (as the "green spir's" of nature's Gothic illustrate) but against a nostalgia for the recent Gothic past that mistakes an apparently sentimental attachment to Gothic architecture for the true meaning of Gothic antiquity.[35] (This is also germane to the serio-comic rejection of mere identification with nature in a postlapsarian world that Marvell himself comes to both in this poem and in "The Garden.") What, then, Marvell takes on in the *narratio* of the convent is not simply antiquarian gothicism, but gothic as a metaphor for the argument between art and nature. My point here is that the poem is at least in part occasional, that it answers to the antiquarian interests both of Dodsworth and Lord Fairfax and in so doing takes on the metaphor of Gothic antiquity that was so commonplace in the mid-seventeenth century.

This aspect of the poem, I would suggest, seems arcane to us only because we have lost the sense of the potency of the Gothic metaphor in the seventeenth century—or perhaps have been persuaded that the so-called Gothic Revival did not occur until the middle of the eighteenth century. Whether what I am talking about is a Gothic Revival or not, however, is irrelevant to the point that an argument from the Gothic was central to the political debate of the parliamentary settlement. It informs the very image that Marvell himself employs politically (though for different purposes) in *The Rehearsal Transpros'd* (1672): "So this Jewel of the Crown was for several hundred of years imbezel'd till *Henry* the 8*th.* and other Princes found it again by chance in the ruines of an old Monastery at the Reformation."[36]

In this context it makes perfect sense that Marvell should pass from the *narratio* of the convent to a lament not only for lost Paradise but for Fairfax's withdrawal to the "five imaginary Forts" of his garden. If it would be wrong to see this passage as a criticism of Fairfax, however, it would not be wrong, I believe, to see it as a critique of the process of withdrawal and engagement in a moral universe.[37] Marvell did not need Milton to instruct him in the dangers of a "fugitive and cloistered vertue, unexercis'd and unbreath'd, that never sallies out and sees her adversary, but slinks out of the race, where that immortall garland is to be run for."[38] His persona enacts just that process in this poem and his Mary Fairfax finds herself in a natural landscape as morally potent as the wood of *Comus* is for Milton's Lady.

35. The argument about the true meaning of Gothic has a long history subsequently. Certainly the debate about whether Gothic is stylistic or organic is central to Pugin's rebuke to the decorative gothicism of the late eighteenth century and to the campaign waged by Ruskin and Morris against such "Gothic Revivalists" as Gilbert Scott.

36. *The Rehearsal Transpros'd*, ed. Smith, 188.

37. Warren Chernaik has observed that "to retreat within the garden is to abandon the world outside to eternal perdition" (*The Poet's Time*, 40).

38. *Areopagitica*, ed. J. Max Patrick, in *The Prose of John Milton* (New York: New York University Press, 1968), 287.

M. L. Donnelly

"And still new stopps to various time apply'd"
Marvell, Cromwell, and the Problem of
Representation at Midcentury

PLACED IN THE context of their times, Andrew Marvell's strategies of representation in the Cromwell poems contribute significantly to our understanding of the available modes of ideological accommodation to events in England at midcentury. Marvell was a highly cultivated and intelligent observer, no less sensitive to moral discriminations than to aesthetic nuance. In a period when the traditional symbolic systems and the received order of things had been thrown into confusion, his choices of how to represent Cromwell's person and acts indicate what identifications, symbolisms, and beliefs he judged his contemporaries most likely to find plausible and persuasive as structures of explanation and understanding. In addition, in a narrower perspective, the kinds of images and figures deployed and the belief systems they imply can clarify for us the pattern of Marvell's own response and eventual commitment to Cromwell and his cause.

Two general observations need to be made at the outset concerning Marvell's range of choices among images, symbols, allusions, types, and figures of representation in these poems. First, while the poet theoretically could levy his examples from a wide spectrum of possibilities more or less apt for his purpose, many of the available particular options have a history of application and ideological associations that vitiate them for Marvell. This is particularly true of the standard repertoire of royalist images of power and political rank and function used before the civil wars. Second, I would postulate for Marvell and the intended audiences of his poems an implicit hierarchy of felt seriousness and weight ranging through the differing grounds of allusion and imagery: classical myth, classical history, Christian history and legend, and scriptural narrative. A certain amount of "truth-value" inheres for the poet and his audience even in the images of pagan, classical deities and heroes. That is, epideictic identification of a public figure with Jupiter or Mars can figure forth real values of majesty, power, and justice, on the one hand, or military prowess on the other, that the recipient of praise is actually felt to have. The affective significance of such identification can (but does not always) go far beyond the function of a mere code of predication, in which for "Mars" one reads the quality of "martial prowess." In a sufficiently cohesive social and ideological context, as for the Caroline court circle and its poets, such representations could transcend the decorative and suggest figural identification, the repetition in the represented person of eternal truths.[1] Identification with historical personages from the classical world would have for self-consciously "realistic" and pragmatic minds (minds like Bacon's, who concludes an analysis of the capabilities of human imagination with the dismissive phrase, "But it is not good to stay too long in the theatre"[2]) less of the potential taint of poetic fictions. Some representations, like the identification with Augustus so beloved to the Stuart courts, had been as resonant a validation of power as the evocation of myth, but their associations with the fallen monarchy as well as the changed facts and relations of political life in the 1650s rendered their use problematical. A new repertoire of models was required. Of the types of imagery deployed by Marvell and other Protestant writers, nonscriptural Christian history and legend plays the smallest role; the prestige and resonance of medieval kings and heroes was less in general than that of the greatest classical figures, and the taint of papist hagiography hung over too many saints and champions of the Middle Ages. Again, the cultivation by the Stuart line of associations with chivalry in general and the Arthurian legend in particular left their successors generally cool to such allusions.

The most potent representations, the associations or identifications evocative of the greatest convincing force and drawing upon the deepest reserves of personal belief, however, were scriptural allusions: the types and figures drawn from the sacred narratives. In *Eikon Basilike*, the signal propaganda success of the royalist identification of the martyred king with Christ provides the cardinal instance. If the Renaissance allegorist "is concerned to veil, or obscurely point to, or in some way render a truth which inheres in the nature of things," that truth evoked and appropriated from the explicit Word of God has an imme-

---

1. See my discussion of this kind of representation in "Caroline Royalist Panegyric and the Disintegration of a Symbolic Mode," in *"The Muses Common-Weale": Poetry and Politics in the Seventeenth Century,* ed. Claude J. Summers and Ted-Larry Pebworth (Columbia: University of Missouri Press, 1988), esp. 164–65.

2. *The Works of Francis Bacon,* ed. James Spedding et al., vol. 3 (London, 1859; rpt. Stuttgart–Bad Cannstatt, 1963), 346.

diacy and imperative claim upon the believer far beyond that to which
the more mundane and obscure signs of the natural order or profane
history and pagan myth can aspire. Elucidating the nature and tendencies of Protestant typology, Barbara Lewalski adduces "Luther's development of a future-oriented typological system in which the words of
scripture, regarded as God's promises, are seen to refer to the three
advents of Christ—in the flesh, in our souls by grace, and in glory—
with the eschatological advent, rather than Christ's life, serving as the
great antitype."[3] In an earlier article, Lewalski examined in Milton uses
of what she calls the concept of " 'correlative typology'—the disposi-
tion of many Protestants and especially Puritans to regard the contemporary Christian and the events of his life as correlative types with Old
Testament personages and events, both exemplars existing on essentially the same spiritual plane and alike looking for fulfillment at the
end of time."[4] The heightened value and significance lent to the contemporary, particular life and event, through its assimilation both to its
scriptural type and its eschatological completion, make the application
of scriptural types and figures the most potent poetic identifications
imaginable for this time, particularly in the context of the rising excitement of millenarianism that gathered force through the midcentury. As
a man and poet who scrupulously weighed his words and the engagements he made with them,[5] for Marvell to use representations based
on scriptural types at all tells much about the degree of his personal
commitment to the cause and person he celebrates; the particular selection of types he mobilizes tells even more about the way he understood
Cromwell and Cromwell's career, and about how he hoped to be able to
justify them to his countrymen.

The first of Marvell's poems specifically associated with Cromwell,
"An Horatian Ode," was written in the early summer of 1650.[6] The

3. Barbara K. Lewalski, *Donne's Anniversaries and the Poetry of Praise* (Princeton:
Princeton University Press, 1973), 144, 163. Lewalski cites J. S. Preus, *From Shadow to
Promise: Old Testament Interpretation from Augustine to the Young Luther* (Cambridge:
Harvard University Press, 1969), 185–94, for the formulation on p. 163. On Protestant
typology, cf. Murray Roston on "postfiguration" in *Biblical Drama in England* (Evan-
ston: Northwestern University Press, 1968), 67–78. Lewalski shows how Protestant
typology differs considerably from the medieval Catholic kind in its tendency to see
the individual, contemporary Christian as antitype. *Donne's Anniversaries*, chap. 5
passim, and *Protestant Poetics and the Seventeenth-Century Religious Lyric* (Princeton:
Princeton University Press, 1979), chaps. 3 and 4.
4. Lewalski's own summary of her article from *Donne's Anniversaries*, 160, n. 39; see
"*Samson Agonistes* and the 'Tragedy' of the Apocalypse," *PMLA* 85 (1970): 1050–61.
5. Annabel Patterson, *Marvell and the Civic Crown* (Princeton: Princeton University Press, 1978), 54ff.
6. I am disinclined to see "An Elegy upon the Death of My Lord Francis Villiers" as

delicate poise or detachment of Marvell's judgment in this piece has often been noted.[7] It is true that the facts of Cromwell's career up to 1650 are singularly resistant to treatment in terms of the established vocabulary of state poems of praise. Confronted by the resignation of Fairfax, Leveller agitation in the army, and the threat of Scottish invasion, Cromwell's position at the time of the poem was awkward to dramatize or legitimate in any terms. He was an astoundingly successful general; as commander of the army, he held a virtual monopoly on effective power in England either to defend the state or to subvert it. His deeds had not the slightest shadow of legitimacy, despite the justificatory rhetoric manufactured by Parliament; but on the other hand, they had the irrefragable sanction of success, which for the seventeenth century raised delicate questions about the cooperation or sufferance of providence. His purposes, as always, were inscrutable. The celebration of so ambiguous a phenomenon demands of the poet who would weigh his words against truth virtually the invention of a new language of representation.

In contrast to the Stuart royalist panegyric mode, the most striking thing about the "Horatian Ode," written before the poet knew the Lord General personally, is its relentless commitment to activity and movement. In this feature, the first Cromwell poem anticipates the strategy of praise in all the rest. Cromwell is never static in the poem: he "could not cease / In the inglorious Arts of Peace, / But through adventrous War / Urged his active Star." The dominant mood of the poem is awe or wonder, at times content to record in astonishment, at others attempting to find among traditional materials a vocabulary that will explain and accommodate what is being witnessed. All the traditional materials levied, however, are comparisons with natural phenomena, or evocations of historical events and personages. Marvell thus significantly eschews the discredited royalist iconography of mythical allusion in his scrupulous effort to celebrate Cromwell's unprecedented achievements in the most "realistic" and historically grounded terms possible.

More interesting in the light of his strategy in the later Cromwell poems, and more significant of the degree of commitment he felt toward his subject at this time, he forgoes the sanction of religious and scriptural figures. In 1650, typology was busily being turned to service

---

a plausible attribution to Marvell. It lacks his usual poetic economy; some passages sound more like secondhand Donne, others like weak Clevelandism. Even were it his, the single direct and bitter reference to Cromwell would have interest in this study only as evidence of the distance traveled by the writer in his political sympathies between July 1648 and March 1654.

7. See headnote to the poem in *Poems and Letters* 1:295, for example.

by both the discomfited royalists and the triumphant but embattled sectaries. Marvell, however, manages to inscribe a poem celebrating national victories and as it were, yielding the praise extorted by his *virtù* to the man "that does both act and know," without ever warmly drawing near him in approval or declaring forthrightly in final ethical approval that such success must be the work of the favored agent of Providence.[8] We can only conjecture about the reason Marvell renounces typological representations and invocations of providential design in this poem, at this time; he may have simply regarded as imprudent the polemic invocation of such ultimate sanctions, especially when conclusions were still in doubt and providence hard to discern in the shifting pattern of events.

Whatever the reason, in poems by Marvell touching on Cromwell there is a noticeable shift in allusions and images: in the "Horatian Ode" natural and historical comparisons and identifications preponderate; in "A Letter to Dr. Ingelo," allusions to classical mythology carry Marvell's compliments to Queen Christina for the first three-fifths of the poem. The final shift in figural authorization from pagan Classical to Christian sacred text or history is marked at line 83 of the "Letter to Dr. Ingelo," written probably in early March 1654,[9] with an echo of Virgil's Messianic eclogue, "Ad Pollio": "*Upsalides Musae nunc et majora canemus.*" The transition to Christian and scriptural typology to represent the Protector marks a significant intensification of ideological commitment for Marvell, while the attributes of motion and process continue as the appropriate tropes of power, as in all Marvell's panegyrics to Cromwell.

In "The First Anniversary of the Government under O. C.," his climactic exercise in ideological justification and mythopoesis for the Protector,[10] Marvell entertains a surmise consummating the marriage

8. "The force of angry Heavens flame" (26) could describe God's scourge (like Attila or Nebuchadnezzar) as well as His minister, the favored agent of divine design (like Moses or David).

9. See *Poems and Letters* 1:315, for dating.

10. However much he may have been "haranguing an empty room" in "An Horatian Ode" [John Carey's phrase on "Tom May's Death," *Andrew Marvell: A Critical Anthology* (Baltimore: Penguin Books, 1969), 22] and addressing courtly compliment and diplomatic persuasion to a private audience of few or one in the poems to Queen Christina, "The First Anniversary" was a public piece and apparently viewed by the government as edifying propaganda for the people: first printed by the government's printer, Thomas Newcomb, sold by Samuel Gellibrand, it was also advertised in the government's own newspaper, *Mercurius Politicus*, no. 240, 11–18 January 1654/5; see *Poems and Letters* 1:319, 320; also Derek Hirst, " 'That Sober Liberty': Marvell's Cromwell in 1654," in *The Golden & The Brazen World: Papers in Literature and History, 1650–1800*, ed. John M. Wallace (Berkeley: University of California Press, 1985), 18.

of historical process and a Christian version of world order by sub-stituting for the repetitive types and icons of royalist *figura* the fiercely active images of chiliasm, moving history relentlessly toward its cul-minating acts. The governing conceits of "The First Anniversary" intertwine one of the most potent of traditional Classical and Christian ideas, represented in a cluster of metaphors engendered by the con-cept of harmony, with reflections on time and history dominated by a Protestant typology.

In asserting at the very beginning of the poem man's victimization by time and Cromwell's mastery of it, Marvell challenges the royalist trope of a timeless universe of static qualities. The opening movement repre-sents Cromwell's active *vis* as the agency that "the force of scatter'd Time contracts / And in one Year the work of Ages acts" (13–14), and contrasts with this an almost parodic version of the Caroline royalist images of monarchy in terms of static, frozen, repetitive gestures (13–44). The "heavy Monarchs" with whom Cromwell is contrasted fight by proxy, beg false renown for the deeds of their agents, oppress their subjects but fight no glorious foreign wars (like the crusade rec-ommended to Christina). "Image-like," "an useless time they tell," as irrelevant as the carved head on a viol is to the harmony actually pro-duced by the strings. In an allusion foreshadowing the ideological core of the poem, "They neither build the Temple in their dayes, / Nor Matter for succeeding Founders raise" (33–34).[11]

"Indefatigible" Cromwell, however, "hyes, / And cuts his way still nearer to the Skyes," where he learns a music "to tune this lower to that higher Sphere" (45–48). Cromwell's active enterprise, as well as the fact that his activities are in tune with heavenly designs, justifies the appro-priation to him of the Amphion image, which was a stock-in-trade of the Caroline courtly panegyrists. I want to emphasize here how Mar-vell lays the groundwork for his appropriation of the image, and by anatomizing the *process* and depicting it in a vocabulary redolent of design, volition, and motion, justifies its application in a way quite foreign to Waller's royalist panegyrics that supply the model. Specific recollection of the occasion of Waller's original praise of Charles I as

11. For detailed examination of some of the telling specific hits at contemporary events and rival ideologies and symbolic sanctions, see Patterson, *Marvell and the Civic Crown*, 74–90; and Hirst, "Marvell's Cromwell in 1654," *passim*. However, nei-ther gives due weight to the fact that the classical imagery fades and all but disap-pears after the first 102 lines of the poem, to be replaced (as in the "Letter to Doctor Ingelo") with scriptural typology and allusions. In fact, almost all the classical mate-rial in the poem is related to the extended elaboration of the Amphion figure, while Marvell carries out his climactic and conclusive appeal to Christian Protestant typology through a copious proliferation of allusions to scriptural texts and heroes.

Amphion in comparison with Cromwell's programs and accomplish-
ments heightens the praise of the Protector.[12] It is Time, history, which
royalist ideology denied, that serves (punning on the Instrument of
Government) as Cromwell's medium or instrument:

> The listning Structures he with Wonder ey'd,
> And still new Stopps to various Time apply'd.
> . . . .
> Such was that wondrous Order and Consent,
> When *Cromwell* tun'd the ruling Instrument.
> (57–58, 67–68)

The harmonic conceit that Marvell deploys here embraces allusions to
music, architecture, geometry, policy, and morals to assert the revolutionary government's mastery of the very liberal arts and ornaments of
life its detractors claimed it lacked.

The representation of Cromwell's government of the state as a balancing of forces, like the construction of an arch in the frozen harmony
of architecture (87–98), suggests Archimedes, who boasted that, if he
had a place to stand, he could move the earth (99–100). Cromwell has
"moved the earth" in terms of the innovations he has effected. The
transition from this recognition of a revolutionary alteration of fundamental givens to ideological support for the Protectorate is made easy,
bridged by Marvell's appropriation of the imagery of millennialist fervor
that was approaching a climax in England about this time. In the context of earth-shaking change, Marvell draws from the apocalyptic passages in Daniel and Revelation a representation of Cromwell as a pattern teaching "observing Princes" to bend to accommodate the coming
of Christ as Final Judge promised in the language of Psalm 2:10–12
(105–8). The visionary millennialist hope articulated in lines 131–44 then
climaxes the first celebratory movement of the poem and the theme of
harmony.

These apocalyptic hopes serve, however, as far more than rhetorical
ornament or a convenient strategy of hyperbolic praise.[13] Hirst pains-

12. Patterson, *Marvell and the Civic Crown*, 74–77; Hirst, "Marvell's Cromwell in
1654," 33–34.
13. "Legitimation was, of course, the most urgent goal of all the parliamentarian
regimes after the execution of Charles. . . . The prophetic dimension legitimates the
Machiavellian founder of a new state. . . . Cromwell's role as the 'prophet armed'
transforms actions that might have had negative political significance" (Hirst, "Marvell's Cromwell in 1654," 38, 39, citing J. G. A. Pocock, ed., *The Political Works of James
Harrington* [Cambridge: Cambridge University Press, 1977] 15–76, esp. 23, 30–31, 37).
Again, I do not believe that recognition of the legitimating power of typology
requires us to see its use as cynical or merely calculating.

takingly shows how the Fifth Monarchy men, having hailed Cromwell in terms much like Marvell's "before that watershed summer of 1653," by the end of 1653 "were branding him as the horn of the Beast" and generating considerable fear among constitutionalist gentry and moderates that their agitation would stir up a radical coup by the army. To counter millenarian rhetoric that might unsettle the army, Marvell's representations offered a counterhermeneutic, "to teach the soldiery the correct meaning of Revelation in order to lessen the damage done by the Fifth Monarchists" (a strategy being pursued at the same time by "Marvell's friend" Marchamont Nedham in *The Observator*). "Marvell attempted to limit potential damage by reclaiming the high religious ground for the Protector, warning the radical saints that they had got the meaning of the 'holy Oracles' all wrong and that they should abandon their hostility, for Oliver was still the great captain." Finally, Hirst suggests, like Wallace and Patterson, that counsel is at the same time offered to the object of praise. In addition to quelling the rising millenarian opposition to Cromwell and reassuring "constitutionalist gentlemen," Marvell was also attempting, in a discreet Horatian manner, to convince Cromwell to resist both the capitulation to a lesser power and role by accepting the crown, and to resist open espousal of a role proclaimed by hare-brained prophets.[14]

This is not to suggest that Marvell is calculatedly using a convenient stick to beat a dog. Modern scholars, perhaps reading their diffidence and skepticism back into their poet, are generally reluctant to credit Marvell's millennialism very far. They cite the abrupt termination of the happy conjecture:

> But a thick Cloud about that Morning lyes,
> And intercepts the Beams of Mortal eyes.
> (141–42)

But Hirst asserts that "even textually its apparent doubts are close to the language of the book," citing the clouds of heaven that accompany the Son of man in Daniel, and noting that "if we look at what saints who were not rabid Fifth Monarchists were saying, Marvell does not seem at all backward."[15] As an example of the emotionally and intellectually effective mobilization of imagery in the service of ideology, the passage holds considerable interest rhetorically. Marvell's success lies in his

---

14. "Marvell's Cromwell in 1654," 42–46.
15. Ibid., 35–36. Cromwell himself, Hirst notes, addressing Barebone's Parliament in the summer of 1653 "sounded almost like a paraphrase of Marvell."

ability to qualify with a subjunctive mood vividly realized and busily active scenes painted with strong verbs, and his retention of a tough-minded realism that refuses to omit the "buts." While the *enargeia* of figure and image elicits emotional assent, and the plausible grounds for the conjecture are firmly drawn, the skeptical intellect is never insulted by a dogmatic assertion of what cannot be positively known.[16] Nevertheless, as praise for Cromwell, the ethical and persuasive force of Marvell's qualified judgment on the proximity of the latest day is not diminished by the inclusion of the cautious "if":

> That 'tis the most which we determine can,
> If these the Times, then this must be the Man.
>
> (143–44)

The contemplation of the carelessness and unpreparedness of his countrymen prompts Marvell's interruption of these chiliastic conceits and engenders a counterpoised speculation: from contemplation of the day of respiration to the just, ushered in by Cromwell as Angel of the Apocalypse, he falls to reflection on Cromwell's possible fulfillment of another type, the sacrificial victim for the sins of men. The accident to the Protector's coach in Hyde Park, September 29, 1654, provides the vehicle for this exercise. In his management of this material, Marvell again discreetly coopts the royalist trope representing the martyred king as suffering servant and Christ-figure. The episode also presents an extended evasion of the obvious allusion to Plato's Phaedrian charioteer. Direct evocation of that figure here would not do, as it might imply the Protector's inability to fulfill the role of the rational soul as controller of the irrational passions and appetites. Marvell instead excuses "the poor Beasts," Cromwell's runaway horses, and lays the blame on "Our Sins," "Our brutish fury strugling to be Free," which "Hurry'd thy Horses while they hurry'd thee" (174, 177–78). In both what he voices and what he sinks in silence, Marvell's adaptation and adjustment of the traditional representations reveal an active judgment and restless intellectual energy at work interpreting events and appropriating (and excluding) meanings.

The sense of incompletion and frustration with which Marvell contemplates the present state of man's life in history finds its appropriate

16. Marvell's strategy here is distinctly reminiscent of Milton's in "On the Morning of Christ's Nativity," stanzas 9–18, which in fact Marvell echoes in lines 151–52. Both poets pull back from ecstatic anticipation of glory to reflect, like orthodox mainline protestants, on the limiting conditions of human frailty and sin and the inscrutable trials of history.

crystallization in reflections on the awkward fact of the recent accident in Hyde Park. The vision of the millennial harmonization and completion of history evokes the balancing recognition of the actual state of man *in* history, called to act, though required to rely on conjecture by dark lights. In each case, the result is glorification of Cromwell, whose imagined death results in his triumphant inclusion in the feast of the Lamb, while his thankless countrymen mourn below, and whose commitment to forward-looking action in life presents the only solution to the doubts that otherwise would paralyze the commonwealth:

> And well he therefore does, and well has guest,
> Who in his Age has always forward prest.
>
> (145–46)

Likewise the image of Cromwell's saintlike mother's living out an Age, which ought to suggest similar hopes for the son, instead evokes the contradictory awareness of how tenuous his hold on life indeed is, further warning his fractious fellow citizens to make the most of his strength and talents while they may.

This chiaroscuro effect, introducing into the poem unharmonious sounds—shrieks of despair and fear and the dying Chorus to the deaf seas and ruthless tempests—forces the poet to imitate the composing, ordering, tuning, and harmonizing power he celebrates in his subject:

> Let this one Sorrow interweave among
> The other Glories of our yearly Song.
> Like skilful Looms which through the costly thred
> Of purling Ore, a shining wave do shed:
> So shall the Tears we on past Grief employ,
> Still as they trickle, glitter in our Joy.
> So with more Modesty we may be True,
> And speak as of the Dead the Praises due.
>
> (181–88)

The violent emotions evoked by the fall, it turns out, are all ours, not Cromwell's. He is superior even to his imagined and inevitable death, having attained a Stoic immunity to private pleasure and pains. Or rather, Marvell attributes to the Protector the resignation of a Platonic philosopher-king, dearly bought

> When to Command, thou didst thy self Depose;
> Resigning up thy Privacy so dear,
> To turn the headstrong Peoples Charioteer;

> For to be *Cromwell* was a greater thing,
> Than ought below, or yet above a King:
> Therefore thou rather didst thy Self depress,
> Yielding to Rule, because it made thee Less.
>
> (222–28)

Concerning the Protector's marvelous superiority to human passions and weaknesses, we may turn for comparison to Waller's "Upon His Majesty's Receiving the News of the Duke of Buckingham's Death." But where Waller overplays hyperbolic comparison to literary and biblical figures outdone by Charles's composed magnanimity, Marvell delicately alludes to associations that, teased out, *explain* the qualities represented in his hero. From lines 220–64, and again in lines 283–320, a dominant thread of biblical allusion supports the ethos that the poem evokes and advertises. From the historical books of First and Second Kings and Judges, and then from the story of the patriarch Noah in Genesis, Marvell draws elements that highlight and counterpoint his representation of Cromwell. Various suggested interpretations of the typological arguments presented by these Old Testament figures may be found in Patterson, Hirst, and Stephen Zwicker. Stella P. Revard sees them as simply illustrations of "successful leadership and comment on its sometimes problematical consequences," but the weight of Protestant concepts of "correlative typology" or "postfiguration" assures that they carry more freight than that commonsensical interpretation—that they are in fact central to the poem's meaning.[17]

The Protector and his family are "like *Noah's* Eight," the mob of ranters, levellers, Fifth Monarchy men, and troublers of the commonwealth "such a *Chammish* issue." Marvell adapts his embedded stories to the contemporary situation. When Elijah was taken up into heaven in a fiery chariot, he left his mantle behind to Elisha whole, but Elisha rent his own garments in grief at his master's departure. Marvell's adaptation of the figure emphasizes the fact that, to vary the metaphor, no one can fill Cromwell's shoes; the mantle of sovereignty is torn asunder if left to others by the Protector (219–20). Marvell presents selected details of the story of Gideon, a great warrior prospered by God, who, like Cromwell, defeated two kings in battle, refused the regal power offered to himself and his sons, and chastised civilian

---

17. Patterson, *Marvell and the Civic Crown*, 81–88; Hirst, "Marvell's Cromwell in 1654," 25–27, 29–32, 39–44; Zwicker, "Models of Governance in Marvell's 'The First Anniversary,'" *Criticism* 16 (1974): 1–12; Revard, "Building the Foundations of a Good Commonwealth: Marvell, Pindar, and the Power of Music," in *"Muses Common-Weale,"* 189.

authorities who refused to assist his military policies or supply his army with its needed rations. The reader familiar with both stories can easily work out the suggested analogies, while in effect conflating the motivating design in the two narratives. The highlighted homologies leave the reader little choice in the conclusions he can draw:

> What since he did, an higher Force him push'd
> Still from behind, and it before him rush'd,
> Though undiscern'd among the tumult blind,
> Who think those high Decrees by Man design'd.
> 'Twas Heav'n would not that his Pow'r should cease,
> But walk still middle betwixt War and Peace;
> Choosing each Stone, and poysing every weight,
> Trying the Measures of the Bredth and Height;
> Here pulling down, and there erecting New,
> Founding a firm State by Proportions true.
>
> (239–48)

Similarly, Marvell's allusions to the apologue or fable of Jotham (257–64) would be lost on anyone not familiar with the scriptural passage; but for the knowledgeable, the oblique reference serves, in effect, to incorporate the whole scripture fable and its glosses into Marvell's text—a particularly effective use of intertextuality. Moreover, familiarity with the ground of the allusion induces a further intertextual relation: the behavior of the olive, fig, and vine in Jotham's fable recalls the natural response of the man fitted to be a philosopher-king in Plato's *Republic*, just as the association of Cromwell with Elijah as "charioteer" (224) automatically suggests not only the passage in Plato's *Republic* referred to in the notes to the standard edition, but more aptly, in a typical Marvellian adaptation of others' material, the Phaedrian charioteer (9.246a–47c, 15.253c–56e)[18] who controls the horses of the soul, the worse—the darker, recalcitrant one—being in the state analogous to the headstrong people of Marvell's line. Thus, by indirections and obliquities Marvell undergirds his praise of Cromwell with an ideology combining two of the strongest, most privileged texts in his tradition, and spells out in carefully selected details the ways in which their moral core may be interpreted and applied to the man he honors for his right

18. These passages are "the earliest intimation of the central doctrine of Plato's theology. . . . The priority of soul to body is either indistinguishable from or immediately involves its control of body (892a, 896c)," according to R. Hackforth, Commentary on Plato's *Phaedrus* (Cambridge: Cambridge University Press, 1979), 71. This doctrine that the best soul should rule is obviously relevant to "The First Anniversary."

knowing and well doing in history. By another kind of obliquity, the testimony of the anxious watching princes in lines 349–94 recapitulates Cromwell's praise in terms of the images, figures, oxymoronic transcendence of categories, and myths of pre–civil war royalist panegyric. Cromwell benefits from the hyperbolic but seemingly extorted praise, while the excesses of the monarchist ideology are distanced and "placed" by being put in the mouths of such witnesses.

Drawing into the imitative economy of his poem such elements as the depiction of the jealous kings, giving reluctant testimony to Cromwell's greatness even as they wish his death, and his representations of the mad enthusiasms of sectarian heretics and levellers, Marvell reproduces Cromwell's art of regiment by harmonizing (or at least holding in artistic tension) the cacophonous elements of the contemporary situation. The final trope of the poem, yet another scriptural allusion, ties the whole survey together, recalling the troubled "Watry maze" of "flowing Time" in the opening lines. As the sectarians represent febrile and chaotic energy, and the heavy kings, suddenly awakened from their slumbering dream of Cromwell's death, represent stasis, both accomplishing nothing, the poem ends with Cromwell himself again, the only stirrer or agitator who brings anything about. His activity is the agency of Grace; its object the disorders the poem has presented, disorders that through his means God will heal:

> thou thy venerable Head dost raise
> As far above their Malice as my Praise.
> And as the *Angel* of our Commonweal,
> Troubling the Waters, yearly mak'st them Heal.
>   (399–402)

The last two lines of the poem refer to the angel who stirred the water of the pool of Bethesda in John 5:4, so that whoever first stepped in after the motion of the water, was healed ("made whole"—Geneva) of whatever malady he had. Cornelius à Lapide glossing this miracle makes much of the fact of the *motion* of the water, first as a sign that the healing power is not a natural property of the water but an effect of God's beneficence and miraculous power given *with* the entry into the water (like Grace in a sacrament); second because "life consists in motion; death in quietness and torpor." Likewise, vigorous motion, conflicting with the nature of illness, may overcome it and expel it. A figurative application to the effect of Cromwell's restless energy on the fevered and diseased commonwealth of England is obvious. Identified by Chrysostum and others as a paralytic, the man who had suffered thirty-eight years with an infirmity was therefore, according to Ambrose, a type of the human race, tropologically paralyzed by the habit of inveterate sin. Even such is the English nation, awaiting the health-giving impetus of the Protector. Set against the paralysis and passive suffering of the sick sinner, the healing angel stirring the waters, a type of Christ, becomes the final version of the Marvellian trope of Cromwell's *vis* and virtue.[19]

"The First Anniversary of the Government under O. C." carried Marvell's exploration of the Protector's moral and historical role as far as he ever would go in the appropriation of religious types and images. Even such cautiously expressed millenarian hopes as Marvell's were decisively foreclosed, first by the inability of the Protectorate to reestablish a constitutional footing for continuity in government and finally by the removal by death of the Protector himself. Thus was the *novus ordo saeclorum* seemingly left high and dry as a freak of history, a missed chance, rather than the foundation of a new order or the precursor of history's end.

Though never a radical Republican like Milton, and far from a Fifth Monarchy man, Marvell was moved to revolutionary enthusiasm by the active force and virtue that he saw in Cromwell and Cromwell's personal rule. He had used to bolster his own conviction and had deployed as the most potent available argument to galvanize the support of his countrymen—as the final argument, really—the legitimating power of a divine mandate fulfilling millennial hopes. With the demise of the "lusty Mate" who had seized the helm and saved the ship of state from disaster, there were simply no available images or types, no *mythos* carrying conviction, that the poet could mobilize to mourn the hero and comfort the nation with the promise of continuity and succession. "A Poem upon the Death of O. C." is among Marvell's works a comparatively unsuccessful piece, rising in only a few places to memorable weight and power. Significantly, one is certainly the *Quantum mutatus ab illo Hectore* passage beginning, in the best strong-lined style, with the flatly prosaic but powerful personal testimony, "I saw him dead" (247). Perhaps we need seek no further for the poetic failure of this piece than the impossibility of giving any kind of intellectual or emotional coherence or promise to the event of Cromwell's death in the generic terms available to funeral panegyric. The ideology of Cromwell

10. Cornelius à Lapide, *Commentarius in quatuor Evangelia*, Tom. 2 (Antwerp, 1605), 317–18. See Hirst, "Marvell's Cromwell in 1654," 40–41, on the multiple valences of this type for Cromwell. If, however, his speculation that "heal" may be intransitive and refer to Cromwell's expulsion of the Rump is accepted, how are we to read "yearly"?

that Marvell had adopted and enthusiastically represented in "The First Anniversary" hinged upon the Protector's being *sui generis*, something greater than a king, the Man of Destiny and the chosen agent of Providence Divine. Clearly, finding the right words to cover the departure of such a figure from the stage is no easy task; the usual recourse in the case of mere hereditary monarchs, the shift of focus to the rising sun of succession, is rendered nearly impossible, although Marvell gamely tries. But if Cromwell *is* indeed *sui generis*, the promise that "A Cromwell in an houre a prince will grow" (312) rings singularly false. Every epithet and predication about Richard merely increases the reader's sense that he is a lesser man who cannot assume his father's mantle: "where his great parent led," he "Beats on the rugged track"; he "revives" and "assures" virtue "by his milder beams" (305-7). Even the hopeful last line seems to confess Richard's lesser force in a way that subverts its intended promise of renewed life-giving rain instead of the scriptural "great Justice that did first suspend / The world by Sin" ("The First Anniversary," 153-54) in the Flood: "He threats no deluge, yet foretells a showre" (325).

In this final tribute to the man who had seemed to him for a time able to change the course of history, Marvell's commitment to tact and truth forces him away from the mythopoesis—in his case, through the skillful adaptation of Protestant typology—that characterizes the panegyric exercise in the construction and validation of ideology. Where the poem seems poetically vital, the poet retreats to the terms of private virtue that upon closer acquaintance had convinced him of the man's greatness in the first place, and had justified the Platonic and biblical allusions and associations that authorized his rule. It is only in terms of the poet's private grief and testimony as one man to another—valor, religion, friendship, prudence—that the poem achieves its successful moments. With this effort, Marvell abandoned the field of panegyric and in the years ahead turned his talents to the less exalted but, as circumstances dictated, more necessary task of healing the commonwealth by chastising corruption and vice in satire—the obverse of the epideictic image in "the Poet's time," the time, not of the millennial "happy Hour," but of fallen history.

Richard Todd

Equilibrium and National Stereotyping in "The Character of Holland"

IN THE THIRD QUARTER of the seventeenth century, three short conflicts occurred between England and the United Provinces of the Netherlands. During the last part of the sixteenth century these countries had been allied against the Spanish imperialist cause, but by the time England herself had briefly become a Protestant republic at the middle of the seventeenth century, relations between them had worsened. Each of the Anglo–Dutch wars of 1652–1654, 1665–1667, and 1672–1674 arose from dissimilar circumstances. In the first two confrontations, the second of which was waged by an England in which the monarchy had already been restored, the rivalries were frankly mercantile and colonial. The third Anglo–Dutch war was rendered more complex by the political strains that had been initiated by Louis XIV's Triple Alliance with Sweden and the Netherlands in 1668. Hostilities were to continue, principally between the Netherlands and France, until the signing of a series of treaties in 1678–1679. Different in nature as their causes were, all three Anglo–Dutch wars provoked sustained outbreaks of political propaganda in which national stereotyping of the Dutch by the English played an important part.

From the English point of view, this propaganda was least assertive during the mid-1660s, and it must be assumed that the domestic disasters of those years—a recrudescence of bubonic plague in 1665 and the Great Fire of 1666—were primarily responsible. Whereas Dutch propaganda of the period is relatively mild, and its tone one of aggrieved surprise, propagandist portrayals *of* the Dutch *by* the English, whether they belong to 1652 or 1672, are more outspoken and play on a limited repertoire of offensive national stereotypes. Even when a specific historical event does occur in these years, the hostile reaction is far from innovative: thus, the lynching of the De Witt brothers at The Hague on August 20, 1672 N.S. gave rise to a restatement of familiar prejudice based on the view that the race as a whole

was savage and barbarous.[1] Prior to 1672 the basis for this view had
been the Amboyna massacre of 1623, when an English settlement in the
East Indies had been destroyed by the Dutch. The issues this massacre
had highlighted were to remain topical during the intervening half-
century; indeed, in 1652 they formed the principal *casus belli.*

After the Treaty of Westminster of 1674, England and the United
Provinces settled once more into a period of calm, now endorsed by
royal recognition in the dynastic marriage between Prince William of
Orange and Princess Mary Stuart in 1677. The couple acceded to the
English throne as joint heads of state in 1689 and reigned together until
Mary II's death from smallpox in 1694. There were no further military or
maritime confrontations involving the English and the Dutch until
after the death of William III in 1702. The intensity of anti-Dutch propaganda during the War of the Spanish Succession (1702–1713) fluctuated
considerably, and it has been suggested that the last years of that pan-
European conflict seemed to constitute "a sort of epilogue to the classic
period of Anglo-Dutch rivalry" of 1652–1674. By now the balance of
power in maritime western Europe had shifted decisively in England's
favor, and this, together with the fact that the personally unpopular
William III had been succeeded to the English throne by his late wife's
younger sister Anne (1702–1714), the last monarch of the Stuart dynasty,
played an important part in palliating English xenophobia.[2]

* * *

Andrew Marvell's 152-line satire "The Character of Holland" must be
situated in this broad historical context. This paper will address Marvell's response to that context. His poem has had few admirers since
the end of the seventeenth century, and some of the most enthusiastic
response on record comes from the nineteenth century. Although
Leigh Hunt and Charles Lamb both tried unavailingly to make William
Hazlitt see its humor, Alfred Lord Tennyson succeeded spectacularly
with Thomas Carlyle, who is reputed to have laughed "for half-an-
hour" at the line: "They with mad labour fish'd the *Land* to *Shoar*" (10);
later Hallam Tennyson would read the poem aloud to his father.[3] In our

1. "Strange Newes from Holland, being a true Character of the Country and the
People; with the putting to Death of De Wit and his Brother . . . by the Burgers at the
Hague, and how cruely they stript them, cutting off their Eares, Fingers and Toes"
(London: E. Crowch, 1672).
2. Douglas Coombs, *The Conduct of the Dutch* (The Hague & Achimota: Martinus
Nijhoff, 1958), 2, 381.
3. *Marvell: Modern Judgements,* ed. Michael Wilding (London: Macmillan, 1969),
19, 30. Wilding attributes the Carlyle anecdote to the mirth-making powers of Hallam Tennyson. But the 1887–1888 memoir quoted in *Marvell: The Critical Heritage,* ed.

own time the poem has certainly received some sensitive commentary,[4] but it has also and more typically been dismissed as containing
little else than "simple-minded jingoism."[5]

Certainly it has proved extraordinarily difficult to find consensus
terms that would readily grant "The Character of Holland" the intellectual rigor of Marvell's better-known occasional and political verse.
Warren Chernaik is one of the few recent commentators to have given
the poem some sustained attention, yet even he is forced to accord it no
more than "a loose thematic unity."[6] In consequence, "The Character of
Holland" has usually been seen as little other than an inferior and more
frivolous political poem than (say) "An Horatian Ode," a work that
owes its particularly high esteem to a number of features. These
include the ode's reticent stance as well as the value that has been
accorded to Marvell's capacity to lift the single and indeed, as its poet
perceives it, unique occasion that inspired it into a statement of permanent accessibility. To be sure, there is a generic difference between the
two poems: the "Horatian Ode" is (at least on the surface) a panegyric,
whereas "The Character of Holland" is (for the most part) a satire. Yet,
although the panegyric of the "Horatian Ode" has proved endlessly
fascinating to commentators wishing to assert Marvell's "exquisite
impartiality,"[7] the satire of "The Character of Holland" has seemed
much more simple-minded, even unworthy of its writer. The implications of this view of each poem provide troubling evidence of the
persistence of a nostalgic, crypto-Royalist school of Marvell commentary, but to dismiss "The Character of Holland" as an early potboiler
will not do, since it postdates by nearly three years the "Horatian
Ode," which celebrates Cromwell's triumphant return from Ireland in
May and June 1650.[8] "The Character of Holland" ends, albeit complexly,

Elizabeth Story Donno (London: Routledge and Kegan Paul, 1978), 246, makes clear
that Hallam is recording his father's achievement and not his own. The material
assembled by Donno provides many other instances of critical acclaim for "The
Character of Holland" throughout the nineteenth century. For Leigh Hunt's approv-
ing comments see Donno, *Critical Heritage,* 138, 140. Atypically for his time, Hazlitt
regarded the poem as "forced" and "far-fetched" (*Critical Heritage,* 133).

4. Some of the most perceptive commentary is to be found in *Poems and Letters*
1:309–13, yet no editor, as I shall argue, has yet done sufficient justice to the wealth of
bilingual (Dutch–English) wordplay in the poem.

5. Annabel M. Patterson, *Marvell and the Civic Crown* (Princeton: Princeton University Press, 1978), 123.

6. *The Poet's Time* (Cambridge: Cambridge University Press, 1983), 162–63.

7. An attitude quoted and censured by Margarita Stocker: see her *Apocalyptic Marvell* (Brighton: Harvester, 1986), xiii, 67–104.

8. The historical context has recently been reexamined in Blair Worden, "The Politics of Marvell's Horatian Ode," *The Historical Journal* 27.3 (1984): 525–46, who (while
fully admitting its enigmatic complexity) argues for a greater sense of republicanism

172

Richard Todd

with a topical reference to the English victory over the Dutch in the sea battle off Portland Bill (February 18–20, 1652/3 O.S.), in which admirals Deane, Monck, and Blake played heroic roles. The poem must therefore be assigned to between February and June 1652/3, Deane's death having taken place on June 3, 1653, O.S.

A conventional reading of "The Character of Holland" might well point to a commonplace satirical history of the development of the nation, one that evidences several mid-seventeenth-century anti-Dutch stereotypes. Even though many of the sentiments concerning the people of Holland, their customs and their history, sound familiar to the student of the anti-Dutch propaganda of the period, a more cautious reader may be alerted to the way the satirical historiography in particular is couched in terms that reflect a constant interdependence of theme with strategy. Both the Aesop-like fable of classical antiquity as well as a more Christian providential view are deployed to chart the history of the United Provinces. The argument progresses through the evolution of the singular landscape of Holland toward a fascinated obsession with the notion that it is precisely that evolution that has led, and uniquely so, to the particular kind of republican government it now enjoys.[9] The very claims of "Holland" to be *land* are examined throughout, and Marvell's poem goes on to satirize the Dutch republic's religious freedom and tolerance. He self-consciously places those eirenic qualities in the disturbing context of a series of hostile naval engagements with a neighboring Christian power. Yet here, too, the irony involved is complex, and again that complexity is located in both theme and strategy. For not only is England a former Protestant ally, but the very presumptuousness of the United Provinces in taking on England *at sea*—against better providential judgment, as it were—does not escape comment. The point concerning the ingratitude of the United Provinces' stance is reached only belatedly, through meandering syntax that digressively undercuts what initially presents itself as a brutally economic *exemplum*:

---

in the poem than is usually granted. Worden also offers the salutary reminder that Marvell was only 29 in 1650: "What will [he] do with his life?" (545). An amended version of Worden's essay is reprinted in *The Politics of Discourse: The Literature and History of Seventeenth-Century England*, ed. Kevin Sharpe and Steven N. Zwicker (Berkeley and Los Angeles: University of California Press, 1987). I quote from the original journal publication.

9. Throughout, the topographical descriptions best fit the provinces of Holland and Zeeland, but the poem itself makes clear that all seven United Provinces are being satirized (see line 137). The saying "God made the world, but the Dutch made Holland" remains proverbial.

> Let this one court'sie witness all the rest;
> When their whole Navy they together prest,
> Not Christian Captives to redeem from Bands:
> Or intercept the Western golden Sands:
> No, but all ancient Rights and Leagues must vail,
> Rather then to the *English* strike their sail;
> To whom their weather-beaten *Province* ows
> It self, when as some greater Vessel tows
> A Cock-boat tost with the same wind and fate;
> We buoy'd so often up their *sinking State*.
>
> (103–12)

Only in the last words do theme and strategy manage to coalesce, an achievement insultingly reflected in alliterative bathos. The vicissitudes surrounding the naval engagements prior to Portland Bill (resulting in part, it seems, from adverse weather conditions) are then briefly dwelt on, and the poem's climax is reached in a passage (145–52) to whose complexity I shall return. That climax is prepared for by concise presentation of the paradox whereby an *"Infant Hercules"* (138)—the young English republic—proves capable of defeating the *"Hydra"* (137) of the seven United Provinces off Portland Bill, and it is triumphantly—if equivocally—celebrated.

* * *

Even this brief summary will have served its purpose if it has managed to suggest that, although Carlyle's somewhat histrionic enthusiasm is to be preferred over blunt dismissal of "The Character of Holland," a proper response to the poem is still wanting. The neo-historicist and historiographical climate of recent years seems to offer a more appropriate political context than that suggested by much commentary hitherto, so that the Marvell of the first half of the 1650s has been seen as publicly committed to the republican cause, forced like his compatriots to take sides on the Engagement of Loyalty, though finding it, as a former Royalist sympathizer, "a more searching test" than it may have been to some of his less scrupulous contemporaries.[10] To accept Marvell's republicanism as an official rather than a subversive position is to be enabled to argue that there *is* a consistent line running from the

---

10. Worden, "Politics," 533. Discussion of Marvell's achievement in this recent context, of which both Worden and Stocker provide good examples, does have a precursor in John M. Wallace, *Destiny His Choice: The Loyalism of Andrew Marvell* (Cambridge: Cambridge University Press, 1968). Despite his claim that "Marvell was never a republican" (89), Wallace's case is presented realistically and without nostalgia.

reticence of the "Horatian Ode" through the more uncompromising public stances, satiric and panegyric respectively, of "The Character of Holland" and "The First Anniversary." Commentators have not customarily borne in mind what it means to realize that these poems are situated in the period covering the Engagement of Loyalty at the beginning of 1649/50 O.S. through early 1654/5, a year after the proclamation of the Protectorate on December 16, 1653 O.S. Yet Marvell's political poetry of the Commonwealth period up to early 1654/5 seems suspended at that point where his speakers are capable of *envisaging* an act of crowning, one that completes a constitutional reform without at the same time ushering in the tyranny that its hero is seen to have overthrown, as in "The First Anniversary":

> Hence oft I think, if in some happy Hour
> High Grace should meet in one with highest Pow'r,
> And then a seasonable People still
> Should bend to his, as he to Heavens will,
> What we might hope, what wonderful Effect
> From such a wish'd Conjuncture might reflect.
> Sure, the mysterious Work, where none withstand,
> Would forthwith finish under such a Hand.
>
> (131–38)[11]

For in reducing the Commonwealth decade to a monolithic entity we may forget how in its early years there was no way of foreseeing that public perceptions of Cromwell would change by the later 1650s or of anticipating the forms that change might take. John M. Wallace reminds us how in the "Horatian Ode" Marvell documents Cromwell's *refusal* to take the crown in 1650, despite public pressure to do so.[12] By the end of the period 1655–1658, however, Cromwell could no longer be seen as "still in the *Republick's* hand" (82).

Be that as it may, whatever kind of poem "The Character of Holland" may have seemed to those who read it in 1653, it was clearly perceived as sufficiently in tune with national feeling to warrant truncated reissue in 1665 and 1672.[13] In manuscript form, as John Kenyon has suggested, it may well originally have been used, together with Milton's letter of

---

11. It is frequently possible to gloss "work" in Marvell's political poetry as referring to the English Constitution as a phenomenon of accretion.

12. *Destiny His Choice*, 90–92, discusses the perceived parallels with Caesar in this stance of forbearance.

13. The 1665 and 1672 reprints consist only of the poem's first 100 lines; that of 1665 is spuriously followed by "an eight-line conclusion suitable to the circumstances of the Dutch War of 1665-7" (*Poems and Letters* 1:309).

February 21, 1652/3 O.S. to Lord President Bradshaw, to support Marvell's application for a post in the service of the republican government.[14] Quite apart from its innate interest, the letter to Bradshaw provides contemporary evidence of Marvell's fluency in Dutch, French, Italian, and Spanish, in addition to his proven competence in Latin and Greek. Kenyon regards this testimony as having come first-hand from Marvell himself; endorsed by someone of Milton's linguistic capabilities, it suggests that the two poets knew that they possessed a grasp of foreign languages remarkable even for their time. The testimony has naturally bred the tradition that Marvell had actually visited Holland in the 1640s during a period of his life that is assumed to have been spent away from England but remains meagerly documented. Given that Marvell *was* in Europe at the time of the first civil war, it is fair to conclude that he was not so much undertaking a Grand Tour (for which, following his father's unexpected death in January 1641/2, he is unlikely to have had the financial resources) as supporting himself through private tuition while self-consciously constructing a diplomatic career through the acquisition of these modern vernaculars.[15] Kenyon's connection of the letter to Bradshaw and "The Character of Holland" is attractive because it suggests the possibility of narrowing down further the date of the poem's composition to nearer the beginning than the end of the period February through June 1652/3—indeed, it may well have been *inspired by* the naval engagement off Portland Bill.[16] This, if true, would give the references to Deane, Monck, and Blake interesting panegyric overtones. Whatever the facts may turn out to be, the poem's first appearance in print in the form in which Marvell

14. John Kenyon, "Andrew Marvell: Life and Times," in R. L. Brett, ed., *Andrew Marvell: Essays on the Tercentenary of his Death* (Hull: Oxford University Press, 1979), 12, 33. For the letter to Bradshaw, see *Calendar of State Papers, Domestic, 1653*.

15. See Michael Craze, *The Life and Lyrics of Andrew Marvell* (London: Macmillan, 1979), 7–8, who has argued, on the basis of Milton's listing of Marvell's foreign languages in chronological order, and of Marvell's likely presence in Rome during the first half of 1646, that Marvell left London for Holland in the spring of 1643 and spent about a year there. Edward Chaney, *The Grand Tour and the Great Rebellion: Richard Lassels and the "Voyage of Italy" in the Seventeenth Century* (Geneva: Slatkine, 1985), 347–50, offers a thorough account of Marvell's presence in Rome, deducing from the available evidence that Marvell arrived there "not later than the winter of 1645–46," and that he may have "received . . . some patronage from the 2nd Duke of Buckingham and his brother, Lord Francis Villiers," in a contact that may have stemmed from Trinity College, Cambridge, as early as the summer of 1641.

16. Circumstantial evidence may be suggested in Marvell's surely certain awareness that the tutelary deity variously associated with the zodiacal signs of Aquarius and Pisces is Neptune (see Charlotte R. Long, *The Twelve Gods of Greece and Rome* [Leiden: E. J. Brill, 1987], 266ff.); the Portland Bill encounter took place more or less on the cusp of these two signs. Neptune, as I shall stress, is actively, even violently present at the end of the poem.

had composed it cannot be traced earlier than to the posthumous *Miscellaneous Poems* of 1681.[17]

The customary generic view is that the ancestry of "The Character of Holland" is to be found in the satiric poems of John Cleveland (1613–1658), although in writing his own poem, Marvell fused the Clevelandesque satire with the prose "character."[18] Ruth Nevo has noted Marvell's Clevelandesque use of "the burlesque conceit and the pun," although in Marvell's hands their logic is finer and their tone harsher. Nevo is unusual in rating the poem highly; for her it is "one of the least characteristic and most distinguished philippics of the period."[19] Annabel M. Patterson, iconoclastically asserting that when he wrote the poem "Marvell had not yet established personal connections with Holland," sees in it, although it is "based on that cheapest of jokes, the abuse of national character, particularly as that can be represented in cartoons," evidence of "a critical intelligence struggling to emerge from this stereotypical shell," especially in the reference in line 113 to Grotius's *De jure belli et* [or *ac*] *pacis* (1625).[20]

My own argument in what follows addresses the significance of the fact that "The Character of Holland" dates from the early years of the Commonwealth. (The scope of this paper does not, unfortunately, permit consideration of the more diffuse anti-Dutch matter in Marvell's "The last Instructions to a Painter" [373–834], a long passage that dwells on the maritime engagement of 1667.) My proposition is that, although "The Character of Holland" *is* a patriotic poem, its reissue on those two occasions during Marvell's lifetime, both of them after the Restoration, shows that even his contemporaries could get the nature of that patriotism wrong. This proposition stems from my attempt to define the poem's argument in terms that resist unexamined assertions of Marvell's "exquisite impartiality." I shall identify and examine instead the distinctive *balance* that operates in "The Character of Holland."

I have already suggested how strategy and theme are, broadly speaking, dynamically set off against each other in the poem: constantly and

17. *Poems and Letters* 1:100–103, follows (with minor emendations) the text of the 1681 *Miscellaneous Poems*.

18. Chernaik, *Poet's Time*, 161.

19. *The Dial of Virtue* (Princeton: Princeton University Press, 1963), 70, 72.

20. *Marvell and the Civic Crown*, 120; Wallace, *Destiny His Choice*, 30–43, discusses Grotius's work in the context of the civil wars debates and the Engagement controversy of the late 1640s not in terms of a specific relationship with "The Character of Holland" but as a source for a drastic reworking of Grotius in English; see Anthony Ascham's *A Discourse: Wherein is Examined, What is Particularly Lawfull during the Confusions and Revolutions of Government* (1648).

varyingly intermingled, they are controlled by Marvell in such a way as sometimes to coalesce with each other (as in *"sinking State"*) and sometimes, as we shall see, to undermine each other. After presenting more contextual material concerning mid-seventeenth-century national stereotyping of the Dutch by the English, I shall be studying more minutely the implications for our sense of the poem as a whole of the balance I have indicated. Even though an extensive reading at the desired level of particularity is not possible in the space available, the quality alluded to by the term *balance* is wholly Marvellian. It leads poet and reader toward profounder discoveries about national identity than those having simply to do with hostile stereotyping of the enemy. I shall show that the poem delivers a view of the evolution of Holland, both as landscape and as republic, that is seen paradoxically as a developed yet ceaseless process. Suspended uneasily in place and time, in ways I shall explore toward the end of this paper, this process finally confronts the immutable force of an invincible rival in the existence of the fledgling English republic. Marvell's balanced presentation of that confrontational process is intimately connected with a largely unacknowledged facet of his achievement that has to do with his use of language. I shall show that those linguistic talents attested to by Milton in his 1653 letter to Bradshaw allow Marvell to force the Dutch language itself into participating in the act in which the providential histories of the rival republics meet. That is to say, Marvell is just as capable of punning bilingually in a modern vernacular as he is of playing, for example, on Latin assonances in a poem such as "Dialogue between the Soul and Body."

* * *

Midcentury propagandists could conscript a wide range of anti-Dutch expression. The scale comprises scatological coarseness pure and simple at one end to a subtlety (albeit still frequently offensive) that depends for its effect on quite complex political allegory and wordplay at the other. Although the material used as propaganda includes a mass of pamphlet writing, it is also graced by the presence of a more substantial kind of work altogether. The essay *A Brief Character of the Low-Countries*, first printed in authorized form in 1652 and usually ascribed to Owen Felltham (?1604–1667/8), seems an appropriate touchstone.[21] Felltham's extended appropriation of the early seventeenth-

---

21. The full title of this remarkable work is *A brief Character of the Low-Countries under the States. Being three weeks observation of the Vices and Vertues of the Inhabitants;* all subsequent quotations from and references to it will be taken from the author-

century fashion for the Theophrastan "character" to anatomize national (rather than individual) types may have been innovatory,[22] but
the use of national caricature as such during the early modern period
can be traced back at least as far as Erasmus and the *Encomium Moriae*
(1509). If it does belong to the late 1620s, surviving in manuscript before
being published under mysterious circumstances, first in 1648 and
then twice in 1652, Felltham's treatise certainly provides the first
instance of the "character" genre being applied to a nation through the
work's title.[23] In 1651 appeared the anonymous *A Character of England*,
purporting to be written by a Frenchman but customarily attributed to
John Evelyn; this work was in turn followed in 1659 by a strangely
humorless riposte, *A Character of France. To which is added, Gallus Cas-
tratus. Or an Answer to a late Slanderous Pamphlet, called the Character of
England*, which is also anonymous. Belonging as it does to 1653, Marvell's poem falls between the composition of these two, neither of
which (unlike Felltham's work as printed by Seile in 1652) was conceived of as a diptych. Felltham's diptychal construction offers first a
hostile and then a sympathetic view of the Hollanders' character and
habitat.[24]

---

itative text issued by Henry Seile (London, 1652). I am not the first to cite Felltham in
the context of Marvell's "The Character of Holland"; see *Poems and Letters* 1:313 for
comment by E. E. Duncan-Jones. Simon Schama, *The Embarrassment of Riches* (London: Collins, 1987), 257ff., persuasively locates the "rancor" in the rich and underin-
vestigated anti-Dutch pamphlet literature as "stemm[ing] from the behavior of the
Dutch subverting the consoling cliché of meanness" (258, 662–64), but I must dis-
agree with Schama's judgments concerning Felltham and Marvell, whose work he
reads as straightforward anti-Dutch polemic.

    22. It is true that there is a brief Theophrastan "character" in *Sir Thomas Overbury
His Observations in his Travailes upon the State of the XVII. Provinces as They Stood
Anno Dom. 1609. The Treatie of Peace being then on Foote* (1626), but Overbury's remarks
are judicious and flattering and contain no trace of hostile stereotyping. Both Felltham and Marvell were of course to concentrate on the coastal provinces of Holland
and Zeeland, whereas Overbury's scope encompasses the entirety of the present-
day Benelux countries.

    23. Ted-Larry Pebworth, *Owen Felltham* (Boston: Twayne, 1976), 71–73. Pebworth
assigns Felltham's visit to the Low Countries to some time between 1623 and 1628 and
concludes that "truncated manuscript copies [of the *Brief Character* that] circulated
widely" (72) date from not long after 1628. William Ley was responsible for the
pirated and incomplete versions of Felltham's work that had appeared in 1648 and
earlier in 1652. Felltham's work was later to be translated into Dutch.

    24. The unsigned preface to Seile's 1652 printing of Felltham is disingenuous,
implying that the work had previously been known only for its first (scurrilous) part
(*Brief Character* [London, 1652], sig. A3v–4r). No reading of Seile's reissue of Felltham's *Brief Character* can answer Schama's description of it as an "irresistibly abus-
ive tract" (*Embarrassment of Riches*, 639): Schama appears to be confusing the two
1652 imprints. Nor—unhappily for a work of such magnificent scope and suggestiveness—is Schama's description (262–63) of the publishing history of Marvell's
poem accurate.

Reading Felltham's essay in its authoritative form enriches Marvell's poem for us; indeed, from now on I shall modernize Felltham's richer term *Æquilibrium* to convey what I have so far been calling "balance." For Marvell's portrayal of the United Provinces in "The Character of Holland" represents a generic refinement as a result of which Felltham's diptychal view is transformed into a series of balanced rhetorical antitheses involving the poem's themes and strategies. Marvell manages to show that the elements making up the character of Holland, understood both as its inhabitants and as the terrain they inhabit, exist in an equilibrium that we may think of, in Felltham's spirit, as "amphibious." Although Marvell does employ available national and topographical stereotypes concerning Holland, he presents them (like Felltham in the hostile part of his *Brief Character*) in terms of their suspension in a form of limbo. In consequence it is more illuminating to think of Marvell's poem *synchronically,* as part of a genre that was undergoing midcentury refinement, than to try to locate it *diachronically* within the totality of Marvell's own achievement. Viewed in this way the poem's surface, ostensibly patriotic and propagandist, would seem to conceal subversive use of official stereotypes of the Dutch: the 1665 and 1672 reprints are thus perhaps best thought of as oversimplifications dissimilar only in degree from the kind of critical dismissal and superficial commentary the poem has undergone in our own century.

As a superficial reading of Marvell's poem shows, the period's stereotyping of the Dutch by the English focuses on mercantile greed, ingratitude to a former ally, and a religious tolerance skeptically viewed as a sectarianism conducing to anarchy. Yet it is difficult to reduce the mass of specific racial insults to a manageable list. Many involve references to the Hollanders' bestiality. To the pamphleteer the word *boer* (farmer, peasant) as a general term for the populace allowed felicitous play on "boar." But the patriciate was not spared reduction to porcine terms either. The frequently encountered insulting abbreviation "Hogen-Mogen," for the customary form of address (*hoogmogend*) to a member of the States General, not only proffered the crude but effectively pejorative translation "high and mighty"; it became itself further abbreviated, suggesting to more than one pamphleteer as well as to Marvell himself (80) the collocation "hogs and boars" to cover both rulers and subjects. This kind of wordplay never seems to pall. Less winsome is that suggested in a title such as: *The Dutch Boare Dissected, or a Description of Hogg-Land.* The title goes on at some length to provide eloquent testimony to some fairly typical prejudicial expressions of the bestiality of the Hollanders:

> A Dutch man is a Lusty, Fat, two Legged Cheese-Worm: A Crea-
> ture, that is so addicted to Eating Butter, Drinking fat Drink, and
> Sliding [i.e., skating], that all the World knows him for a slip-
> pery Fellow. An *Hollander* is not an *High-lander*, but a *Low-
> lander;* for he loves to be down in the Dirt, and *Boar*-like, to wallow
> therein.

This publication (London, 1665), one of the relatively few that does date
from the plague year, launches into an attack on Dutch acquisitiveness
and greed, expressed in heroic couplets. Its insults are not in themselves novel, and indeed remarkably few writers seem to have recognized the full firepower of the weapon they were holding. Felltham and
Marvell both belong to this small but discerning company: in Marvell's
case I shall show how *his* portrayal of the Dutch character and landscape contrives to contain an implicit assertion of his *own* national
identity. A stereotype may be lethally potent if it can suggest not just
national differences but the *uniqueness* of some aspect of the stereo-
typed nation. And it was the Hollanders' terrain that was unique in its
inhospitability. In describing it, Marvell (perhaps actually using Felltham as a model) succeeded in representing himself to his readership
as both an observer and a foreigner. Marvell achieves this success by
balancing satirical recognition of the providential power behind the
uniqueness he discerns against a much more thoughtful admission
that this power must force the English to confront the uniqueness of
their historical moment.

Throughout the Anglo–Dutch wars there was a great deal of interest
in the terrain occupied by the Hollanders. At times this interest becomes acute, and references to "lowness" abound, some considerably
more sophisticated than that just quoted from *The Dutch Boare Dissected*. Thus, "The Low Estate of the Low-Countrey Countess of Holland on her Death-bed, with the advice of her Doctors, and Confessor"
(London, 1672) offers a series of diagnoses of the present state of the
United Provinces. The remedy finally prescribed is an "Orange": to
appreciate the full point of this we need to remember that the post-
humously born Prince William III, the future joint head of state of
England, had inherited the princedom of Orange in 1650 upon the
unexpected death of his father Prince William II. Up until 1672, William
III's life had been overshadowed by internecine conflict between Hol-
land (including Amsterdam) and the six remaining United Provinces
(Groningen, Friesland, Overijssel, Gelderland, Utrecht, and Zeeland).
It was Holland that had become determined to prevent a Prince of
Orange from ever again occupying the position of Stadholder, as Wil-
liam II had done. A stalemate was ended when, in response to Anglo–

French aggression, legislation was rescinded on July 8, 1672 N.S. As a result, William III, duly proclaimed Stadholder of the United Provinces, was in a position to be appointed Captain General in command of the Dutch army as well. One of the first acts of his successful campaign, in a Netherlandic scorched-earth policy equivalent, was to open the dikes around Amsterdam and other cities, protecting them against invasion by means of a so-called "water line." It is likely that this policy is referred to in the grotesque physiological hyperbole of the following lines from the *Low Estate:*

> Hold, quoth a soberer Doctor, she's too Old,
> She's just a hundred, and her days are told.
> Her blood is turn'd to a Pituitous Matter,
> She's Dropical [*sic*], and Drown'd in her own *Water,*
> She makes it freely, but no ease at all,
> Although it *overflow the Urinal.*

The lines, enhanced by their likely historical context, reflect a horrified fascination with what has since become ennobled. Our twentieth-century admiration for the achievements of the seventeenth-century Dutch masters makes it hard for us to appreciate that seventeenth-century propagandists had no such aestheticized view of the Holland-ers' landscape. One reason for their attitude may well be sought in the descriptive professionalism that Svetlana Alpers has brilliantly perceived to be a form of what she has termed "the mapping impulse" in Dutch art.[25] At the time when Felltham's *Brief Character* is likely to have been written, much of the landscape of Holland had still to be drained. Felltham's figurative description is especially vivid:

> They are a general Sea-Land, The great Bog of *Europe.* There is not such another Marsh in the world; that's flat. They are an universall Quagmire, Epitomized, *A green Cheese in pickle.* There is in them an *Æquilibrium* of mud and water. (sigs. A5r-v)

The "lowness" of the landscape meant to many propagandists that Holland was as close to Hell as could be imagined. Felltham gives the

---

25. *The Art of Describing: Dutch Art in the Seventeenth Century* (Chicago: University of Chicago Press, 1983), 119–68. Recent neo-historicist scholarship is recognizing the propagandist potential of cartography; see for example Richard Helgerson, "The Land Speaks: Cartography, Chorography, and Subversion in Renaissance England," *Representations* 16 (Fall 1986): 51–85; reprinted in *Representing the English Renaissance,* ed. Stephen Greenblatt (Berkeley and Los Angeles: University of California Press, 1988), 327–61.

commonplace an anatomical twist: in the hostile first part of his diptych he portrays Holland as "the Buttock of the World, full of veins and
bloud, but no bones in't" (sig. A7r). Earlier he has deflected another set
of commonplace beliefs relating to lowness and Hell:

> if [the Hollanders] dye in perdition, they are so low, that they have
> a shorter cut to Hell than the rest of their neighbours. And for this
> cause, perhaps all strange Religions throng thither, as naturally
> inclining toward their Center. Besides, their Riches shewes them
> to be *Pluto*'s Region, and you all know what part that was which
> the Poets did of old assign him. (sig. A6v-r)

The association of Holland with proximity to Hell, and by implication the idea that the Hollanders enjoyed a special league with the
Devil, was widespread. In this context, anatomical conceit can revert
to scatology: thus, *The Dutchmen's Pedigree, or A Relation, Shewing how
they were first Bred, and descended from a Horse-Turd, which was enclosed
in a Butter-Box* (London, 1653) fancifully derives the name "Belgia"
from "bel-regia" or "Beelzebub's realm." The peroration reminds us (as
does Marvell's poem, with its reference to "Brand wine" [115]) of the
mercantile rivalries that had helped spark off the first Anglo–Dutch
war:

> do not wonder that the Dutch have acted as Hellishly like Devils as
> they have . . . [d]o not wonder at their wicked traiterous and
> unjust wringing of all Trade out of other mens hands: Nay do not
> wonder at their barbarous and Inhumane cruelties, since from
> Hell they came, and thither without doubt they must return again.

In this bizarre coprophiliac fantasy Beelzebub had charged a mon-
strous horse (the progeny of a devil and a mermaid) to drain the North
Sea. Meeting with an accident, the horse died of "a fit of shiting,"
remaining in Hell to this day. The excrement was placed in a box
smeared inside with butter. From this butter box filled with dung
"within nine days space sprung forth men, women, and children; the
offspring whereof are yet alive to this day, and now commonly known
by the name of Dutchmen." The term *butter box* was current to describe
the Dutch in the period. In "The Character of Holland" the collocation
"*Skipper gross, / A Water-Hercules Butter-Coloss*" (93–94) offers a typically
Marvellian variation on the insult. Through antithesis there is a double
solidification: the element of water is as it were literally transformed
into a metonymic version ("*Butter*") of that of the earth; while quasi-
mythological weight is given to the process as the muscular prowess of

Hercules solidifies into the lapidary mass of the Colossus. The point is worth stressing because a similar process can elsewhere actually conclude a Marvell poem: Elsie Duncan-Jones has pointed out how "The Nymph Complaining for the Death of Her *Faun*" begins with natural language about a real event and "end[s] in the frozen world of statuary."[26] The ending of "The Mower against Gardens" seems to invert the strategy.

> Their Statues polish'd by some ancient hand,
> May to adorn the Gardens stand:
> But howso'ere the Figures do excel,
> The *Gods* themselves with us do dwell.
>
> (37–40)

The crude engraving accompanying *The Dutchmens Pedigree* ("Van Trump" and "De Witte" are portrayed inside the butter box, to the right of the shitting horse) bears no comparison with a much more refined one attributed by Edward Hodnett to the illustrator Francis Barlow (?1626–1704). I quote Hodnett:

> The Dutch are ridiculed as spawn of the Devil and are shown inside and issuing from a large cut-out egg, on top of which the horrible Devil himself crouches. As he seizes one of the men from around a table inside, he says, "What thou may'st be, as yet I cannott tell / But Butterbox is the worst food in Hell."[27]

Hodnett rightly defends the craftsmanship of the illustration, which probably dates from 1673, without attempting to gloss over the coarseness of the verse. If the illustration suggests that the egg is voided rather than laid, the verse makes the suggestion explicit:

> Doe but observe this Cacodæmon's bum,
> And thence you'll find, whence Th'High & Mighty's come[;]
> Though Nature never did such method use
> Maggotts, and Flyes with shape of Toad t'abuse.

* * *

26. "A Great Master of Words: Some Aspects of Marvell's Poems of Praise and Blame" in *Proceedings of the British Academy* (Oxford: Oxford University Press, 1975), 4.

27. *Francis Barlow: First Master of English Book Illustration* (London: The Scolar Press, 1978), 28. The subsequent quotation is from p. 29. I am indebted to Jeremy Maule, Trinity College, Cambridge, for the reference.

What sets apart Marvell's uses of elements such as these, so common to the propagandist literature? If the ending of "The Character of Holland" dwells on the hellishness of the inhabitants of Holland, its opening inverts, with characteristic temperateness, the theme of coprophilia. Yet the figure whereby *"Holland,* that scarce deserves the name of *Land"* (1) is portrayed as "This indigested vomit of the Sea" (7), is neither arbitrary nor gratuitous. The frugal industry of the Dutch in redeeming even excrement to serve as land is grudgingly praised:

> Glad then, as Miners that have found the Oar,
> They with mad labour fish'd the *Land* to *Shoar;*
> And div'd as desperately for each piece
> Of Earth, as if't had been of *Ambergreece;*
> Collecting anxiously small Loads of Clay,
> Less then what building Swallows bear away;
> Or then those Pills which sordid Beetles roul,
> Tran[s]fusing into them their Dunghil Soul.
>
> (9–16)

As remarked earlier, the strategies of classical fabulation intermingle with the theme of providential history, and that providential portrayal comes into conflict with a single unprecedented moment in English history. The triumphant note on which the poem originally ended—historical events, in the form of Deane's death in June 1653, however, intervened to remove one prong of Neptune's trident—expands the small scale and satirical tone of the enterprise of the opening lines to more cosmic realms whose representation reveals a strikingly expressed sense of responsibility mingled with disdain:

> For now of nothing may our *State* despair,
> Darling of Heaven, and of Men the Care;
> Provided that they be what they have been,
> Watchful abroad, and honest still within.
> For while our *Neptune* doth a *Trident* shake,
> Steel'd with those piercing Heads, *Dean, Monck* and *Blake,*
> And while *Jove* governs in the highest Sphere,
> Vainly in *Hell* let *Pluto* domineer.
>
> (145–52)

Commentators have noted the grotesqueness of the figure of Neptune's trident. The violence of the conceit may be attributed to Marvell's characteristic capacity for allowing his figurative language to *drift;* therefore, one's first response to the impaling on Neptune's trident of the heads of England's naval triumvirate is to think in terms of punitive, even criminal associations. Such a response immediately comes to seem insufficient, however, in the light of the active and assertive choice of "pierci*ng*." Subjecting these lines briefly to scrutiny, we see that by the time we have reached the poem's conclusion, an insistence on triplication has begun to muddy Marvell's clearly diptychal view of his subject matter. That is to say, as long as Holland can be identified with Hell, Pluto's role is fairly straightforward; but it is hard to allegorize these triple personages (Neptune, Jove, and Pluto) with any real precision, although their portrayal in a group may be traced back indirectly to Plato (*Laws*, 828 B-D). Neoplatonic theory would come to associate the three gods Zeus, Poseidon, and Hephaistos (or Pluto) with creative forces within a quadripartite framework.[28] Some Roman iconography, however, groups Jove, Neptune, and Pluto together, and it is worth recalling that there had traditionally been a blurring of the distinction between Pluto and Plutus (the god of wealth), perhaps through intermediary association with Hephaistos (Vulcan). The concepts of Hell, mining, and wealth thus drift into and out of collocation in Marvell's poem. Pluto/Vulcan's female counterpart is Proserpina/Ceres: sterile acquisitiveness is played off against fertile achievement.

Nevertheless, Marvell continues to operate preeminently with *pairs* that persist chiasmically or by means of other kinds of rhetorical balance right up until Neptune's introduction ("Darling of Heaven, and of Men the Care" [146]; "Watchful abroad, and honest still within" [148]). Another instance of (rhetorical) equilibrium contributes to our uncertainty as to how to read the final couplet, and it is possible to overlook a buried pun in the last word. To begin to feel something of the full resonance of the lines we must recall Felltham. The wealth of the Dutch is something they have been actively acquiring throughout the providentially historical pageant portrayed in Marvell's poem with the frugal eagerness suggested in the simile "Glad . . . as Miners that have found the Oar" (9); as Felltham's devil's advocate puts it, this wealth "shewes them to be *Pluto*'s Region." Yet the surface sense of "domineer" is plainly being set off against "governs" in the preceding line, and this ploy forces us to ask how we are to *feel* about the way the Dutch have acquired their wealth during the history portrayed in quasi-providential terms throughout the poem. We recall the near parody of biblical history in which the building of a "*watry Babel*" (21) is followed by the inevitable "deluge" that is punitively "daily" (27); instead of the rise of the kingdom of Israel, "*Necessity,* that first made *Kings,* / Something like *Government* among them brings" (37-38); the revelations of the New Testament are vouchsafed in terms of the "Ark" of "*Religion*" mistakenly "splitting on this unknown ground" (67-69) whose inhabitants are (naturally) "converted" by "Th' *Apostles* [who] were so many Fishermen" (57-58). Yet the poem's last line appears to be suggesting that the Dutch will be allowed to get on with their mercantilism, working away at the very existence of a Hell of their own making, unaffected by English prowess at sea, and that however hard Pluto tries, he will be unable to "do" (or do for [i.e., vanquish]) "Mynheer."

* * *

One final extended example of Marvell's fascination with Felltham's evident absorption with what he terms "an *Æquilibrium* of mud and water," and with the way in which the various elements seem to coexist in that terrain, must serve to conclude the argument of this paper. The most fascinating passage (23-54) in the entire poem is the one in which Marvell completely transforms Felltham's conceptualization of elements in equilibrium and arrives at his own quite unique portrayal of the character of both the terrain and the inhabitants of Holland—the fabled development of their landscape and the providential character of their history—in terms of what he evidently saw as the relationship between the two. In doing so, Marvell adumbrates the discovery of national identity that the poem's problematic ending celebrates.

Felltham's "epitomizing" of the Hollanders' landscape as "*A green Cheese in Pickle*" visualizes a terrain, in itself both recognizable and fertile, transformed by being suspended in a sterilizing medium. Not only does the figure convey equilibrium between earth ("mud") and water, but it relies for fullest effect on *defamiliarizing* the earth by portraying it as surrounded by water in limbo. In this way the landscape is rendered simultaneously familiar and alien; it is recognizable in terms of ours but is fundamentally different from it. In such a way some of Felltham's most arresting passages explore elemental equilibrium in the Hollanders' habitat in terms of anarchic transformations within the natural world:

> Some things they do that seem Wonders. 'Tis ordinary to see them fish for fire in water, which they Catch in nets and transport to land in their boats. . . . The Elements are here at variance, the subtile overswaying the grosser, The fire consumes the earth, and the air the water, they burn Turffs, and drain their ground with Windmills. . . . And they would prove against Philosophy the

Worlds Conflagration to be natural, even shewing thereby that the very Element of the Earth is Combustible. (sigs. A8v-9r, A11v)

Felltham, seeing the elements of earth and water in a state of war such that they threaten to annihilate each other, seems to have influenced the writer of *Strange Newes from Holland* (1672), who affirms that "had it been meant as a habitation of men . . . the four Elements would not have conspired together to be there all naught."[29]

Yet Marvell "epitomizes" this extraordinary landscape not with Felltham's sense of suspenseful wonder but in terms of ongoing historical process. The "daily deluge" (27) to which the Hollanders are subjected is presented as nothing less than a continuing parodic reenactment of Noah's flood.[30] In so viewing historical providence as it must appear to the Hollanders, Marvell employs *"Level-coyl"* (28) to describe the process by which at one time the sea and another the land gains victory. The word is a bastardization of *faire lever le cul à quelqu'un.* It describes what we might term "musical chairs"; that is, the game "leve-cul" or "leve-le-cul" (literally, "hitch buttock"). *"Level-coyl"* becomes "coil" or turmoil involving earth and water, which are "leveled" both "with" and "at" each other. Confining *his* attention to the leveling effect of water on earth, Marvell describes the "Injur'd Ocean" playing "Leapfrog ore their [the Hollanders'] Steeples" (23–24).[31] The phrase is given particular piquancy by the realization that the appellation "frogs" was often used to describe the Dutch in the seventeenth century; its application by the English to the French (as in customary parlance) is much more recent. Marvell's disorder quickly turns civic: "The Fish oft-times the Burger dispossest, / And sat not as a Meat but as a Guest" (29–30). J. B. Leishman senses a profane inversion of John Donne's "digest" of his 19/29 December 1619 sermon preached at The Hague: "This is the net, with which if yee are willing to be caught . . . then you are fishes reserved for that great Marriage-feast, which is the Kingdom of Heaven; where whosoever is a dish, is a ghest too; whosoever is caught

---

29. See note 1 above; the quotation is from sig. A2v.

30. In arguing the parodic character of this passage, I should not want to overlook Simon Schama's quite proper emphasis on the powerfully lingering effect exerted on the collective folk memory of Holland and Zeeland as late as the Dutch "Golden Century" of the tidal deluges of the fifteenth century. Schama likens this effect to that of memories of the Black Death on sixteenth-century Flanders and Italy (*Embarrassment of Riches*, 37).

31. Cornelis D. van Strien, *British Travellers in Holland During the Stuart Period: Edward Browne and John Locke as Tourists in the United Provinces* (Amsterdam: Vrije Universiteit, 1989), 60, points out that steeples standing in flooded land in Zeeland and near Dordt (Dordrecht) are regularly mentioned in the travel literature of the period.

by this net, is called to this feast."[32] Marvell's citizens are "serv'd up for
Cabillau" (32). The modern Dutch form *kabeljauw* (cod) is nothing other
than a phonetic rendering of the French, and Marvell constructs a
chiasmus whereby the metamorphosis of land into sea and vice versa is
seen to have a metonymic counterpart in the "dispossession" of "Burger" or citizen by "Fish." But the metonymy that brings about the
chiasmus is destabilized lexically by a process in which the English and
Dutch languages themselves are made to participate ("land/citizen . . .
sea/fish; . . . sea/fish . . . land/citizen" becomes "*Dutch . . . Cabillau;*
. . . *Herring . . . Heeren*"):

> And oft the *Tritons* and the *Sea-Nymphs* saw
> Whole sholes of *Dutch* serv'd up for *Cabillau;*
> Or as they over the new Level rang'd
> For pickled *Herring,* pickled *Heeren* chang'd.
>
> (31-34)

The "*Duck* and *Drake*" with which "Nature . . . asham'd of her mistake
/ Would throw their Land away" (35-36) again reinforces through strategy
and theme the idea of the unstable coexistence where the elements are
suspended within each other. While the game of skimming flat stones
across a still expanse of water is alliteratively pointed up, both fabled and
providential views of historical process are once again intermingled and
examined in Nature's vacillating response to her "mistake." In the 1681
Miscellaneous Poems most of the antitheses in the passage that follows are
indicated typographically by italicization. The Hollanders are compelled
by the state of "level coil" to arrive at "Something like *Government*" (38);
rhyme, balanced repetition, and various forms of assonance, all typographically highlighted, help sketch out this unwilling process:

> For as with *Pygmees* who best kills the *Crane,*
> Among the *hungry* he that treasures *Grain,*
> Among the *blind* the one-ey'd *blinkard* reigns,
> So rules among the *drowned* he that *draines.*
> Not who first see the *rising Sun* commands,
> But who could first discern the *rising Lands.*
>
> (39-44)

32. *The Art of Marvell's Poetry* (London: Hutchinson, 1966), 24-25n; *The Sermons of
John Donne,* ed. George R. Potter and Evelyn M. Simpson, 10 vols. (Berkeley and Los
Angeles: University of California Press, 1962), 2:309-10. For a recent account of this
sermon in its historical and diplomatic context, see Paul R. Sellin, *So Doth, So Is
Religion: John Donne and Diplomatic Contexts in the Reformed Netherlands, 1619-1620*
(Columbia: University of Missouri Press, 1988), 109-34.

Particularly striking here is the way in which the expected "drunkard" (another stereotype repeatedly applied to the Hollanders) is finessed: it drifts through collocation with *"blind"* into *"blinkard."* In the poverty bestowed by an inhospitable terrain, a poverty that lends its very terms to those of the processes of hierarchical government, the acquisition of wealth is identified with that of power. Neither is to be had except by means of the practical activity of extricating the element of earth from that of water, but the labor involved in this activity—once begun—is perpetual. One might try to envision Sisyphus condemned to torture on flat ground. It seems to me that the passage provides yet one more gloss on the famous closing words of the "Horatian Ode" (119–20, usually taken to refer to the destruction of the English constitution): "The same *Arts* that did *gain* / A *Pow'r,* must it *maintain."* Thus, whoever can construct a dike ("make a *Bank,"* 47) achieves success not just at the level of bare sustenance; he will also, in due course, "make a *Bank"* financially. Such power and wealth are available both individually and communally. On the individual level, whoever can "pump an Earth so leak" (45),[33] or build a dike, or "Invent a *Shov'l"* (48) can rise to power and wealth, assuming in the process a role to which he was not born: the "unperceiv'd" transformation from *"Dyke-grave"* to *"King of Spades"* (49–50) conceals a bilingual wordplay that renders the antithesis between the two terms particularly satisfying.[34] *"Dyke-grave"* refers, by analogy with the title "Graaf" (Count), to an official position and, thus, chiasmically balances *"King,"* which is in republican terms meaningless. The verb *"graven"* (to dig) cannot have been absent from Marvell's mind, yet he does more than explore a bilingual pun on "grave." In its Dutch form, the office of "dijkgraaf" formed a collocation with "heemraad" ("local council"). The "dijkgraaf en heemraad" were entrusted with responsibility for the upkeep of the polders; the "heemraadschap" carried out its duties under the chairmanship of the "dijkgraaf." It is these Dutch terms that Marvell is rendering in English with his *"Commission of the Sewers"* (itself a formal term; see *"sewer"*

33. To suggest that with the form "leak" Marvell may be recalling Dutch *"lek"* ("leaky" or "leaking") is in the present context more significant than to learn that this form of the adjective in English is the latest recorded in the *OED* (*Poems and Letters* 1:310).

34. None of what follows here is to deny that, as Cornelis D. van Strien has privately suggested, there are coded underlying references to the (rebellious) "rising" of Holland against the "King of Spain" under the leadership of some small *"Dyke-grave"* (the Prince of Orange, Count ["Graaf"] of Nassau, whose power is limited by the States General [*"joynt states"*]). Van Strien points out that a reader familiar with the travel literature of the period could not fail to make subliminal associations such as these.

OED 3a). "Sewer" was at this time only beginning to acquire the pejorative associations that the term now exclusively possesses. In pre–civil war and post–Restoration England, a royal commission of the sewers (or waterways) could be invested with temporary authority within any given area susceptible to inundation from sea or river. The patrician dignitaries ("*joynt States*") who collectively make up "a *Commission of the Sewers*" are thus set off by both antithesis and alliteration from the "*King of Spades*" into which the upstart ("small") "*Dyke-grave*" has been transformed. *This* is the way in which "*Necessity*" has quasi-providentially brought about democratization, described as "Something like *Government*" (37–38).

The effect of all this conceited thought is consummated in a word-play on the very identity of the inhabitants themselves. With his excursion on "Hollanders" Marvell goes further than does the anonymous pamphleteer of 1665 who was to equate "Holland" with "Hogg-land." Although Marvell's latent pun is on "Whole-[l]anders," its full force can be comprehended only with some knowledge of the language of the people whose national character he is portraying:

> these *Half-anders,* half wet, half dry,
> Nor bear *strict service,* nor *pure Liberty.*
>
> (53–54)

Keen to spot an allusion to the famed religious tolerance of the Holland-ers, something Marvell will go on to pursue later in the poem with his ludicrous allusion to the inverted diaspora that follows the splitting of the ark of religion "on this unknown ground" (67ff.), commentators have missed the incisive effect of "*Half-anders.*" The latent pun, which Marvell once more finesses, would have suggested what all too many propagandists of the national stereotype would have wanted to hear, yet "*anders*" in Dutch is "other[wise]," "different." Marvell's chosen coinage thus goes far beyond the imputation that the country's inhabi-tants, the "true" Hollanders, are neither one thing nor the other, lukewarm in their convictions.[35] His point is that it is only *in part* that they are a different kind of creature altogether. To be like the English, that is, wholly dry, they would need to "bear . . . *Pure liberty.*" To assert

---

35. Cf. the rebuke to the Laodiceans in Rev. 3:16. In personal communications, Douglas D. C. Chambers has suggested a further subliminal play on a Greek ety-mology, so that "Half-anders" might also be read as "half-[hu]man," and Michael C. Schoenfeldt yet a further subliminal play on, or part anagram of, or indeed finessing of, "half Flanders."

that they are not, and do not, is to state that the quasi-providence, which has cast the Hollanders ashore and set them perpetually to work to reclaim their earth from the water, has also denied them the capacity to "bear [either] *strict service,* [or] *pure Liberty.*" This quasi-providential force will be seen by the poem's end to be a parodic reflection of the true providential force it finally and implacably comes into conflict with, a force that has brought about not a state of suspension and perpetuity but on the contrary, the unprecedented events being experienced in the England ("Our sore new circumcised *Common wealth,*" 118) of 1653. Now freed from the tyranny of regal autocracy through Divine Right, and still to face the increasing tyranny of the Protectorate, the English no longer "bear *strict service.*"

It is in this way that the Hollanders can be portrayed as "*Mairmaids* with . . . *Tails of Fish*" (85), that is to say, as creatures that themselves figure a mythical transformation of the amphibious lifestyle forced on them by the elements. For the fabled evolution of their terrain and the tortuously farcical way providence has operated in their history have combined to consign them to a perpetual limbo. This state is less the hell of the propagandists than a purgatory in which the equilibrium that must be maintained if the Hollanders are to survive can be brought about only by sustained, continued, and active confrontation with the elements. They can never successfully engage the English at sea because all hands are needed on land, or what passes for it. To portray one's neighbors in this way, similar to oneself but at the same time "*Half-anders,*" is thus to realize what it is to be oneself. In his profound understanding of what it is that enables the English to stereotype the Dutch in this way, and what, at the same time, absolutely elementally divides the two nations from each other, Marvell certainly managed to provide fuel for the anti-Dutch propaganda campaigns of 1665 and 1672. Yet the susceptibility of his poem to propagandist use does not ultimately offer the most compelling account of it available to us once it is located within its cultural context. To perceive *that* urgency we must conclude that Marvell's portrayal of elemental equilibrium between earth and water in "The Character of Holland" argues nothing less than his sense of what it was to be English in 1653 at a providentially unique historical moment during the Interregnum.

Diana Treviño Benet

"The Loyall Scot" and the Hidden Narcissus

IN 1611, TEN YEARS before the birth of Andrew Marvell, John Donne lamented in "The First Anniversary" that the "new Philosophy cals all in doubt":

> 'Tis all in pieces, all cohaerence gone;
> All just supply, and all Relation:
> Prince, Subject, Father, Sonne, are things forgot,
> For every man alone thinkes he hath got
> To be a Phoenix, and that there can bee
> None of that kinde, of which he is, but hee.
>
> (ll. 213–18)[1]

According to Donne, the collapse of the geocentric perspective caused a radical disorientation loosing the individual into solitary self-regard. In fact, several of the major guiding stars slipped from their accustomed places, contributing to a new inwardness in the Renaissance: "The Sun," as Donne says, was "lost, and th'earth"; the one, infallible Church had been rejected; and (in Marvell's day) the head of the body politic was cut off. Given this "world of new explorations, new politics, and new thinking, which had blurred the familiar shapes," many "chose to withdraw into the one haven remaining"—the self.[2]

The Roman Catholic emphasis on meditation, from the sixteenth century forward, had simultaneously reflected and encouraged a "newly-valued individualism" that led the worshiper to look into himself;[3] and ironically, reformers rejected the forms of the institutional Church by urging the Protestant also to find faith and to practice piety by looking within, into his own heart. Consequently, the pervasive self-centered-

---

1. Quotations of Donne are from *The Complete Poetry of John Donne*, ed. John T. Shawcross (Garden City, N.Y.: Anchor, 1967), and of other authors from *The Later Renaissance in England: Nondramatic Verse and Prose, 1600–1660*, ed. Herschel Baker (Boston: Houghton Mifflin, 1975).

2. Paul Zweig, *The Heresy of Self-Love: A Study of Subversive Individualism* (1968; rpt. Princeton: Princeton University Press, 1980), 125, 126.

3. Ibid., 52.

ness of many seventeenth-century authors still serves to locate the self in the uncertain world according to religion. Thomas Browne asserts, for example, "The world that I regard is myself," but loves his "O *altitudo*" and remembers in his "solitary and retired imagination" that he is not alone. Thomas Traherne glories that "Long time before / I in my mother's womb was born, / A GOD, preparing, did this glorious store, / The world, for me adorn," but he looks within to find the child again that was God's pure and particular object. Others of a more secular bent also use inwardness to achieve outward connectedness. Richard Lovelace, for instance, admires the "Wise emblem of our politic world, / Sage snail, within thine own self curl'd," but he curls into himself to create the "genuine summer" of cavalier fellowship that defines and anchors him. Inwardness in Marvell's poetry, however, is different. It is often the refuge of the divided self lacking a foundation against which to organize and stabilize itself.

Writing some years ago about Marvell and the science of optics, Donald M. Friedman remarked that the poet explores "the moral effort that goes into maintaining one's sense of self as distinguished from the world around" and suggested that identity is "the problem that attracts Marvell." Following these and other hints from Friedman and from Christopher Ricks's remarks on reflexive imagery,[4] I shall argue that the problem of a cohesive, stable self underlies Marvell's poetry. Overriding our critical division of lyrical and political poems, this central concern surfaces in the recurring (and complementary) figures of the Actor and Narcissus. Since both figures are essential to "The Loyall Scot," the poem will organize our examination of the images, themes, and techniques that comprise Marvell's exploration of the fragmented self and of the relation of art to this fragmentation. The tale of Narcissus is Marvell's informing myth, one of those idiosyncratic clusters of concerns and motifs resulting from the convergence of cultural materials and individual experience and sensibility. For Marvell as for Jacques Lacan, the story of Narcissus is fundamental as an account of the divided self. Although Lacan uses the object closely associated with narcissism, the mirror, and the poet especially uses the human figure in a self-regarding attitude, both use the myth's components to indicate and explore the nature and the vicissitudes of the divided human subject. In part, "The Loyall Scot," a narrative-satirical poem, treats some mirror-stage effects, such as the subject's desire to experience the illu-

4. Donald M. Friedman, "Sight and Insight in Marvell's Poetry" in *Approaches to Marvell: The York Tercentenary Lectures*, ed. C. A. Patrides (London: Routledge & Kegan Paul, 1978), 314, 321. See Christopher Ricks, "'Its own resemblance'" in *Approaches to Marvell*, 108–35.

sion of unity, the fearful production of a disintegrating or fragmented body image, and the yearning for a reified image of a supposedly stable self.

Readers in general agree that Marvell gives a particular emphasis to "the dance of contradictions" and oppositions characterizing life and man.[5] His fascination with the self divided by contraries is everywhere apparent: in "A Dialogue, between the Resolved Soul and Created Pleasure" and "A Dialogue Between the Soul and Body" the spiritual and sensual aspects of a man argue their opposing claims and threaten to tear him apart. In "Upon Appleton House," Fairfax "retired here to Peace, / [but] His warlike Studies could not cease" (283–84). Similarly, Cromwell has "sev'ral Aspects, like a Star, / Here shines in Peace, and thither shoots a War" ("The First Anniversary," 101–2). But perhaps Marvell's definitive description of self-division occurs in "The Garden," where the soul actually splits off from the body in the experience of ecstasy. Capt. Archibald Douglas, the loyal Scot, is another of Marvell's fragmented selves.

We owe "The Loyall Scot" to John Cleveland and the English Parliament: in 1644, Cleveland had written "The Rebel Scot," and in 1669–1670, the Parliament discussed the union between England and Scotland. Initially, the two nations had come together in the person of Elizabeth's Stuart successor. But James I of England and VI of Scotland did not achieve his desire to join the two countries formally. In 1643 the Scots, discontented with the rule of an English king, entered the civil war on the parliamentary side; in 1644 their assistance led to victory at the battle of Marston Moor. This disloyalty to Charles I was the basis of Cleveland's royalist satire. After Charles was defeated, the Scots made no progress in governmental independence; instead, Cromwell "simply annexed Scotland by military force." At the Restoration, when this "temporary incorporation was abandoned,"[6] Scotland was back where it had begun with James: a nation ruled by an absentee king and his foreign government. Like his grandfather, Charles II hoped to consolidate the two countries, and the English Parliament in 1669–1670 discussed ways to bring the nations together in a united governing body. Marvell wrote "The Loyall Scot" in support of this union, and he made "Cleveland's Ghost" do a "favourable penance" for "The Rebel Scot" by making him the speaker of the poem.

5. Frank Warnke, "Play and Metamorphosis in Marvell's Poetry," *Studies in English Literature* 5 (1965): 25–30. Rpt. in *Seventeenth-Century English Poetry: Modern Essays in Criticism*, ed. William R. Keast (London: Oxford University Press, 1971), 354.
6. P. H. Scott, *1707: The Union of Scotland and England* (Edinburgh: Chambers, 1979), 5.

Captain Douglas had commanded a Scottish regiment whose task was to defend the *Royal Oak,* an English ship, against the Dutch in 1667. According to Marvell, this defense was the Captain's hour of glory. The seductive images of Douglas encourage the reader to linger over and return to "The Loyall Scot." The poet, too, felt compelled to revert to the images he had created for, and already exhibited in, "The Last Instructions to a Painter." The secretive and evasive poet's singular repetition of forty-eight lines from an earlier poem is his acknowledgment of the power of these images. By detaching Douglas's story from one context and placing it in another, Marvell demonstrates that its meaning is multifaceted; moreover, by elaborating on his first version, he indicates that the tale has not exhausted its interest or significance for himself. The obvious importance that Marvell attaches to his story and its resonance with other poems suggest that this is a personal and a personally significant version of the Narcissus myth.[7]

Marvell's Douglas is androgynous, uniting opposites in a single body. He appeals tremendously to women; however, his self-reflexive bent is obvious from the outset:

> modest beauty yet his sex did vail,
> Whilst Envious virgins hope hee is a Male.
> His shady locks Curl back themselves to seek
> Nor other Courtship knew but to his Cheek.
>
> (17–20)

Swimming by night, the young man was often seen and desired by admiring nymphs: "To bee espy'd by him, / The Nymphs would Rustle, [but] hee would forward swim" (23–24). Douglas's attentions were all to and for himself: his frequent swims in "chill" waters were exercises that "Hardned and Cool'd those Limbs soe soft, soe white" (22). The virginal youth is not interested in seeing the eager girls. Instead, his concern is to rectify his androgynous softness; his attention is for

---

7. Some editors do not believe the entire poem to be Marvell's work. George de F. Lord, for example, does not print ll. 63–64, 93–100, and 105–236. See his *Andrew Marvell: Complete Poetry* (New York: Random House, 1968), 188. I will not consider the question of Marvell's authorship of "The Loyall Scot" explicitly; however, in the course of commenting on the poem, I glance at echoes, parallels, and other structures of internal consistency that themselves constitute an argument for Marvell's authorship. See also Elizabeth Story Donno on this subject: *Andrew Marvell: The Complete Poems* (1972; rpt. Middlesex: Penguin, 1976), 295; and Warren L. Chernaik, *The Poet's Time: Politics and Religion in the Work of Andrew Marvell* (Cambridge: Cambridge University Press, 1983), 210–11: "the strong probability is that both the shorter and the longer versions [of the poem] are authentic" (211n).

himself as object of admiration and as image of another's sight. During the battle with the Dutch, Marvell remarks that the Scot's only fear is "least Heaven fall ere thither hee Ascend" (30). When the Dutch fire the *Royal Oak* and the other sailors flee, he "disdaines" to save his life:

> Much him the glories of his Antient Race
> Inspire, nor cold hee his own Deeds deface;
> And secrett Joy in his own soul doth Rise
> That Monk lookes on to see how Douglass dies.
>   (39–42)

Douglas did not return the regard of the women who admired his none-too-solid self. But amidst his performance of a death that identifies him as a hero, he joyfully regards himself in the gaze of his chief. General Monck, a former Cromwellian, was now duke of Albemarle and leader of the English fleet. Elsie Duncan-Jones remarks on the "stagey" aspect of Douglas's story and wonders if Marvell is "hinting not unintentionally at the self-love and self-congratulation, not to say narcissism, that might be part of a heroic suicide, however sanctioned by naval tradition."[8] More supporting details follow, but these lines, stressing Douglas's need to be seen in his extremity, identify him as Actor and Narcissus.

In subtle guises, these figures often appear in conjunction with each other, almost interchangeably, in Marvell's poems. They are closely related, if not quite identical. Both are called into existence by vision, by being seen: Narcissus must see himself and the Actor must be seen by an audience. (Narcissus *is* an Actor, inasmuch as the mirror splits him into performer-image and his own audience.) The two figures are paradigms of the fragmented subject: Narcissus represents the split of body and image (and the yearning for an impossible union), and the Actor represents the split between the self and the personality, the subject of being and the subject of speech, the inward subject and the outward, projected image. As these oppositions suggest, both figures raise the question of substance versus representation, of truth versus inauthenticity. As Marvell puts it in "Upon Appleton House," those seeing themselves in a mirror wonder "If they be in it or without" (638).

Both figures were familiar in the seventeenth century, but perhaps the Actor was the more popularly accessible and culturally freighted of the two during Marvell's lifetime. The Actor was outlawed with the

---

8. "Marvell: A Great Master of Words" in *Proceedings of the British Academy* 61 (1975): 278.

closing of the theaters in 1642, and readmitted into the kingdom only after this period of banishment, during the Restoration. Moreover, the Actor is the avatar under which the puritanical part of Marvell's society for awhile acknowledged, criticized, and (temporarily) ostracized the fragmented self.[9] Donald Lupton detailed some reasons for the general fear and disapproval of actors: "A player often changes; now he acts a monarch, to-morrow a beggar; now a soldier, next a tailor. Their speech is loud, but never extempore; he seldom speaks his own mind, or in his owne name. . . . All their care is to be like apes, to imitate and express other men's actions in their own persons."[10] The anonymous author of "A Short Treatise," writing in 1625, believes the Actor's falsehood is contagious: "And many goe honest thither [to the theater], which returne home dishonest." He objects that actors "never come on the Stage in theire owne name, but some in the name and person of a divell, others of a foole, others of a bawde, others of a tyrant, others of other men, which beseemeth not a Christian . . . but is contrarie to Christian profession."[11] William Prynne is horrified by actors wearing women's clothes: "The verdict of human nature condemnes men degenerating into women; so from the selfsame grounds, it deeply censures the aspiring of women above the limits of their female sex, & their metamorphosis into the shapes of men, either in haire, or apparell."[12] As the quotations suggest, a part of seventeenth-century society disapproves of the Actor because he dissolves, by his unpredictable metamorphoses, the boundaries or classifications that render the social world comprehensible. Each person must have a coherent and consistent identity in order for others to interact comfortably with him, but the Actor changes gender and appropriates identities at will. He evokes such strong fears because he makes manifest the problems and dangers attending the duality of flesh and spirit acknowledged by all Christians. Representing inwardness in the service of "falsehood" rather

9. Jonas Barish cautions us that not all the people who opposed or criticized actors and the stage were Puritans; "Nevertheless, the term has come to stand, with some justice, for a complex of attitudes best represented by those strictly designated as Puritans." See *The Antitheatrical Prejudice* (Berkeley and Los Angeles: University of California Press, 1981), 82n.

10. *London and the Countrey Carbonadoed.* 1632. Rpt. in *Every One a Witness: The Stuart Age: Commentaries of an Era*, ed. A. F. Scott (New York: Thomas Y. Crowell, 1975), 108.

11. "A short treatise against stage-plays." 1625. Rpt. in *Critics and Apologists of the English Theatre: A Selection of Seventeenth-Century Pamphlets in Facsimile*, ed. Peter Davison (New York: Johnson Reprint Co., 1972), 19, 18.

12. *Histrio-Mastix. The Players Scourge or Actors Tragaedie* (London, 1633), 200. Prynne also quotes, on page 141 of *Histrio-Mastix*, "I. G." in *Refutation of the Apologie for Actors* (London, 1615): "A iust man cannot endure hypocrisie, but all the acts of Players is dissimulation, and the proper name of Player . . . is *hypocrite.*"

than piety, the Actor is the Christian who exploits the discontinuity between body and spirit for purposes of deception, the man who defaces the divine image in himself, obscuring it with false and multiple images. In short, the Actor threatens some seventeenth-century men because they understand, on some level, that he is a reflection of themselves. By the Restoration, when the theaters reopened, the clamor against players had ceased. But, as we shall see, it is for Marvell himself as it had been earlier for an influential segment of the population: at best, *Actor* is a word for doubleness; at worst, a name for hypocrisy and inauthenticity.

We have observed that Archibald Douglas, "The Loyall Scot," is something of an Actor, filled with "secrett Joy" that he can perform his definitive death scene before the appreciative audience of General Monck. The significance of his status as Actor-Narcissus we shall consider shortly; for the moment, we observe that the Anglican prelates Marvell criticizes in the poem are Actors, too. This entire poem, arguing for unity, is concerned with unnecessary or reprehensible divisions, and all of the clergy's sins have to do with division: bishops divide Scotland and England as well as "the world" at large (99). For their own advantage, they try to split the royal power so that "Kings head saith this, But Bishops head that doe" (196); for their enjoyment, they split morality into matters necessary òr indifferent: " 'Tis necessary Lambeth never wed, / Indifferent to have a wench in bed" (218–19). But their essential sin involves being Actors:

> Their Companyes the worst that ever playd,
> And their Religion all but Masquerade.
> The Conscious Prelate therefore did not Err,
> When for a Church hee built a Theatre.
>   (166–69)

The theater at Oxford financed by Gilbert Sheldon, the Archbishop of Canterbury, enables Marvell to imply that the divisions promoted by the Anglican hierarchy have nothing to do with faith. As Actors, the bishops sever their behavior from the truth of their hearts.[13] Such is their power, however, that the deceptive clergy undergo a lucrative metamorphosis: "A Hungry Chaplain and a Starved Rat / Eating their brethren Bishop Turn and Cat" (174–75).

---

13. The connection between (supposedly insincere) prelates and actors goes back at least as far as the mid-sixteenth century. William Tyndale criticized the Roman Catholics, for instance: "So that in one thing or other, what in the garments, and what in the gestures all [is] played" (quoted in Barish, *Antitheatrical Prejudice*, 160).

Division, dissolution, and metamorphosis link Archibald Douglas, the Anglican bishops, Narcissus, and the Actor. The nymphs Douglas ignored had wondered if he fled love's fires because he was "reserv'd for other flame" (26). Marvell's indication of Douglas's narcissism is artfully buried, but not far from the surface as the Scot dies in a blazing, self-directed passion.

> Like a glad lover the fierce Flames hee meets
> And tries his first Imbraces in their sheets.
> ·
> And on his flaming Planks soe rests his head
> As one that Huggs himself in a Warm bed.
>
> (43–44, 55–56)

Like another youth who rejected an importunate girl, Douglas can be a glad lover only when he can hug himself, and the embrace must kill him. The hidden association between Douglas and Narcissus is underscored by watery allusions: "his reliques" sink and the "sad stream" drinks his ashes (57–58), though the Scot burns to death, dissolving and beginning to assume a new identity in fire.

Douglas is split beyond the usual immortal mind and mortal form. We have noted that he is "brave" but his limbs are "soe soft, soe white"—manly but feminine, desirable but undesiring, inspired by his "Antient Race" but eager for present approval, heroically sacrificing but tragically self-regarding. This complex of oppositions was the living Douglas, but he joyed, at last, in the opportunity to present the unified image of a hero. The text indicates that this was Douglas's dearest aim. Notwithstanding his performance as a complete hero, however, the Scot finally experiences his radically divided nature as the literal incoherence of death. Curiously, the final dissolution sounds gorgeous:

> His shape Exact which the bright flames enfold
> Like the sun's Statue stands of burnisht Gold:
> Round the Transparent fire about him Glowes
> As the Clear Amber on the bee doth Close;
> And as on Angells head their Glories shine
> His burning Locks Adorn his face divine.
> But when in his Imortall mind hee felt
> His Altred form and sodred Limbs to Melt,
> Down on the Deck hee laid him down and dy'd
> With his dear sword reposing by his side.
>
> (45–54)

The fire fixes the image of Douglas, catches his "shape Exact" as if he were a solid object, like a golden statue of Apollo. Like clear amber, the flames at once capture, preserve, and display the fragile living form. Finally, they clothe him in divine glory. In the process of burning, Douglas undergoes metamorphosis: the sun, a golden statue, an amber-enclosed bee, an angel with a brilliant, dazzling corona. Not to cohere is, first, not to exist as a stable identity and, finally, to die; but as Douglas melts from one identity to another to another yet more remarkable one, Marvell emphasizes the wonder and beauty of his metamorphosis.[14]

It would seem that Douglas, having ceased to cohere and, therefore, to exist as a unified subject could be no more. But such is not the case. His metamorphosis is not yet complete.

> Fortunate Boy, if ere my verse may Claim
> That Matchless grace to propagate thy fame,
> When Oeta and Alcides are forgott,
> Our English youth shall sing the valiant Scott.
> . . . .
> Shall not a death soe Generous now when told
> Unite our distance, fill the breaches old?
> Such in the Roman forum Curtius brave
> Galloping down Clos'd up the Gaping Cave.
> Noe more discourse of Scotch or English Race
> Nor Chaunt the fabulous hunt of Chivy Chase:
> Mixt in Corinthian Mettall at thy Flame
> Our nations Melting thy Colossus Frame,
> Shall fix a foot on either neighbouring Shore
> And Joyn those Lands that seemed to part before.
> (59–62, 65–74)

Thanks to the poet's fire, the "Fortunate Boy" is transformed into the "valiant Scott." Additionally, in lines 65–74 above, the section that Marvell adds to his first version of Douglas's death (in "The Last Instructions"), the Captain is transformed into a unitive story to replace the ballad of Chevy Chase, the old divisive tale about hostilities on the English–Scottish border. Finally, Douglas is the agent capable of melting the two countries, the Colossus whose gigantic frame spans the two nations and joins them. Marvell presents Douglas's life as a prepara-

14. Warren Chernaik relates Marvell's treatment of Douglas's story to "the Renaissance epyllion, the Ovidian mythological narrative" and remarks that "the strained imagery seeks to depict the exact moment of metamorphosis, the interpretation of the earthly and the spiritual" (*Poet's Time*, 154).

tion for his heroic death and transformation: the limbs whose softness and whiteness the Scot sought to alter by swimming in "Chill Eske or Seyne" (21) are "Hardned and Cool'd" best by his metamorphosis into the colossal bronze statue of Apollo, the god of the sun and of poetry. Archibald Douglas at last achieves the stability unavailable to him in life. No longer a self-regarding, fragmented human subject, he is translated into a coherent and unified work of art.

Earlier, I stated that for Marvell, *Actor* is a word for doubleness, at best, and a name for hypocrisy or inauthenticity, at worst. Subsequently, I noted that, according to the poem, Archibald Douglas and the Anglican Bishops are alike in being Actors. In "The Loyall Scot," hypocrisy taints only the Bishops, but doubleness or division characterizes every human being. This awareness of the subject's fragmentation enables Marvell to link Douglas, the Anglican Bishops, Narcissus, and the Actor. And the connections between them go beyond fragmentation. Douglas's story shows the seemingly whole Scot undergoing metamorphosis in a radical dissolution followed by a reification of a glorified unitary self. The villainous Bishops are subject to the same processes. They, too, seem unified wholes, identities reified in fixed, solid shapes: "Ah! like Lotts wife they still look Back and Halt, / And surplic'd shew like Pillars too of salt" (124–25). But because of their error what seems solid is susceptible to dissolution or disintegration: "All Mischeifs Moulded by those state divines; / Aaron Casts Calves but Moses them Calcines" (134–35).

> The good will bravely, bad will basely doe;
> And few indeed can paralell our Climes
> For Worth Heroick or Heroick Crimes.
> The Tryell would however bee too nice
> Which stronger were, a Scotch or English vice,
> Or whether the same vertue would reflect
> From Scotch or English heart the same effect.
>   (239–45)

The Scots and the English, the heroes and the villains, Douglas and the bishops—all are actuated by the same vices and virtues and, more importantly, all partake of the same nature. All are fragmented, hampered and moved by the same instability and incoherence. Given that fragmentation or division is the nature of the human subject, dissolution seems a possibility and reification a desirable aim—for those of "Worth Heroick" like the brave Douglas; for the base Bishops, guilty of "Heroick Crimes," reification is a threat of entrapment in shapes of sin or punishment.

In addition to these thematic repetitions, Marvell uses certain technical devices related to Narcissus and the Actor. Just as the apprehension of fragmentation, the act of reflection, and the metamorphosis are essential aspects of the Narcissus myth, the principles of mirroring and of twin or matched images are important in Marvell's poems. "The Loyall Scot," for example, echoes its literary source in several ways: Cleveland's "The Rebel Scot" refers to "Hocus" (26), the juggler, and so does Marvell (106). As Elizabeth Donno remarks, Marvell also echoes Cleveland's "most popular lines" in his own lines 108–9: "had Bishops come, / Pharoah at first would have sent Israell home."[15] In addition, Marvell's poem reverses the images of Cleveland's in several ways: the rebel becomes a loyalist; the figurative flame of Cleveland's "I am all on fire" (5) in "The Rebel Scot" becomes literal, underlining the difference between mere, blustering indignation and true, fiery loyalty. Cleveland's poem criticizes the Scottish Presbyterians while Marvell's lambastes the Anglican clergy.

Within "The Loyall Scot" itself, the Colossus that joins together the two countries has its reverse-image in the "scotch Twin headed man / With single body" who is a "Living Embleme" for the division of one country-body by two governors-heads (186–89). The two-headed Scot is also, perhaps, the quintessential fragmented subject, since his divisions are multiple. By having two heads, he is divided not simply into body and mind, but into body and mind and mind: he is the man whose nature is to be always and inevitably of (at least) two minds. Marvell indulges his quirky sense of humor with the two-headed man, who is a perverse double of Narcissus. Narcissus loves his image and hates being separated from it; the monster's two heads have "wild disputes" and hate being joined. The poet plays here with the mirroring so essential to the Narcissus myth.

While "The Loyall Scot" insists that division is the condition of human identity, it also demonstrates the power of art to alter those discontinuities, its ability to unify and transform incoherence. This Marvellian development corresponds to the third section of the myth, after the boy dies, when Narcissus "disappears as a self to come back as a flower."[16] "The Loyall Scot" itself enacts Douglas's metamorphosis, transforming him (seemingly) from a divided being into a golden Colossus solidly beyond fragmentation. Marvell's art makes him into a brilliant symbol for two previously divided countries finally becoming

---

15. *Complete Poems*, 297n.
16. Carol Armstrong, "Reflections on the Mirror: Painting, Photography, and the Self-Portraits of Edgar Degas," *Representations* 22 (1988): 126.

a unified entity whose beauty far surpasses their fragmented incarnations. The poem concludes with an emphasis on union: the great soul of Charles II looks forward to joining England and Scotland, and John Cleveland and Douglas, who were on opposing sides in life, come together in friendship. The poet-ghost apologizes for his first, critical poem. In a reciprocal gesture, the ghost Scot warns Cleveland of a possible consequence of his new sympathies: his soul might be transferred into the body of a Scottish Presbyterian, his former nemesis. Suitably, Douglas's playful mention of transmigration is Marvell's final word in this poem (and it is not Marvell's word at all).

Retrospectively, the divided subject dominates the poem because of two points. First, for all that Douglas seemed unified into a conciliatory tale and the giant Colossus, the poet shows his division persisting into death: his body disposed of, Douglas's ghost speaks in Elysium. We could say that death enables the loyal Scot to be his own double: one Scot, sacrificed to the heroic ideal of his "Antient Race," dies, but the other Scot lives contentedly forever in Elysium. Then there is Marvell's own appropriation of another poetic identity. For it is not he, Andrew Marvell, or even he the anonymous-author-of-this-poem who speaks "The Loyall Scot." Instead, as we have remarked, a disembodied voice sets the scene and immediately appropriates the identity of John Cleveland's ghost. This is not Marvell's only such poem. Ben Jonson's ghost speaks a large part of "Tom May's Death," and a foreign Prince speaks a part of "The First Anniversary of the Government." By this device, Marvell may be suggesting that he "wants to be free to change his stance without inconvenience, either because he had been forced to take it without conviction or because the conviction from which it resulted was only provisional." He may be a "chameleon poet" who writes from "an experimental curiosity—to see what this part was like to play."[17] This may be the poet engaging in one of his infrequent "acts of self-definition, confirming that in his own eyes his own personality was split."[18] The philosopher of "Appleton House" who is yet "easy" indicates self-division as does the speaker of "The First Anniversary":

> If gracious Heaven to my Life give length,
> Leisure to Time, and to my Weakness Strength,

17. John Klause, *The Unfortunate Fall: Theodicy and the Moral Imagination of Andrew Marvell* (Hamden, Conn.: Shoe String Press, 1983), 5; John Dixon Hunt, *Andrew Marvell: His Life and Writings* (London: Paul Elek, 1978), 118.

18. Annabel Patterson, *Marvell and the Civic Crown* (Princeton: Princeton University Press, 1978), 27.

> Then shall I once with graver Accents shake
> Your Regal sloth, and your long Slumbers wake.
>   (119–22)

We know that this poet had a trick "of speaking of himself in the third person" in his personal letters, and "found it easier to correct or modify other men's statements than formulate his own." But whatever else he is doing, by borrowing Cleveland's identity, Marvell deliberately indicates yet again the absence of a whole, unitary subject.[19]

I suggested initially that the hidden Narcissus images reveal Marvell's concern about identity in a world without a center upon which the subject can found unity or stability. Religion is not a unitary principle in his poetry; instead, as the "Dialogue" poems suggest, it is part of the problem, with its emphasis on man's divided nature. Narcissus figures indicate other areas of experience that fail to provide a foundation for a unified self. Love does not last and so Clora "courts her self in am'rous Rain; / Her self both *Danae* and the Showr"—herself both lover and beloved ("Mourning," 19–20). The world fails to value ethical qualities that matter, so Maria Fairfax retreats behind a screen of trees to reflect, alone, on her own kind of beauties ("Upon Appleton House," st. 88). Political and military success fail to satisfy Oliver Cromwell, so he regards himself in his daughter Eliza whose illness makes her "his tortur'd Image" ("Upon the Death," 54). Cromwell appropriates Eliza's identity to the extent that her every pang is felt in *his* "steely Brest," which is "Like polish'd Mirrours" (73). And when "the dear image fled, the mirror broke" (78)—Eliza's death means his death; there can be no self without reflection. "The Loyall Scot" may be the purest of Marvell's hidden narcissists since the poem provides no particular clue to Douglas's introverted split: the division of the subject is simply assumed.

In these and other poems, the poet's hidden Narcissus embeds an account of the self generally consistent with the conception of identity that Jacques Lacan describes in "The Mirror Stage." One topic of "The Loyall Scot" is the mirror stage drama, to which belong fantasies extending "from a fragmented body-image to a form of its totality" that Lacan calls "orthopaedic," or "the statue in which man projects himself."[20] The subject's experience of fragmentation, his subsequent, joyous experience of wholeness or completeness in a specular image,

19. Ibid., 10, 13.
20. Jacques Lacan, "The Mirror Stage" in *Ecrits: A Selection,* trans. Alan Sheridan (New York: Norton, 1977), 4, 2.

and his fervent desire for a reified image of a stable self are the psychic structures replicated in the poem. We recall that Douglas longs for solidity, for a substance beyond dissolution or fragmentation, and understand the significance of his performance before Monck: the general's regard reflects the image of the ideal, total hero. Still, Douglas experiences exactly the nightmare he sought to avoid: like the Bosch paintings cited by Lacan in "The Mirror Stage," the poem depicts the fearful disintegration of what would appear to be the Scot's whole, united form. Finally, of course, the terrifying fantasy is succeeded by Marvell's version of the cherished dream: the supposedly stable self is reified in the gigantic, glorious image of the Colossus. These mirror-stage effects are deliberately situated in the domain of art by the poet's intuition that the perception of wholeness in identity is only imaginary, an illusion that can be created or sustained only in the reflection—or in the symbolic order.

Of course, "The Loyall Scot" was a political poem with a political intention: to present a Scottish hero whose defense of an English ship in an English cause would help to bring the two countries together. (I need not mention, perhaps, the particularly marvelous wit of a symbol of unity whose primary characteristic is self-division.) One reason, at least, for Marvell's interest in Archibald Douglas was that the captain's heroism was politically useful to him in his parliamentary aims. But this prosaic truth cannot explain the poet's particular treatment of Douglas or of his death. Margoliouth's notes on "The Last Instructions" inform the reader that Archibald Douglas's widow, Frances, in 1667 petitioned the government "for a prize ship as compensation" for her husband's death, and that she received a sum of money in the same year. Whether or not Marvell knew that Douglas was a married man, his account emphasizes the Scot's virginal purity. He deliberately describes an androgyne rejecting the women who pursue him. Such details and others, like the fiery, melting metamorphosis and the erection of the Colossus, are irrelevant to Douglas's performance of a heroic act; they are indispensable, I have argued, to the description of the fears and desires of the split subject. These operations evoke a greater interest than the original occasion of "The Loyall Scot." A poem urging a political agenda that failed three centuries ago achieves a new aspect, from our perspective, as an account of timeless psychic structures.

The Actor and Narcissus, extricated from the artful contexts in which they are embedded, identify the fundamental preoccupations that underlie Marvell's poetry and explain its power. The poet is keenly aware of the dichotomous subject, a self divided into visible and invisible parts, public and private aspects; he understands the extent to which everyman is consequently factitious. His poetic project seems to be again and again to reconstitute the potentially dissolving or disintegrating subject; his aim in inscribing it, to give a paradoxical substance and unity to what he insists is fluid and manifold. Even while his poetry insists on self-division, it lends coherence to incoherence, wholeness to fragmentation; it transforms deepseated concerns into beautiful forms. Marvell's art effects the metamorphoses by which fears of dissolution and disintegration become birds with silver wings and blazing statues of the sun.

John Rogers

The Great Work of Time
Marvell's Pastoral Historiography

LIKE ADAM IN THE last two books of *Paradise Lost*, the speaker of Marvell's "Upon Appleton House" can be seen to witness a prophetic pageant of world history. Situated comfortably within the forest on General Fairfax's estate, the narrator claims to read "What *Rome, Greece, Palestine*, ere said" in the "light *Mosaick*" of the leaves and feathers he finds scattered in the woods (577–82). But while Adam's prophetic vision is the product of the careful accommodations of a divine agent, Marvell's speaker identifies himself as a proponent of a new, more relaxed, mode of historical knowledge: he is the "*easie Philosopher, / Among the Birds* and *Trees*" (561–62). He simply happens upon a historiographical masque enacted in the woods, remarking of his good fortune, "how Chance's better Wit / Could with a Mask my studies hit!" (585–86). Although few of Marvell's pastoral poems are as explicit as "Upon Appleton House" in their incorporation of a scene of historical interpretation, a persistent interest in historiographical "study" can be seen to mark a number of his pastoral works. The Elizabethan critic George Puttenham located the impetus behind the production of pastoral verse in the poet's desire to "insinuate and glaunce at greater matters," and those critics of Marvell who have attempted to supply a historical understanding of the pastoral poems have proceeded on just this assumption of the possibility of topical analysis.[1] There can be little question that many of Marvell's poems glance, however coyly, at an identifiable world of seventeenth-century persons and events. But in analyzing the relation between Marvell's pastoral poetry and the "greater matter" of history, I will not be attempting merely to unveil

1. *The Arte of English Poesie,* ed. Gladys D. Willcock and Alice Walker (Cambridge: Cambridge University Press, 1936), 38. For political readings of Marvell's pastorals, see, for example, Don Cameron Allen, *Image and Meaning* (Baltimore: Johns Hopkins University Press, 1968), 187–225, and more recently, Michael Wilding, *Dragons Teeth: Literature in the English Revolution* (Oxford: Clarendon Press, 1987), 138–72. I discuss later in this essay the interpretative tradition that sees Marvell's pastoral as socio-political statements on agrarian labor.

Marvell's allegorizations of midcentury politics. It is not precisely "history" as the aggregate of particular past events, or even as the array of current political or socio-economic affairs, that will be viewed as the ultimate concern of Marvell's pastoral poems. It is, I will argue, a more abstract discourse of history as process that frames and situates the historiographical interests of "Upon Appleton House," and of many of the pastoral lyrics as well.

The first scene in the natural masque that the forces of chance bestow upon the speaker reveals two rows of trees in Fairfax's wood. This accidental tableau displays a historiographical paradigm that, we will see, is central to much of Marvell's pastoral verse:

> The double Wood of ancient Stocks
> Link'd in so thick, an Union locks,
> It like two *Pedigrees* appears,
> On one hand *Fairfax,* th' other *Veres*:
> Of whom though many fell in War,
> Yet more to Heaven shooting are:
> And, as they Natures Cradle deckt,
> Will in green Age her Hearse expect.
>
> (489–96)

Most of the trees the speaker surveys emerge from their origins in "Natures Cradle" in a gradual ascent to heaven, expecting as they grow in their domesticized wood the gentle arrival of Nature's "Hearse." The speaker proceeds in his description of the forest to specify the nature of the trees' heavenly ascent:

> When first the Eye this Forrest sees
> It seems indeed as *Wood* not *Trees*:
> As if their Neighbourhood so old
> To one great Trunk them all did mold.
> There the huge Bulk takes place, as ment
> To thrust up a *Fifth Element*.
>
> (497–502)

Behind this image of the "one great Trunk" of Fairfax's forest lies the doctrine of the great chain of being, the gradual scale along which all living matter rests in an unbroken continuity between earthly and divine substance. Marvell's simile, though, shifts this time-honored image of nature's ontological unity from a spatial to a temporal axis, transposing the subtle gradations of matter from their timeless position in an immanent natural hierarchy onto the inexorable motions of a historical process, a process perhaps more recognizable as the trees' natural growth. This organic ascent that catches the speaker's eye involves a natural progress from "trees" to "wood," and from wood to ethereal quintessence, a gradual movement that traces the decidedly linear path of the Christian schemes of salvation and providential fulfillment. While England's Fifth Monarchists had insisted on a violent hastening of providence as they prepared for that fifth, and final, monarchy of Christ, the trees in "Upon Appleton House" strike the speaker as thrusting their way to that final *"Fifth Element"* by kinder, gentler means.

Critics of seventeenth-century literature are too often tempted to reduce the discourse of providential change to the Calvinist conception of God's arbitrary manipulation of the course of human history. But there are some important strands of seventeenth-century scientific discourse that might help us account for what seem to be Marvell's unorthodox figuration of providence. By bracketing the question of the first, or divine, cause behind all physical change, many of the materialist philosophers of the seventeenth century could account for change in the natural world as the movement of physical bodies in time and space. In defining causation as a strictly physical process, materialism challenged the traditional wisdom that God acts as the "constant impelling force" behind all change.[2] Marvell's poetry reflects, of course, a Christian materialism, as he reconciles the theological notion of a providential *telos* with the increasingly common scientific view that change is nothing more than matter in motion. In the seventeenth century the study of the natural world was most commonly called not "science" but "natural philosophy," and sometimes "natural history."[3] And it is in part this notion of the history of physical change, which we might call an early historical materialism, that shapes Marvell's figuration of Christian history. The possibility of a naturalized process of providential change allows Marvell to represent the providential end not as a transcendent revelation of new heavens but as a specifically terrestrial millennium, a redemptive intermingling of nature's atomic particles. As we have seen, the more fortunate trees on the Nunappleton grounds can expect the arrival of Nature's hearse "in green

2. See Basil Willey, *The Seventeenth Century Background* (New York: Columbia University Press, 1934), 11–32; Robert Westfall, *Science and Religion in Seventeenth-Century England* (New Haven: Yale University Press, 1958), 70–105; and Samuel Mintz, *The Hunting of Leviathan* (Cambridge: Cambridge University Press, 1962).

3. Barbara J. Shapiro, *Probability and Certainty in Seventeenth-Century England* (Princeton: Princeton University Press, 1983), 19. I have discussed Milton's engagement of the seventeenth-century philosophy of matter in "Milton and the Mysterious Terms of History," *ELH* 57 (1990): 281–305.

Age." And it is perhaps this phrase, *green age,* which best names Marvell's naturalistic vision of the promised end, a final state of spiritual
and vegetative union to which the whole creation moves.

However absurd the attention in this poem to the soteriological destiny of Lord Fairfax's trees, Marvell's employment of this religious conceit should signal the general solemnity attending this doubled historical vision. I want to look now at that other element in Marvell's
dialectical tableau, those trees within the speaker's ken which, like the
members of the Fairfax and Vere families who fought in the English
revolution and in earlier wars, have been felled in war. The poem
suggests an antithetical relation between those trees shooting to
heaven and those trees destroyed by the soldier's axe, and the logical
implication of this antithesis is that the trees fallen in war are, quite
simply, dead and irredeemable.[4] The description of the "double Wood,"
which "like two *Pedigrees* appears," delineates in an emblematic form
two competing approaches to historical change and political reformation. On the one hand, the figure of the heaven-bound arbor, representing the natural process of continual development and growth, suggests
the potential for a gradual historical progress toward an ultimate state
of "redemption." The picture of the trees fallen in war, on the other
hand, introduces a considerably different, though perhaps more familiar, notion of historical change: the fact of the destruction of these trees
assumes a prior act of militant human assertion, an exercise of human
agency which not only threatens natural process, but which seems to
jeopardize a soterial future as well. While the image of trees growing
endlessly heavenward promises the redemptive potential of nature
itself, the image of trees irredeemably destroyed by soldiers or vandals
implies an argument for the futility of human attempts at change and
political reform.

Here we touch on what is perhaps the most pervasive thematic paradigm behind Marvell's poem: the intersection of a narrative of recent
English history with a Christian discourse of the spiritual history of
man. Marvell's image of the trees' salvation, I would argue, functions

4. The destruction of trees on both public and private property was in fact a common radical political gesture even after the war during the 1650s; the early modern
conservationist John Evelyn went so far as to claim that much of the "magazine of
timber" in England and Ireland was "destroyed by the Cromwellian rebels" (*Sylva,
or a Discourse of Forest Trees,* 2 vols. [1664; London: Doubleday, 1908], 2:169). Keith
Thomas has written that "during the Interregnum no actions aroused more passion
than the felling of groves on Royalist estates. The supporters of Root and Branch
even planned to cut down the royal walk of elms in St. James's Park, 'a living gallery
of aged trees,' as Edmund Waller described them" (*Man and the Natural World: A
History of the Modern Sensibility* [New York: Pantheon, 1983], 218–19).

in the poem as an element in the larger framework of a universal Christian history. As Maren-Sofie Røstvig has demonstrated, the narrative of "Upon Appleton House" is structured, to a significant degree, by some of the most foundational elements of Christian historiography—the state of innocence, the fall, and that final, compensatory, event of redemption. We need not, of course, conclude with Røstvig that Marvell's use of an essentially Christian vocabulary removes the poem to the realm of religious allegory, or that it suggests "the existence of a possible anagogical interpretation leading to a perception of absolute truth."[5] We can see, rather, that the recurrent images of innocence, fall, and redemption function in "Upon Appleton House" as indispensable units of a broader cultural discourse of history and change. Taking advantage of the urgent theological controversies surrounding certain key moments in Christian history, Marvell explores the problem of the reformation and change of the existing social order. It has been argued that it was in the seventeenth century that Europeans began to conceptualize their experience of social and political upheaval in terms of historical *crisis*.[6] The argument of this essay is focused in particular on Marvell's use of the scriptural fall from grace to represent the recent national crisis of the civil wars, the revolution he depicts as the "wasting" of the "*Paradise* of four Seas" (321–28).[7] Given that the English garden has "fallen," what remains for the poem to explore, within the terms of Marvell's politico-theological discourse, is the problem of "redemption," that action or set of actions that will somehow recover the lost natural—and, by extension, political—order.

The most striking, and certainly the most elaborate, historiographical lesson to "hit" the speaker in his naturalized study concerns itself with just this problem of a political redemption. Like the earlier vision of the trees on the Nunappleton estate, the episode of the oak and the woodpecker features the important image of the processes of natural growth:

5. "'Upon Appleton House' and the Universal History of Man," *English Studies* (Netherlands) 42 (1961): 338. A more recent, perhaps unwitting, avatar of Røstvig's spiritualist critique can be found by Marshall Grossman, "Authoring the Boundary: Allegory, Irony, and the Rebus in 'Upon Appleton House,'" in "*The Muses Common-Weale*": *Poetry and Politics in the Seventeenth Century*, ed. Claude J. Summers and Ted-Larry Pebworth (Columbia: University of Missouri Press, 1988), 191–206.

6. José Antonio Maravall, *The Culture of the Baroque: Analysis of a Historical Structure*, trans. Terry Cochran (Minneapolis: University of Minnesota Press, 1986), 19–53.

7. James Turner has provided a number of examples of the midcentury use of the image of the Fall to suggest contemporary political upheaval in *The Politics of Landscape: Rural Scenery and Society in English Poetry 1630–1660* (Cambridge: Harvard University Press, 1979), 91.

But most the *Hewel's* wonders are,
Who here has the *Holt-felsters* care.
He walks still upright from the Root,
Meas'ring the Timber with his Foot;
And all the way, to keep it clean,
Doth from the Bark the Wood-moths glean.
He, with his Beak, examines well
Which fit to stand and which to fell.

The good he numbers up, and hacks;
As if he mark'd them with the Ax.
But where he, tinkling with his Beak,
Does find the hollow Oak to speak
That for his building he designs,
And through the tainted Side he mines.
Who could have thought the *tallest Oak*
Should fall by such a *feeble Strok'*!

                                        (537–52)

Critics have for some time identified this passage as Marvell's oblique rendering of the political event that seems most deeply to have affected him, the execution of Charles Stuart, the Royal Oak.[8] Indeed, it could be argued that one of the central images of the "Horatian Ode," the execution of Charles I on the "tragick scaffold," generates for Marvell a tropological structure that appears in numerous guises throughout his work. There can be little question that this passage in "Upon Appleton House" resounds with some of the clamor of the English revolution. But I propose that we articulate more precisely the particular relation this narrative strikes with that crucial event of 1649. We can discern Marvell's nod to the actual event of the beheading not in the description of the oak, but in a brief simile that brings together the activity of the hewel and that of the English regicides: the hewel hacks the trees "As if he mark'd them with the Ax." I would argue that it is against this embedded image of the axe and its evocation of the decidedly human act of regicide that Marvell arrives at his narrative of the hewel and oak; it is in contradistinction to this image of deliberate human action that Marvell develops a fable of the processes of natural selection in the judicious activity of the hewel's tinkling beak. The story of the oak gestures toward the beheading of Charles, but this gesture is dialectical, as Marvell limns a vision of an alternative regicide that functions

8. Allen, *Image and Meaning*, 218; Harold Toliver, *Marvell's Ironic Vision* (New Haven: Yale University Press, 1965), 122.

not as the result of purposive human action, but as a link in the causal chain of a natural course of events.

We can perhaps see more clearly the historical dialectic Marvell is articulating if we juxtapose the hewel story with the evocation of the regicide we have already observed, the narrator's sight of a row of ancient trees, "Of whom . . . many fell in war." Both modes of arboreal destruction—the axing of trees, and the hewel's gradual pecking—lead to the same result, the clearing of the forest. But if we consider these passages as models of woodland reformation, they affirm substantially different positions on the possibility of historical progress: the first passage suggests the willful, and plainly human, destruction of trees by military fiat, while the second, far more elaborate, fable imagines this clearing as the exercise of a justice that operates on principles internal to the natural world. The vision of the oak and the hewel represents a utopian notion of historical reformation, one in which the corrupt historical subject itself invites its own destruction. The oak would not have fallen, the narrator insists, had it not already been internally corrupt, "had the Tree not fed / A *Traitor-Worm*, within it bred" (553–54). Trees in this idealized forest participate in the inevitable forces of a natural history: the solid oaks find their proper end as they shoot to heaven, while the corrupt trees seem "to fall content," in gracious recognition of their own corruption.

Although all of the elements in Marvell's story, including the "*Traitor-Worm*," have been identified as specific historical personages, the narrative of the hewel works less as an explicit political allegory than as a myth of political change. We can measure the complexity of this myth by examining the remarkable parenthetical suggestion that the corrupted oak itself solicits the salutary reformations of the modest hewel. A worm-tainted tree, Marvell argues by analogy, will invite its own destruction by a woodpecker,

> (As first our *Flesh* corrupt within
> Tempts impotent and bashful *Sin*).
> (555–56)

Marvell amplifies his fable with a theological analogy that reverses the conventional wisdom that it is sin which tempts the flesh. According to Marvell's refiguration, "Sin," in the sense of a reified external agent, is practically powerless; indeed, as a quaintly retiring and bashful figure, Sin, paradoxically, is almost innocent. With this startling inversion of passive and active forces, Marvell questions the validity of any conventional notion of an external agent in a historical process. Sin in Marvell's analogy may participate in a historical change, but only as a *passive agent*, one that merely enables the operation of a natural process already set in motion: like a woodpecker that merely hollows further an already decaying tree, Sin here can do no more than facilitate the pre-existent internal corruption of the flesh.

As an allegory of historical reformation—or the gradual clearing away of corruption—the fable of the hewel is perhaps most striking in its attribution of cause to the bird's utterly inadvertent behavior: although the hewel fells a corrupted oak of tremendous size, there is nothing resembling a larger political intent behind the mechanical motions of its beak. At the same time, however, the hewel is not altogether will-less, and we misunderstand the thrust of the episode if we fail to recognize the sphere of action to which this bird is assigned. Marvell's woodpecker is a father, and his primary purpose is to fulfill the immediate needs of his household. In his role as *paterfamilias*, the hewel mines through the tainted side of the oak to design shelter for his young, gleaning "from the Bark the Wood-moths" and the worms for sustenance. In characterizing the hewel as the servant of household necessity, Marvell invokes the traditional political wisdom that the basis of the household sphere lies not in the decisive, intentional acts most often attributed to the political world, but in the inevitable, naturally determined labor required for maintaining life in the household. Hannah Arendt has usefully described an important distinction assumed throughout classical political philosophy between the natural "labor" of the household and the unnatural, almost supererogatory, "work" and "action" that were seen to take place outside the private realm.[9] According to Aristotle, for example, the household is formed "for the reproduction of the species—not from deliberate intention, but from the natural impulse, which exists in animals generally as it also exists in plants, to leave behind them something of the same nature as themselves."[10] Marvell, I think we can see, attempts to ground the hewel's authority in precisely this natural household impulse the bird shares with plants and other animals. As the father of a family, assuming "the *Holt-felsters* care," the hewel is engaged in the activity Arendt would

9. In describing the Aristotelian distinction between the private and public spheres, Arendt writes in *Between Past and Future: Eight Exercises in Political Thought* (Harmondsworth: Penguin, 1968), 117: "Only the household community was concerned with keeping alive as such and coping with the physical necessities . . . involved in maintaining individual life and guaranteeing the survival of the species." For an extended treatment of her distinctions among the concepts "labor," "work," and "action," see Arendt's *The Human Condition* (Chicago: University of Chicago Press, 1958).

10. *The Politics of Aristotle*, trans. Ernest Baker (Oxford: Clarendon, 1946), 3.

denote not as "action" or "work," but as "labor," limiting his exertions to the creation and the maintenance of his tree-trunk nursery.

It is through the hewel's role as household architect that we are invited, I think, to associate the woodpecker with the poem's most important architect, Thomas Fairfax. In his "*Humility* [which] alone designs / Those short but admirable Lines" of Appleton House (41–42), Fairfax has modeled his domestic space on the sober dwellings, like the hewel's, he has found in the natural world, imitating the "Beasts [who] are by their Denns exprest: / And Birds [who] contrive an equal Nest" (11–12). As Marvell implies in the "Horatian Ode," Fairfax had served, in his capacity as Lord General of the Parliamentary Army, as a far more august architect in the political arena; however, after he had helped "design / The *Capitols* first Line, / A bleeding Head where they begun, / Did fright the Architects to run" (68–70), and thus Marvell's employer retired from civic life to his family estate, protesting at once the act of regicide and the prospect of a military invasion of Scotland.[11] Fairfax had chosen the private labor of the *oikos* over the public action of the *polis.*

In an earlier stanza of "Upon Appleton House," which many readers have interpreted as Marvell's implicit criticism of his patron, Marvell accounts for the consequences of this retirement by enlisting the classical subordination of the private to the public realm: had Fairfax maintained his power as military commander, he "Might once have made our Gardens spring / Fresh as his own and flourishing" (339–40). According to this formulation, the choice of public duty and military commitment holds at least the promise of a political reformation, while retirement holds the considerably diminished prospect of the flourishing of Fairfax's own garden. Marvell's fable of the hewel, however, remaps the conventional boundaries separating the civic from the private sphere of action, reassessing the domestic retreat as a new locus of historical change. In this story it is precisely the necessary labor associated with the household that serves the purpose of a sweeping societal reform, the kind of change most often assigned to the realm of public action. In his vision of the utopian political economy within the Nunappleton wood, Marvell seems to advocate a revival of the Aristotelian ideal of the "political order as a natural association that did not depend on deliberate human actions."[12] He depicts the reformation of the cor-

---

11. See Claude J. Summers, "The Frightened Architects of Marvell's 'Horatian Ode,'" *Seventeenth-Century News* 28 (1970): 5.

12. Gordon Schochet, *Patriarchalism in Political Thought: The Authoritarian Family and Political Speculation and Attitudes Especially in Seventeenth-Century England* (Oxford: Basil Blackwell, 1975), 23.

rupt English state as if it were occurring in a wholly naturalized political order that could reform itself without the purposeful interventions
of man and axe. Historical progress is simply the result of the feeble
strokes of a creature who, concerned only for his young, unwittingly
serves the political function of preserving the values of the forest at
large. The absence of political motive behind the hewel's action situates
this scene as a fable for the politically redemptive consequences of a
simple domestic retirement.

In 1655, Richard Baxter had advised his fellow ministers, "You are like
to see no general reformation till you procure family reformation."[13] In
the idealized universe sketched out in the fable of the hewel, Marvell
relies on the same system of values informing Baxter's comment, the
belief that all social relationships and, by extension, all social changes
should be grounded in the moral economy of the household. Marvell's
story of the hewel imagines that Fairfax, in his retirement, devoted
solely to the values of the household, has without the least trace of
aggression or violence purged England of its corrupt monarchy. Looking to his own house, this domesticated hero serves the needs of the
entire body politic, effecting a gradual purification of society by a
domestic, rather than a directly public, and military, revolution. The
fable articulates a fantasy alternative to the English revolution, a natural revolution whereby the domestic sphere subsumes the political. It is
retirement rather than action, the household rather than the political
realm, that enables man's participation in the real movement of history,
his integration into the moral realm of nature that ultimately subordi-
nates all public acts of human assertion.

Having established in Marvell's country-house poem a culturally
specific figuration of history as redemptive process, we might now
juxtapose these images of natural progress and human prodding with a
famous passage from the prose satire Marvell would write twenty years
later. In *The Rehearsal Transpros'd*, Marvell reconsiders the Good Old
Cause of the Parliamentarians in the light of a broader view of historical
cause and effect: "but upon considering all, I think the Cause was too
good to have been fought for. . . . For men may spare their pains where
Nature is at work, and the world will not go the faster for our driving.
Even as his present Majesties happy Restauration did it self, so all
things else happen in their best and proper time, without any need of
our officiousness."[14] It is most commonly suggested that this expres-

---

13. *The Reformed Pastor* (London, 1655), quoted in Christopher Hill, *Society and Puritanism in Pre-Revolutionary England* (London: Continuum, 1964), 445.
14. Andrew Marvell, *The Rehearsal Transpros'd and The Rehearsal Transpros'd. The*

sion of political passivity is the result of Marvell's disappointment after the Restoration. Marvell's notion that the movement of world history does not respond to man's driving voices a providentialism that denies the efficacy of any human action, a view fundamentally opposed to his earlier, more positivistic identification of the vigorous Cromwell with "the force of angry Heavens flame." What is perhaps most striking about Marvell's providentialism in this passage is his stated reliance not on God but on "Nature." In his political poetry, Marvell often identifies the source of providential control with the traditionally anthropomorphic deity of the Old Testament: it is almost the arbitrary God of Calvinist theology that impels Cromwell's power. But Marvell's claim in *The Rehearsal Transpros'd* is rather that men may spare their pains where a providential *nature* is at work. We can see, I think, how Marvell's Restoration critique of political action intersects in an important way with the country-house poem of the Fairfax period. In both the early work and the Restoration satire, "Nature" functions for Marvell as a temporal process, a force of history that labors to direct man toward his proper Christian end.

In his retreat to the Fairfacian wood, the narrator seems to validate the mode of historical causation most closely allied with natural development and growth. We can see in the speaker's sensuous engagement of the natural world an attempt to force an integration with the natural forces behind the living world. Entering the "yet green, yet growing Ark" of Fairfax's wood, he identifies his immersion in natural process with the redemptive mission of a Noah, hoping to purify a world corrupted by war. As if to internalize that law of nature, which sends the ancient trees shooting to heaven, and which impels the hewel's instinctive, salvific motions, the narrator imagines that he himself has merged with the stream of natural providence, in possession of the naturally redemptive powers of both the "*Fowles*" and the "*Plants*" (565).

It is not, however, the narrator's Hermetic and organicist reverie that constitutes the poem's final vision of nature or of history. For just as he seems almost fully to dissolve into the elemental forces of the natural world—"Stretcht as a Bank unto the Tide" (644)—the speaker grows conscious that "The *young Maria* walks to night." As his pupil, Mary Fairfax, proceeds through the landscape, the narrator's idle fantasy of a descent into a vegetative state evaporates abruptly in the numinous presence of a girl who is none other than the "*Law* / Of all her *Sex*, her *Ages Aw*" (649–56). Representing a new force of historical change,

Second Part (Oxford: Oxford University Press, 1971), 135. Further references to this work will be included in the text.

Maria is likened to the mythical halcyon, the bird believed capable of transfixing the troubled forces of nature:

> The modest *Halcyon* comes in sight,
> Flying betwixt the Day and Night;
> And such an horror calm and dumb,
> *Admiring Nature* does benum.
>
>   (669–72)

A magically exosmotic presence, soaring through a porous, and importunate, body of air that "Follows and sucks her Azure dy" (674), Maria is seen to illuminate the darkening landscape of her father's estate. With the preternatural force of Marvell's Cromwell, the modest Maria seems able to "contract the scattered force of time," calling a halt to the natural rhythms that bring the evening upon the Nunappleton estate.

Marvell is careful to distinguish the particular quality of Maria's supernatural power from the other wonders that have hit the speaker. Maria embodies a providential force that clearly transcends the mundane operations of natural law:

> *Maria* such, and so doth hush
> The *World,* and through the *Ev'ning* rush.
> No new-born *Comet* such a Train
> Draws through the Skie, nor Star new-Slain.
> For streight those giddy Rockets fail,
> Which from the putrid Earth exhale,
> But by her *Flames,* in *Heaven* try'd,
> *Nature* is wholly *vitrifi'd.*
>
>   (681–88)

Marvell charges his description here with the rhetoric of divine intervention and extraordinary providential control, taking pains to differentiate Maria's prodigious powers, "in *Heaven* try'd," from those meteorous flames that "from the putrid Earth exhale." From the moral perspective introduced at Maria's entrance, the idealized fusion of man and nature is dismissed as delusory and self-indulgent. Just as Maria's entrance interrupts the narrator's natural streamside languor, the poem signals a startling repudiation of its investment in vegetable growth, affirming a new supernatural force that interrupts and transcends the ordinary processes of nature. The autonomy that the narrator granted earlier to "*Natures mystick Book*" gives way now to a new order of divinity, as Maria replaces the narrator's attempts at a natural language

(569–76) with the *"Wisdome"* of *"Heavens Dialect"* (710–11). Most important, perhaps, Maria's appearance marks the poem's engagement of contemporary millenarian discourse, a new consciousness of the imminent culmination of Christian history. Whereas the narrator had participated in a natural world that seemed to move by a gradual, terrestrial progression toward a final heavenly end, Maria's entrance introduces to the poem what is perhaps a more orthodox understanding of Christian history, a concession to the violent discontinuity of apocalypse: in her presence, *"Nature* is wholly *vitrifi'd,"* reduced, as if by the final conflagration, to the crystalline state thought by many Renaissance thinkers to be "the untainted substance left after the earth has been tried by fire."[15]

In view of what is surely the inappropriate application of chiliastic rhetoric to Fairfax's very young daughter, it is not unreasonable for us to ask on what basis the speaker invests Maria with this surcharge of divinity. When the narrator asserts Maria's superiority to the other members of her "fond sex," he establishes the source of her powers; it is nothing less than the prospect of her marriage that places Maria in a realm of divinity associated more with grace than nature:

> Hence *She* with Graces more divine
> Supplies beyond her *Sex* the *Line*;
> And, like a *sprig of Misleto,*
> On the *Fairfacian Oak* does grow;
> Whence, for some universal good,
> The *Priest* shall cut the sacred Bud;
> While her *glad Parents* most rejoice,
> And make their *Destiny* their *Choice.*
>
> (737–44)

The final section of "Upon Appleton House" swells in a joyful anticipation of the marriage of General Fairfax's only heir. The choice of Fairfax and his wife to accept the destined marriage of their daughter fulfills the apocalyptic prophecy attached to that first heroic Fairfax, the patriarch "whose Offspring fierce / Shall fight through all the *Universe"* (241–42). By heralding the possibility of the continuation of the Fairfax line, Maria's marriage promises the birth of a future general who, unlike her father, really can make England's garden flourish.

When the narrator claims that the disseverment of Maria the "sacred Bud" will serve "some universal good," the poem affirms a mechanism

---

15. Kitty W. Scoular, *Natural Magic* (Oxford: Clarendon Press, 1965), 178.

of historical change in stark opposition to the gradualist model of organic change imagined earlier. Marvell's figuration of Mary Fairfax's marriage invokes the operation of sacrifice and reward that forms the basis of the Christian Redemption. Like the crucifixion of Christ, which functions in Christian history as a sacrifice that institutes the redemption of fallen man, the Fairfaxes' sacrifice of their daughter on the altar of marriage will institute the redemption of a world fallen in war.[16] The representation of their redemptive act recalls as well that auspicious event to which Marvell so often returns, the execution of the Stuart monarch.[17] The sacrifice of Maria's virginity on the marriage bed retraces in outline the sacrifice of Charles, who in the "Horatian Ode" "bow'd his comely Head / Down, as upon a Bed" (63–64). Like the "bleeding Head" of a king, which augured in the ode the "happy Fate" of a newly designed nation (67–72), the disseverment of Maria's maidenhead will by a mysterious process of sacramental causation usher in a "universal good."

Most critics of the poem have accepted without question the narrator's jubilant claim that the Fairfaxes have blithely made their daughter's destiny their choice. But we should not overlook the degree to which the marriage stanzas represent an unsettling divergence from a complex of values the poem has established. The deliberateness with which Maria's parents embrace their fate recalls one of the most primitive aspects of the Christian crucifixion, the parent's willing sacrifice of the child. Maria's "*glad Parents,*" quite unlike the nurturing hewel, resemble Marvell's insouciant heron, the bird who "from the Ashes top,

16. Marvell's sacramental representation marks a pronounced distance from the contemporary Puritan emphasis on the primacy of companionship in marriage, constituting instead an ironic version of the Catholic association of matrimony with the Christian Redemption. Aligning the sacrament of marriage with the sacrifice of crucifixion, Thomas Aquinas had written that matrimony, like baptism, "is able to touch the body and cleanse the heart . . . through Christ having represented it by His Passion" (*The Summa Theologica of St. Thomas Aquinas*, vol. 3, *Supplement* [New York: Benziger Brothers, 1948], Q. 42, A.3., quoted in James Turner Johnson, *A Society Ordained by God: English Puritan Marriage Doctrine in the First Half of the Seventeenth Century* [Nashville: Abingdon, 1970], 44).

17. Blair Worden, in "Providence and Politics in Cromwellian England," *Past and Present* 109 (1985): 90, argues that it was an inveterate logic of sacrifice among the Puritan revolutionaries that enabled the commitment to regicide: "The execution of Charles I is inexplicable without reference to . . . the biblical theory of blood-guilt which was as potent a force among the regicides in January 1649 as it was to be among Cromwell's soldiers in Ireland later in the year." Robert Cummings, in "The Forest Sequence in Marvell's 'Upon Appleton House': The Imaginative Contexts of a Poetic Episode," *Huntington Library Quarterly* 47 (1984): 192–96, argues persuasively that it is the contemporary understanding of Druidic sacrifice that informs the description of Mary's marriage.

/ The eldest of its young lets drop" (533-34), an image that just begins to convey the horror of a ritual child sacrifice. The priest's druidic dis-severance of the delicate sprig of mistletoe evokes inevitably the vio-lation of nature committed by the wanton cutter of trees, or by the levelling cutters of grass in the poem's harvest section. In a poem that invests so heavily in the ideology of the green age, Marvell's figure for Maria's marriage—the priest's cutting of the "sacred Bud" of mistle-toe—carries a rhetorical burden that nearly overwhelms the speaker's straightforward praise. The moral value attached to all such violent actions is a problem that Marvell's work continually worries. But while the poem seems implicitly to articulate a lament for the loss of Maria's natural innocence, there lurks the obstinate fact that her continued virginity would end the Fairfacian line, thwarting all hope that a future Fairfax could effect a universal salvation. The sacrificial action of Maria's parents is countenanced because it may work not only to redeem "that dear and happy Isle" of England; it might even invite an apocalypse that redeems man by removing him from the temporal world.

Behind this vision of the "*Fairfacian Oak*" in Marvell's description of his pupil's future marriage stands the other oak we have observed in "Upon Appleton House." And it is with the image of the oak tree that Marvell draws the idea of Maria's future marriage into relation with the fable of the hewel, marking the priest and the hewel as distinct types of historical agents, and the two narratives themselves as distinct models of historical reformation. I want now to suggest that the presence in "Upon Appleton House" of the narratives of the Royal Oak and the Fairfacian Oak points to Marvell's familiarity with a type of story that appears to have been in circulation during the years of the Interregnum. In his *Discourse of Forest Trees*, the Restoration writer John Evelyn recounts one of the many "histories of groves that were violated by wicked men, who came to fatal periods; especially those upon which the misselto grew, than which nothing was reputed more sacred":

> I am told of the disasters which happened to the two men who (not long since) fell'd a goodly tree, call'd the Vicar's Oak, standing at Nor-Wood (not far from Croydon) partly belonging to the arch-bishop, and was limit to four parishes, which met in a point; on this oak grew an extraordinary branch of misselto, which in the time of the sacriligious usurpers they were wont to cut and sell to an apothecary of London; and though warn'd of the misfortunes observed to befall those who injured this plant, proceeding not only to cut it quite off, without leaving a sprig remaining, but to demolish and fell the oak it self also: The first soon after lost his

eye, and the other brake his leg; as if the Hamadryads had revenged the indignity.[18]

The popular genre of the "histories of groves that were violated by wicked men" can be seen to supply an imaginative source for the representation of both of the oaks in "Upon Appleton House." Like the oak in the fable of the hewel, the Vicar's Oak (suggestive of the ill-fated Archbishop Laud) evokes the vulnerability of any sanctioned authority, in this "time of sacriligious usurpers," to the deliberate violence of axe-bearing men. Like the "Fairfacian Oak" in the stanza on Maria's marriage, this tree is prized for its "extraordinary branch of misselto" that is purposefully "cut . . . quite off." A look at the relation between this folk history of the destruction of an oak, as related here by Evelyn, and the two oak-tree narratives embedded in Marvell's poem might sharpen our focus on the highly ambivalent representation of the sacrificial action that concludes "Upon Appleton House."

It is easy to see that Marvell would have found himself sympathetic to the general sense in these stories of the sacredness of plants. But he would have had more difficulty subscribing to the faith that there inheres in nature such an aggressive force of self-preservation. Marvell's nature is more fragile and tenuous than the spirit of Evelyn's wood; it is incapable of any act of justice that could be likened to the vengeance wreaked by angry hamadryads. But the folk tale of the oak seems nonetheless to linger behind the plangent narratives of "Upon Appleton House." The story's shadowy presence just behind the text gives shape to the poem's implicit distrust in the value of even the most revered human action. It is with an unmistakable note of regret that Marvell permits the resignation to a society that sanctions such sacrificial rites as regicide and marriage. The submerged history of the grove voices the poem's muted desire, acknowledged to be futile, that nature were sufficiently powerful to defend from injury the progressive potential of natural innocence.

* * *

When Marvell's nymph complains that the "wanton Troopers" have shot her fawn, the intrusion of English soldiers upon the private world of pastoral signals a startling confrontation between the antithetical modes of historical redemption we have explored.[19] I want to conclude

---

18. *Sylva* 2:249–50.
19. The relative contemporaneity of the "wanton Troopers" was first argued by

this essay with a consideration of "The Nymph Complaining for the Death of Her *Faun*," and some of the Mower lyrics, because in many ways these poems provide an important critique of the official historiographical conclusions reached in "Upon Appleton House." While the country-house poem, as we have seen, equivocates on the subject of historical reformation, it seems ultimately to reject the possibility of a naturalistic redemption in favor of Fairfax's sublimer, sacrificial action. But Marvell's "The Nymph Complaining," I will argue, subjects to some scrutiny this final commitment to the necessity of sacrifice and the faith in the ultimate transcendence of the natural world.

I want to begin by specifying the nature of the historical process that the poem posits as its elusive ideal. In a passage that Marvell's aestheticizing critics have spirited away from the realm of ideological investment, the nymph describes the biological transformation the fawn would have undergone had it not been shot; depicting the pleasures derived from her life in the garden, she offers an account of the fawn that begins to edge toward the literary mode of historical prophecy:

> But all its chief delight was still
> On Roses thus its self to fill:
> And its pure virgin Limbs to fold
> In whitest sheets of Lillies cold.
> Had it liv'd long, it would have been
> Lillies without, Roses within.
>
> (87–92)

Imagining what could have been, "had it liv'd long," the gentle metamorphosis of the fawn's body, the nymph describes a gradual regenerative process in direct contrast to the arrested development the fawn has in fact experienced at the hands of the wanton troopers. What is perhaps most striking about the fawn's transformation is Marvell's displacement of the divinely guided Ovidian metamorphosis onto the more familiar terrain of material causation: he situates the interfusion of flora and fauna solidly within the natural world, subjecting it to a process of second causes rather than a transcendent progress governed directly by God or some immanent spiritual realm. It is by nothing more unworldly than the physiological process of ingestion and growth that the fawn would have rarefied its nature to a purer composition of flowers. But despite the erasure of any supernal causes behind

Edward S. Le Comte, who noted that the word *troopers* entered the language in 1640 as a term for the Covenanting army, in "Marvell's 'The Nymph complaining for the death of her Faun,'" *Modern Philology* 50 (1952): 100.

the concrescence of fawn and flower, Marvell frames the nymph's
account within the discourse of Christian soteriology. In his remarkable
naturalization of the highly emblematic images of lillies and roses,
Marvell establishes the possibility of a directed process of change that
we can identify as a form of natural providence.

To read, as I have, the nymph's reverie as a vision of providential
history is not to deny her status in the poem as a naive and, perhaps,
overly excitable youth. The poem's lightness of tone does not necessarily invalidate the nymph's fantasy as Marvell's expression of an
important mode of historical consciousness. It might be instructive to
juxtapose the nymph's highly domesticated, localized vision with a
passage from *Paradise Lost*. In what is surely the century's most famous
account of an imperilled future history, Raphael describes the bodily
transformation the first couple will undergo if they remain sinless:

> from these corporal nutriments perhaps
> Your bodies may at last turn all to Spirit,
> Improv'd by tract of time, and wing'd ascend
> Ethereal.
>
> (5.496–99)[20]

Raphael describes for the unfallen Adam and Eve the mysterious process of digestion, the physical transmutation of "corporal nutriments"
by which the first couple could metabolize themselves into spiritual
creatures and "wing'd ascend / Ethereal." Like the nymph's dream of
her pet's eventual metamorphosis, Milton's physical universe follows a
gradual process of natural providence, moving toward what might best
be described as an alimentary apocalypse.

There are, of course, some important differences between Marvell's
and Milton's ideal future histories. Raphael seems to picture Adam and
Eve as spiritualized bodies enjoying themselves at the heavenly court,
ultimately to be resumed into the entire creation, when God shall be
"All in All." The nymph, on the other hand, locates the ideal end in the
creature's physiological union with the lower end of the natural world,
in a return to the "one first matter all" that many Christian materialists
imagined as the world's condition at the beginning of time.[21] But both

20. John Milton, *Complete Poems and Major Prose*, ed. Merritt Y. Hughes (New York:
Odyssey Press, 1957). Dennis Danielson discusses the contemporary prevalence of
this belief in unfallen perfectibility in *Milton's Good God: A Study in Literary Theodicy*
(Cambridge: Cambridge University Press, 1982), 210–14.

21. See Paolo Rossi, *The Dark Abyss of Time: The History of the Earth and the History
of Nations from Hooke to Vico*, trans. Lydia G. Cochrane (Chicago: University of Chicago Press, 1984), 6–21.

images of transmutation affirm in outline one of the important heretical twists on the Christian doctrine of regeneration: the belief that regeneration operates not through the divine work of grace upon the spirit but through a self-impelled physical renovation of the natural body.[22] Both the first couple's spiritualization and the fawn's floralization share a conceptual debt to the alimentary theory of natural history conceived by Paracelsus, the view whereby the natural world continually improves itself through the purifying process of digestion. The two passages seem boldly to adumbrate the modern axiom, "You are what you eat."

The image of digestion provided the Renaissance with an important conceptual analogue for the abstract notion of a self-contained economy of purposeful motion and change, an autonomous system of material cause and effect.[23] The use of an organic process like digestion as the controlling trope for a theory of all natural change functions to locate the efficient *cause* of any development within the organism itself; it is, for example, a system of forces within the body that impels the motions of digestion. With the figurative conjunction of purgative and salvific ends, Marvell constructs a cosmos in which the determining cause of man's final end rests within man himself: a fully human quality of virtue—figured throughout Marvell's pastoral works as the physical condition of virginity—is itself sufficient to effect man's salvation. Marvell's insistence here on an internally motivated process of development owes more to an Aristotelian conception of change than to any orthodox Christian pattern of providence. The Marvellian body—whether animal or vegetable—functions as Aristotle's *materia prima*, a principle of pure potentiality, and this body is seen to obey an internal form that oversees the actualization of its potential. With this radical subversion of the Protestant emphasis on the primacy of the external force of divine grace, Marvell effectively internalizes the efficient cause of the individual's historical progress.

As we have observed in our reading of "Upon Appleton House," Marvell's pastoral figures often express the rather conventional idealization of their former communion with the natural world. But I would add that this sense of natural reciprocity assumes in many of these

22. For a reading of the importance of natural regeneration to Milton's theology, see Arthur Barker, *Milton and the Puritan Dilemma 1641–1660* (Toronto: University of Toronto Press, 1942).
23. Rossi, in *Dark Abyss of Time,* writes of the effect that the Paracelsian idea of digestion had on the discovery of a system of natural processes that integrated man with the rest of the natural world: the Paracelsian interpretation of the creation in terms of digestive processes "ended up dissolving the specificity of animal and human life into a global vitalism of forms and principles" (9).

poems the force of a providential sense of natural progress. In "The Mower's Song," Damon remembers his union with nature as a historical process, for his mind had been fully attuned to the providential force of natural growth:

> My Mind was once the true survey
> Of all these Medows fresh and gay;
> And in the greenness of the Grass
> Did see its Hopes as in a Glass.
>
> (1–4)

Geoffrey Hartman has suggested that these lines identifying the speaker's *hope* with the "greenness of the Grass" evoke the role of nature St. Paul foresaw in man's ultimate salvation.[24] Both earth and humanity, according to St. Paul, participate in the apocalypse he refers to as "the redemption of our bodies" (Rom. 8:23). As the example of the fawn's potential metamorphosis makes clear, Marvell recasts St. Paul's vision of the promised end of Christian history in the most literal sense imaginable: the final union becomes the actual physiological convergence of creaturely and vegetative bodies.

However ecstatic the images of a utopian future history in Marvell's pastoral poems, they are invariably countered with the recognition of the fact of the radical disruption of natural process. Nearly all of the pastorals evince a dialectic of growth and arrest that hinges on a narrative element roughly assimilable to the founding crisis of human history, the Fall. Like the civil wars, which are seen in "Upon Appleton House" to cause the lapse of an entire nation, the violent eruption of the mower's passion for Juliana, in "Damon the Mower," "The Mower to the Glo-Worms," and "The Mower's Song," instigates a new sundering of man from the rest of the natural world. Having identified Marvell's imposition of the structure of Christian history onto his notion of the providential development of nature, we can hear the historiographical resonance of the rhetorical gesture that constitutes the closure of so many of the pastorals. Marvell's speakers try quite simply to *redeem* their former state, attempting to renew the obstructed development of natural providence with an often alarming degree of vigor. It is, for example, the mower's desperation to recover an idyllic union with nature that impels him to hasten his own demise. In "The Mower's

24. *Beyond Formalism: Literary Essays 1958–1970* (New Haven: Yale University Press, 1970), 166–69. I am indebted throughout to Hartman's association of Marvell's natural theology with the literary form he calls the "interrupted pastoral" (192n).

Song," Damon assumes a prophetic voice when in his frenzy he vows to avenge himself on the unresponsive world around him with an act of violent, apocalyptic mowing: "And Flow'rs, and Grass, and I and all, / Will in one common Ruine fall" (21–22). And in "Damon the Mower," Marvell describes in apocalyptic tones the folly of the mower who in his haste cuts his own ankle with his scythe: "And there among the Grass fell down, / By his own Sythe, the Mower mown" (79–80).

The inevitable self-destruction that accompanies these misguided acts of redemption seems implicitly to reinforce the dictum that man should spare his pains where nature is at work. As Marvell's frequent use of images of *falling* should indicate, these blind attempts at deliverance cannot but recapitulate man's initial destructive lapse. Marvell is most forceful in conveying the utter inefficacy of such bald human action in "The Nymph Complaining," as the nymph dismisses the redemptive potential of the wanton act of the troopers:

> Though they should wash their guilty hands
> In this warm life-blood, which doth part
> From thine, and wound me to the Heart,
> Yet could they not be clean: their Stain
> Is dy'd in such a Purple Grain.
> There is not such another in
> The World, to offer for their Sin.
>
> (18–24)

For the nymph, the troopers are seen to embody what Hartman has described as "the spirit of activism wishing to speed redemption."[25] And as her deeply Christian discourse of guilt and remission makes clear, the act of the fawn's murder seems to have been modeled rather optimistically on that scene of redemptive sacrifice *par excellence*—the crucifixion of Christ. But the nymph hastens to interpret for us the cruel irony that inevitably attends such human acts of sacrifice: while the troopers seem to have sacrificed the fawn in an attempt to redeem themselves and cleanse their "guilty hands," their act serves only to guarantee their irredeemability, making indelible that original sin they were trying to wash away: "their Stain / Is dy'd in such a Purple Grain."

In this context of the politicization of the Christian redemption we can best understand the most notable, and most outrageous, attempt in Marvell's poetry to force an alliance with the forces of nature. I refer to

25. *Beyond Formalism*, 186.

the remarkable stanzas in "Upon Appleton House" in which the narrator
submits himself to the solicitous landscape of the Fairfacian wood:

> Bind me ye *Woodbines* in your twines,
> Curle me about ye gadding *Vines*,
> And Oh so close your Circles lace,
> That I may never leave this Place:
> But, lest your Fetters prove too weak,
> Ere I your Silken Bondage break,
> Do you, *O Brambles*, chain me too,
> And courteous *Briars* nail me through.
>   (609–16)

Critics have taken offense at William Empson's suggestion that the
narrator in this passage "becomes Christ with both the nails and the
thorns."[26] But it is difficult to deny that these images of binding and
nailing conjure a scene of crucifixion. We might fruitfully amplify the
significance of Empson's association by articulating the special status
Marvell lends to this particular attempt at redemption. The narrator's
desire to bind himself so completely to the natural world that he "may
never leave this Place" suggests an attempt to reconcile in one action
both the naturalistic and the sacrificial modes of redemption we have
observed. He seems to try to redeem the estate flooded by war through
a passive resignation to the forces of nature. But his attempt at an
organic, Hermeticist deliverance begins to assume the shape of one of
the most unnatural acts of redemption in world history, the ultimate
sacrifice of Christ on the cross. We can measure the inadequacy of this
admittedly noble gesture by the narrator's final dismissal of his own
solitary communion with nature (649–56). Leaving behind his awkward
attempt at a naturalistic *imitatio Christi*, the speaker proceeds to honor
the more sanctioned, though no less violent, prospect of Maria's public
submission to the sacrifice of marriage.

In the "Horatian Ode," Marvell can claim that the "bleeding Head"
(69) of Charles augurs the success of the new state, and in "Upon
Appleton House," the sacrifice of Maria to the priestly knife in marriage promises "some universal good." But we have examined the way
in which many of Marvell's pastorals question the faith in the
redemptive potential of such sacrificial acts. In fact, what is perhaps
most central to Marvell's pastoral historiography is the way in which

26. *Some Versions of Pastoral* (1936; New York: New Directions, 1968), 123. See Pierre
Legouis's reaction in *Poems and Letters* 1:290n.

these dramatic *coups de grace* function to preclude all hope in an ideal future. The Mower lyrics, for example, suggest the futility of any attempt to precipitate the redemption of nature. Even though the intended goal in the final actions of these poems may be to speed the process of man's reabsorption into nature, the mere fact of human assertion in these lyrics seems to alter fatally the direction of the Marvellian ideal we can call natural history. Like the speaker of "Upon Appleton House," as he importunes the "courteous *Briars*" to subject him to a woodland crucifixion, Marvell's speakers are often placed in the paradoxical position of *actively* forcing themselves into a *passive* relationship with nature, lapsing into a sybaritic buffoonery as they embrace the natural world with perhaps too much erotic intensity.

It is this grim irony that accompanies the idea of human action which informs Marvell's use of the georgic figure of the mower. Anthony Low and Annabel M. Patterson, extending Raymond Williams's analysis of the political content of the first-generation country-house poems, have each recently argued that Marvell's innovative use of the mower figure bespeaks an acute consciousness of what Patterson calls the "question of land-ownership and rural labor."[27] Low and Patterson are, of course, correct in their broader assumption that Marvell's pastorals participate in many of the discursive struggles of their historical moment. But I would argue, against their position, that Marvell exhibits—in both his poetry and prose—considerably less interest in the socio-political status of agrarian labor than we find in his predecessors in the country-house genre: Jonson, Carew, and Herrick. Marvell seems rather to employ the Virgilian dialectic between pastoral and georgic as a symbolic system with which to explore what was for him the more pressing—albeit more abstract—question of the proper attitude toward historical agency and political reform. Surely the dominant irony behind Marvell's use of the mower figure resides in the fact that, even as Damon idealizes the passive reciprocity he once enjoyed with his physical surroundings, his task as mower requires a systematic exercise of violence on that natural world. The work of mowing is, of course, from one perspective a beneficent activity intended to provide fodder for animals. But we should not, I think, imagine with Low that Marvell has attempted to construct in these lyrics an agriculturally viable image of the production of hay. Marvell's representation of a mower who, in the

---

27. Annabel M. Patterson, "Pastoral Versus Georgic: The Politics of Virgilian Quotation," *Renaissance Genres: Essays on Theory, History, and Interpretation,* ed. Barbara Kiefer Lewalski (Cambridge: Harvard University Press, 1986), 262. See Anthony Low, *The Georgic Revolution* (Princeton: Princeton University Press, 1985), 275; and Raymond Williams, *The Country and the City* (New York: Oxford University Press, 1973), 26–34.

violence of his frenzy, shows an unlikely tendency to "cut / Each stroke between the Earth and Root" ("Damon the Mower," 75–76) is more evocative of the many seventeenth-century attempts at political and cultural deracination—such as the riots attending the Root and Branch Petition—than it is immediately suggestive of a tangible rural practice.[28] In the highly emblematic world of Marvell's lyrics, the mower's intervention in the realm of natural process functions as an act of historical hubris that invariably fails.

It is in the context of the failed historical redemption that we should examine the ending of "The Nymph Complaining." Upon recognizing the impossibility of a natural metamorphosis after the fawn's violent death, the nymph consoles herself with yet another future history:

> Now my sweet Faun is vanish'd to
> Whither the Swans and Turtles go:
> In fair *Elizium* to endure,
> With milk-white Lambs, and Ermins pure.
>
> (105–8)

The nymph's vision of the future could not be more opposed to her earlier image of the fawn's gradual, organic immersion into the processes of vegetative growth. The material constitution of the fawn has "vanish'd" in its translation to the transcendent realm of the nymph's pagan heaven. When the nymph imagines her fawn accompanied in its heavenly stay with "milk-white Lambs, and Ermins pure," this fair Elysium sounds peculiarly unendurable, drained as it is of the variegated coloring of the pet's fusion with the flora. But Marvell seems less concerned here with the fact of an ultimate transcendence than he is with the psychology of the nymph's faith in this final apotheosis. The new hope in a heavenly end seems to derive primarily from the nymph's consciousness of the failure of the fawn's materialistic progress; her final lines belie the status of the fawn's putative transcendence as a compensatory mental construction:

> There at my feet shalt thou be laid,
> Of purest Alabaster made:
> For I would have thine Image be
> White as I can, though not as Thee.
>
> (119–22)

28. On the anti-Episcopal movement, Root and Branch, see J. P. Kenyon, *Stuart England* (Harmondsworth: Pelican, 1978), 125.

The nymph's faith in her pet's otherworldly destiny is diminished here to the mere fashioning of a statue. These lines seem to suggest a homology between the apotheosized body of the fawn and an alabaster artifact, hinting that the idea of apotheosis might itself be artificial, a product of the historical consciousness that must fashion a transcendent end for the life narrative.

In "Upon Appleton House," Marvell rejects his highly naturalistic, metamorphic vision of change and affirms that Maria's concession to her marital fate endows her with an apocalyptic power to "vitrify" nature. As we have seen, "The Nymph Complaining" is structured by a related shift in historical values, imagining a fall from the potential of natural history to a final commitment to an alabaster apotheosis. Despite these structural similarities, however, Marvell charges the endings of these two poems with antithetical emotional valencies: the optimism that marks the progressive last movement of the country-house poem could not be farther from the defeated resignation to eternal mourning that concludes the pastoral lament. The two poems affirm conflicting views on the efficacy of sacrifice and on the possibility of man's participation in a historical redemption. Denying any causal power to the act of redemptive sacrifice, "The Nymph Complaining" traces the faith in a transcendent future to a strictly human consciousness. Through the force of its negations, this poem can be viewed as Marvell's own critique of the faith expressed at the end of "Upon Appleton House" that a divine force will sanction a human attempt to redeem, or improve, a given historical state.

It remains now to answer to what end Marvell focuses on the historical processes integral to the natural world. In his pastoral poems, the insistently naturalized shape that providence assumes replaces the anthropomorphic deity of Protestant orthodoxy with an impersonal, yet highly moral, law of nature. I would argue that Marvell's emphasis on an impersonal, naturalized providence works to expose the folly of so many of his zealous reformers and drivers of the eschaton. In *The Rehearsal Transpros'd*, Marvell calls the illiberal clergymen of England "well-meaning Zealots" (135), and I think we can with some justification apply this same term to the figures like the mower and the wanton troopers who seem altogether too eager to hasten the inevitable end. The millenarian goals of the Fifth Monarchists and other radical sects relied heavily on the belief in a personal, willful God who would respond directly to their aggressive attempts to hasten the Last Days. The "well-meaning Zealots" throughout Marvell's work seem to mistake the human imposition on the natural course of events for the willful exercise of God's omnipotence. In focusing on the operations of a natural form of providence, the pastoral lyrics are eager to define a realm of divine determinism that can be distinguished from the belief in the crudely anthropomorphic providence that seems to have deluded so many of Marvell's radical puritan contemporaries. The poems set the ideal of an impersonal, natural providence against the illusory human projection of the divine approval of partisan action.

When in the "Horatian Ode" Marvell recognizes that Cromwell has ruined the "great Work of Time" (34), we seem meant to understand that Cromwell is in some sense England's redeemer, having destroyed the historical aggregate of custom and error. But the pastoral lyrics provide an alternative gloss on that "great Work of Time," suggesting that it is Time itself, a Time identified with natural providence, that has left this great work; from the perspective of this pastoral identification of Time with an ideal natural process, Cromwell's act of ruination is but another reprise of *ruina*, the Fall, that fatal interruption of the ideal progress toward the "green Age."[29] It could be said that the status of the phrase *work of time* concerns Marvell throughout his career. His writing continually poses the question whether that "great Work of Time" is *man's* work over the course of history, or whether it is the work that Time, or a naturalized providence, itself has wrought. Many of Marvell's political panegyrics necessarily approve man's active preparation for the millennial kingdom: Cromwell, for example, is a "Husbandman" in "The First Anniversary," tilling the "large Vale" of England (285–86). "Upon Appleton House" suggests ultimately that the purposive, georgic action of Maria's marriage—the harvesting of her "sacred Bud"—can elicit a divine power that might restore the nation to its unfallen state. But Marvell's shorter pastoral lyrics seem more often to question this "great work" of deliberate human action. Closer to the ideology of peaceful, private labor embedded in the hewel episode, these poems hint at the redemptive potential of a radical historical patience and political passivity. They affirm the decidedly conservative faith in man's acquiescence to nature and providence, historical forces which will effect reform only in the "best and proper time."[30]

29. For this point, I am indebted to K. W. Gransden's comments on the "one common Ruine" of "The Mower's Song," in "Time, Guilt, and Pleasure: A Note on Marvell's Nostalgia," *Ariel* 1.2 (April 1970): 86.

30. I am grateful to Donald Friedman, Peter Goldstein, Cristina Malcolmson, and George Lord for their comments on earlier drafts of this essay.

John Klause
Ann Baynes Coiro
Michael C. Schoenfeldt

The Achievement of Andrew Marvell
Excerpts from a Panel Discussion

[The panel discussion from which the following statements are excerpted was organized by Claude J. Summers and chaired by William V. Nestrick. The excerpts presented here have been edited and, in some cases, augmented by the panelists.]

John Klause

On Emerson Hall, the philosophy building at Harvard, there is an inscription that represents, so a probably apocryphal story goes, the triumph of one ideology over another. When the hall was constructed around the turn of the century, one party in the university wished to proclaim from the building's frieze the heady humanistic ideal of Protagoras: "Man is the measure." That group did not prevail. It was outmaneuvered by a devout party of less "pagan" and anthropocentric views, who arranged to have placed on the frieze the words that now appear there, words of the Psalmist: "What is man, that thou art mindful of him?" The anecdote has its own didactic purposes, of course; but it may also serve an unlikely turn. With only a little teasing, these two mottoes can be made to illustrate opposing and extreme tendencies in assessments of Andrew Marvell's achievement: "The man is the measure" *vs.* "Who (or where) is the man that we should be mindful of him?"

The first motto was the earliest to have currency. In the eighteenth century, the editions of Marvell's works were tributes paid to his personal qualities, which were considered exemplary to a nation. But through the ages, attention shifted from his character, which his life and works revealed to be that of a stalwart Protestant and incorruptible

233

patriot, to his more anonymous status in the nineteenth century as a nature poet, or as a creator of isolated poetic felicities of various kinds, to his yet more anonymous condition, in the mind of T. S. Eliot, as one who embodied in his poetry a "quality of civilization."

It was in the wake of Eliot's pronouncements that the second motto came into its own. More and more, Marvell's achievement became abstracted from the man in a search for the "virtues" of his art: "tough reasonableness beneath the slight lyric grace"; balance and proportion; epistemological sophistication; paradox, irony, and "double vision"; earnest playfulness; "negative capability" and freedom from narrow partisanship. Marvell the man was being annihilated to his thoughts—or perhaps not even to "thoughts" (because his true thoughts began to be considered unknowable), but to procedures. His poetry became a green procedure in a green shade.

Among factors contributing to this analytical approach to Marvell's "remains" was the depreciation of history and biography in the New Criticism, a disparagement that has continued in the hostility of some contemporary theory to the "author" or to authorial "intention." If one might be allowed an instructive simplification, such critical philosophies might be called puritanical, for their advocates have seemed eager to remove from aesthetic creation or experience the contamination of the irrelevant, which in many cases turns out to be the contamination of the "personal." Just as the painterly art might be pure in its disavowal of representation, or of personal statement or confession; just as the novel might be pure in its submersion of the "author" and authorial assessment; so criticism might be pure in quarantining itself from consideration of a poet's "life" or "mind." The desire for purity may have any number of motives, but for the critics who wish to share in the respectability of the scientist, the allure of "hard" knowledge has been especially strong. Thus, after the manner of Plato, they strive to separate knowledge (episteme) from opinion (doxa). With the certitude of logicians they discover and dismiss biographical and intentional "fallacies," consigning much personal literary commentary to the shallow cabinet of idle speculation. They believe that for criticism to be "valid" and therefore indefectible, it must, like the immortal figures on Keats's urn, sever in some ways its connections with life. Concentration on Marvell's "art" has rarely been formulaically pure, however, and has, both in its rigor and its laxity, produced some estimable results (as in the work of Frank Kermode, J. B. Leishman, Rosalie Colie, Donald Friedman, Christopher Ricks, John Carey, and many others who have helped us to appreciate certain artful features of Marvell's achievement). Postmodern criticism has only just begun (as in Jonathan Goldberg's essay on "The Nymph Complaining for the Death of Her *Faun*") to challenge the poetry with its "impertinence." Yet one can appreciate and apply to criticism in general the exasperated response of Graham Greene to the vogue of the "pure novel" of Flaubert and Henry James: "The exclusion of the author can go too far. Even the author, poor devil, has a right to exist."

Another reason for the disallowance of the personal in appreciations of Marvell has been more practical than theoretical: the growing sense that he is too anonymous, cryptic, contradictory, and enigmatic to be visible in his works—many of which cannot be dated, some of which are of uncertain attribution, some of which are propagandistic or polemical and, therefore, unlikely to be wholly ingenuous utterances of a *coeur transparent*. Although to admit defeat in the face of puzzling evidence may be as much a failure of will as of critical method, although to delight in the "aesthetics of inconclusiveness" may be as much an act of personal preference as a necessary consequence of insight (and indeed, those who value contradictions may discover more of them than are to be found), Robert Wilcher, in his recent edition of *Selected Poetry and Prose of Marvell*, speaks for a large, wise congregation of the prudent in advising readers to be "content to admire the brilliance with which [Marvell's] voice is adapted to occasion [and not] to seek for the face behind the mask."

It is clear, however, that despite all of the caveats and proscriptions, criticism of Marvell has continued to be unabashedly impure and incautious. The second motto has not triumphed so completely as has its counterpart chiseled in the stone of Emerson Hall. Scholars of various persuasions have persisted in their conviction that Marvell's achievements should not be depersonalized, or at least that his presence should not be excluded from his works. In the last few decades, for example, there have been many efforts to define, from within and without his writings, Marvell's politics, out of a sense that he was a man of particular and classifiable allegiances. Thus, we have had portraits of him as a "Puritan libertarian" (from Christopher Hill and Warren Chernaik), as a "loyalist" (from John Wallace), as a "trimmer" (from Donal Smith), as a "classical republican" (from Blair Worden—who "gingerly" applies the term, it should be said), as a "moderate chiliast" (from Margarita Stocker), and as an epideictic and polemical writer of strong views not liable to simple taxonomy (from Annabel M. Patterson). My own book on Marvell attempts to reveal something of Marvell's mind, to conceptualize certain premises of his religious and political principles (for even principles may have premises) and to suggest how his "moral imagination" might have been both relevant and irrelevant to his world.

If impure criticism is not merely the product of a blind stubbornness or of a hermeneutical naivete, it must rest on certain assumptions, among which, it might be argued, are these. Such criticism is licit—at least as legitimate as, for it is essentially no different from, any other attempt to know another through signs. The prohibitions *on principle* against biographical readings of Marvell's work have been more forcefully asserted than compellingly argued; and as a matter of inductive *fact*, the problematical evidence in his work about his mind and character is not utterly opaque—with more effort (some of it necessarily but unashamedly speculative) it can be made less so. Such criticism, furthermore, may be valuable. It does not suggest how (as Auden once said in adumbration of some modern approaches to literary study) "The words of a dead man / Are modified in the guts of the living," but how words helped to make a life before an author "became his admirers." May not an imperfect initiation into the mysteries of a life be as momentous as an exquisite experience of the "pleasures of the text"? Finally, impure criticism is in Marvell's case almost inevitable. Even the depersonalizers have, whether they intended to or not, created from his literary remains a version of his character: that of the detached, ironic connoisseur. The portrait may be only of a mostly disembodied Cheshire cat, displaying not a cartoon smile drawn by Tenniel or Disney, but the enigmatic grin of Mona Lisa. Yet it is clear and distinct enough to taunt those who would have the inconvenient author disappear.

That Marvell, in myriad guises, continues to be seen in his poems—despite their multiple personae, their reliance on conventions, their sometimes public themes and "voices," their contradictions (within themselves and with each other), their ironies, feints, and deceits—implies that they are somehow intensely personal. They do not as a rule liturgically suppress all signs of their author's character (as do, for example, medieval lyrics or seventeenth-century political ballads), nor is their art so large and so radically given to the objects of portrayal (as in the plays of Shakespeare) that it retards an "irritable reaching after" the mind and circumstances of its creator. Marvell's poetry may, of course, be read without attending to the "man," but that inattention is at best a refusal to listen to a voice because it is misinterpretable or because it may distract from a specialized pursuit. Thus the neglect is either timid or, even if useful, arbitrary.

There is more in Marvell's utterances than their art. He speaks in his poems with the lyric "I," who may or may not wholly be himself. He populates them with versions of men and women who lived and died outside his mind: Flecknoe, Lovelace, Lord Hastings, the Fairfaxes, King Charles, Cromwell, Tom May, Archibald Douglas, Clarendon, and "little T. C." He writes of politics, war, pieties religious and domestic, love and lust real or imagined, dreams of escape approved and condemned. Marvell, his characters, and world are all, in a sense, like Donne's angels, who take on bodies of "aire" in order to be seen. The visible air is not the reality for which it stands—a reality that it can only caricature and may sometimes hide; but the reality is responsible for the image, and surely one may inquire how. If the angels themselves evoke in us a skepticism like Hotspur's before Glendower's "spirits from the vasty deep"—"But will they come when you do call for them?"— the doubt should not be paralyzing. They will never come, whatever they be, unless called. Only nothing will come of nothing. Understanding relatively little of Marvell's personal mystery, we should at least know enough to sense that it is too valuable to be slighted or ignored. We may judge the punctiliousness misguided that would preserve the integrity of a mystery by forswearing any attempt to comprehend it. And we may wonder if a criticism that refuses to risk superstition has been too hasty in settling for "certitudes," which may not themselves be unassailable.

But the example of Marvell, it must be admitted, might serve to rebuke as well as to encourage quests for the historical poet. Readers who are interested, as was Carlyle, in an author's writings primarily insofar as they form part of that "greatest work of every man, the Life he has led," may let a desire for heroes overcome considerations of truth. Hero-lust (the second-to-last "infirmity of Noble mind"?) has often tempted us to turn Marvell into a champion, to purify him, even in our impure criticism, and canonize him as an exemplary sponsor of some aesthetic or political ideology or other. Richard Marius once told me of his suspicion that he was the first biographer of Thomas More who did not pray to him. It is unlikely that Marvell has been the recipient of prayers. Yet the complexity of his character ought to discourage even a secular devotion to him as a patron whom we might invoke to bless the truth of our own causes—to that extent, the "man" is not the "measure." Marvell offers a different kind of caution to practitioners of the different varieties of New Historicism, which has begun to turn critical attention again to the place of literature in a world larger and ultimately more important than itself. Although in his recent book on Shakespeare, Stephen Greenblatt has expressed a desire to "speak with the dead," it is not yet clear how, given its concern for large statements about "society" or "culture," this criticism might allow such a conversation to become detailed and intimate. It also remains to be seen what features a newly historicized Marvell himself will have. At any rate, there must be something humbling to grand interpretative aspirations in the case of a man so baffling as Marvell. May we be more confident in our interpretations of whole cultures and their codes than we are in our best but doomed efforts to see a single man whole?

Ann Baynes Coiro

Perhaps Marvell's poetry achieves nothing. Marvell has become in our readings and in our classrooms the emblem of compressed ambiguity, of formal virtuosity, and of multiple moral visions suspended. Marvell's poetry is deeply private, even lonely—worked from a personal code of images that we can only partially translate. Indeed it is this marked privacy that has led some recent critics to identify Marvell as a figure on the margin of the emergent modern subjectivity.[1]

Marvell does, however, make significant revelations about his own poetry in his complex, involuted assessment of Milton's achievement in "*On Mr.* Milton's *Paradise Lost.*" Underlying the balanced antithesis of the lines is the larger antithesis the poem insists upon between Milton and Marvell. Most obviously, "*On Mr.* Milton's *Paradise Lost*" is a series of heroic couplets that ends with a particularly fine epigrammatic twist:

> Thy verse created like thy *Theme* sublime,
> In Number, Weight, and Measure, needs not *Rhime.*

The poem's deflating end "points" back to Marvell's own tagged lines in self-mockery certainly, but also with a destabilizing hint of mockery for Milton and his sublime. Marvell's poem, thus, makes wittily clear in its statement and in its form the strong differences between his poetry and Milton's, and this tension between Marvell and Milton, between the inscriber of this prefatory poem and the described, is indeed the principle of construction which underlies the structure of "*On Mr.* Milton's *Paradise Lost.*" Marvell, in the act of bestowing ambiguous praise on Milton—

> Well mightst thou scorn thy Readers to allure
> With tinkling Rhime, of thy own Sense secure

1. See, for example, Catherine Belsey, "Love and Death in 'To his Coy Mistress,'" *Post-Structuralist Readings of English Poetry,* ed. Richard Machin and Christopher Norris (Cambridge: Cambridge University Press, 1987), 105–21; and Lynn Enterline, "The Mirror and the Snake: The Case of Marvell's 'Unfortunate Lover,'" *Critical Quarterly* 29 (1987): 98–112.

—gestures toward his ambivalence about his own poetry and, especially, about published poetry itself. Milton is both admirable for refusing to pander to the reading public *and* shadowed with the hint of a suggestion that his audience will be few indeed. The couplet, with *its* tinkling rhyme, also strongly and disturbingly suggests that it is Marvell who is not secure in his own sense, and that the very security of the form—its shortness, tightness, and highly marshalled lines—reveal *not* the security and control it clamps down on the page, but the very insecurity that needs to cling to patterning. But the strands of irony twist once more, for it is Marvell's restraint, the mysterious, runic quality of his poetry that we value in the late twentieth century, and this compression is a product of his terse, emblematic control. Nor do we have control over the meaning of Marvell's poetry, its sense, a sense that certainly eludes critical consensus.

Within the dialectic of form that *"On Mr. Milton's Paradise Lost"* sets up between Marvell and Milton is also an obsessive interest in sight.[2] Milton's literal blindness becomes a trope of power. The poet-Marvell *sees* and cannot understand; the poet-Milton is blind and prophesies. "I beheld the Poet blind," the poet-speaker begins, beheld "his vast Design, . . . saw him strong" and feared he would overwhelm the world "to revenge his Sight." Then the poet-Marvell "read" and fears Milton's blindness again, fears that some lesser writer will appropriate the epic and "show it in a Play." But Milton transcends sight, sings, flies, and is therefore preserved "inviolate." Sight is clearly a limitation, indeed a violation. The reader's sight of the poem *Paradise Lost* places the poem at considerable risk of being misunderstood, and the poem can escape in large measure because it can escape the finite, the visible, the tangible, material shreds of tagged ends. When Marvell first beheld the poem,

> the Argument
> Held me a while misdoubting his Intent,
> That he would ruine (for I saw him strong)
> The sacred Truths to Fable and old Song,
> (So *Sampson* groap'd the Temples Posts in spight)
> The World o'rewhelming to revenge his Sight.
>
> (5–10)

Paradise Lost escapes Marvell's sight because Milton rewrites the Sam-

---

2. Marvell's use of the emblems and epigrams as crucial models for his poetry is demonstrated by J. B. Leishman, *The Art of Marvell's Poetry* (London: Hutchinson, 1966), esp. 29–100; and Rosalie Colie, *"My Ecchoing Song": Andrew Marvell's Poetry of Criticism* (Princeton: Princeton University Press, 1970), esp. 106–17 and 181–294.

son myth and does not bring the temple down in revenge for his blindness but leaves the temple of sacred truth standing. It is Marvell in his metaphor of Milton as Samson, who changes the sacred Truths, who brings the capacious temple down around the edges of his poem. And it is Marvell who in this poem succeeds in doing to Milton exactly what he says Milton has escaped—he "show[s]" him, he "dare[s] / Within [Milton's] Labours to pretend a Share." He engraves on the front matter of Milton's published poem this epigram. In so doing, he both participates in and makes fearsome the very act of publication.

Indeed, Marvell's antithetical movement in the poem between sight and blindness and between form and sense may be extended to the antithetical movement in the poem and beyond it between Milton's poetry and Marvell's. "*On Mr.* Milton's *Paradise Lost*" is one of the very few poems Marvell published during his lifetime. The great majority of Marvell's poems remained out of print and out of sight until he died. Then they appeared with the teasing announcement:

TO THE
R E A D E R

These are to Certifie every Ingenious Reader, that all these Poems, as also the other things in this Book contained, are Printed according to the exact Copies of my late dear Husband, under his own Hand-Writing, being found since his Death among his other Papers, Witness my Hand this 15*th* day of *October,* 1680.

Mary Marvell.

In arranging the poems' passage from hand and paper and desk, to Reader and Print, this statement of provenance has proven a certification as enigmatic as the poems it prefaces.

I would argue that Marvell's reticence about print, his linkage of sight and disablement in "*On Mr.* Milton's *Paradise Lost,*" is connected in suggestive ways with the obsession throughout his poetry with graven, permanent words, with physical inscriptions that he presents as impossibly and inevitably enigmatic because they remain hard and dead when we try to read them. The very epigrammatic and enigmatic tightness of Marvell's poetry insists upon its textual solidity.

The genre that particularly concerns me here, because it seems to be a key to Marvell's *own* assessment of his poetry, is the inscription, the epitaph on a grave or the memorial or sententious inscription on a building or monument. Marvell wrote a number of poems expressly in this genre—his five extant epitaphs, three in Latin and two in English, for example, and the "Inscribenda Luparae," his six alternative inscriptions which he wrote as entries in an international contest for the best inscription to be carved on the portal of the Louvre.[3] This contest is itself evidence of a broad cultural passion for inscriptions that swept Europe throughout the seventeenth century, but to which little critical attention has been paid.[4] Such epigrammatic inscriptions could serve as memorial epitaphs designed for relatively private spaces or as enormous carved words, with powerful ideological weight, on public buildings and monuments. Inscriptions appear as well in baroque painting, either carved in stone or written on a scroll in capitals, serving as teasing puzzles or as clues to the interpretive depth of the painting. During the sixteenth and seventeenth centuries as printing became more sophisticated there developed a widely popular fashion for books of printed inscriptions laid out on the page so that they looked like they were graven capitals filling a stone.

Evident in Marvell's best-known poems are traces of inscription. "Upon Appleton House," for example, may be read as the inscription circling its walls, completing its design. Certainly the first seven stanzas make elegantly clear that House and poem belong together and that the poem has been crafted in imitation. Architect and poet work together to create a "sober Frame":

> Those short but admirable Lines,
> By which, ungirt and unconstrain'd,
> Things greater are in less contain'd.

But the inscription which is "Upon Appleton House" may be construed as carved upon not only the House but also the grave, for the House is described, in fact, as a grave. Here in Appleton House, "Their Bodies measure out their Place" and do not demand "more room alive

---

3. Sancroft's transcription of what he believed to be the winning inscription is cited in *Poems and Letters* (1:274):

> Regia, Rex, Regnum tria sunt Miracula Mundi:
> Rex animo, Regnum Viribus, arte Domus.

> [The palace, the king, the kingdom are the three wonders of the world / The king in his mind, the kingdom in its strength, and the palace in its art.]

4. I am indebted to John Sparrow's pioneering work on this subject, *Visible Words: A Study of Inscriptions in and as Books and Works of Art* (Cambridge: Cambridge University Press, 1969), and to the work of Armando Petrucci, especially *La Scrittura: Ideologia e rappresentazione* (Torino: Einaudi, 1986).

then dead." The lines of the poem become lines engraved on the walls of a house and of a tomb, the shrine that the poem imagines Appleton House to be when Fairfax is dead and pilgrims come to adore. The poem for all its beauty becomes a sarcophagus for the living, now trapped and dead.

Inscriptions become more sinister in Marvell's poetry when they intrude upon the garden. The mower against gardens, for example, describes artful "Gardens square" that "enclose" "A dead and standing pool of Air," an extraordinarily damning statement since it can clearly be applied to the poem itself. The mower's condemnation of gardens is a terrible condemnation of art, and yet the poem's very enclosure on the page deals "between the Bark and Tree" so that we must remain "in dispute" about the poem and its ending:

> 'Tis all enforc'd; the Fountain and the Grot;
> While the sweet Fields do lye forgot:
>
> . . . .
> [Where] *Fauns* and *Faryes* do the Meadows till,
> More by their presence then their skill.
> Their Statues polish'd by some ancient hand,
> May to adorn the Gardens stand:
> But howso'ere the Figures do excel,
> The *Gods* themselves with us do dwell.
>
> (31–32, 35–40)

Who are "we" and what are the "figures"? As we work our way through the polished skill of the poem, where do we locate ourselves? We are not in the "presence" of the fauns and fairies in the meadows, but in thrall to the skillful hand that has written these words. And where does the poem, the "figure" of the poem itself exist—inside the enclosure it itself imitates or outside with the gods? The *voice* of the mower may dwell outside, but the words on the page are carved on the base of the statue and remain within, "all enforced."[5] It is the poem that is the polished figure in the garden.

Similarly, in his "Song" the mower takes revenge upon a landscape that once reflected his mind, but that now flourishes and luxuriates in spite of his misery. To make the landscape again a mirror of his mind, he cuts it down and uses the greenery cut off from life as "the Heraldry . . . / With which I shall adorn my Tomb." By the end of the poem, we realize that the fields have become a symbolic decoration

---

5. On the tension of voice and inscription I am indebted to Mary Thomas Crane, " 'His Owne Style': Voice and Writing in Jonson's Poems," *Criticism* 32 (1990): 31–50.

upon a grave, and that we have been reading the monument. Indeed, each of the mower poems can be read as the dead heraldry on the tomb of a once green thought. Translated to words on a page, the mower is mown indeed; only the enigmatic words remain, the heraldry on the tomb. They are what we see, and vision is treacherous.

Again, in the garden of lilies and roses, the nymph concludes her complaint upon her fawn "I / Will but bespeak thy Grave, and dye" and the poem becomes in the end a weeping statue upon a grave, her tears carving his epitaph in the stone.[6] She becomes a statue graven with words in a pastoral landscape—and the words are this poem itself. Every act of artifice in Marvell's poetry becomes an act of inscription. The speaker of "The Garden" rejoices in finding there "Fair quiet" and "Innocence," but quiet and innocence are violated and changed even in the act of naming. While others have "Cut in these Trees their Mistress name," the speaker will turn the trees into engraved monuments:

> Fair Trees! where s'eer your barkes I wound,
> No Name shall but your own be found,

standing named in the garden of the poem.

Andrew Marvell eludes us, and he seems to have intended to do so. His poems remained out of print, and yet they are constructed out of a fascination with print. We may now look upon them, but we cannot fully understand. The words stand stark on the outside of the marble vault, portentous and enigmatic. The grave is indeed a fine and private place.

Michael C. Schoenfeldt

I have long admired Marvell's poetry but have also found it to elude the very terms in which I try to convey my admiration. In John Aubrey's gossipy characterization of Marvell, however, may lurk a clue to some of the chronic elusiveness of Marvell's texts. Aubrey suggests that Marvell "was in his conversation very modest, and of very few words: and though he loved wine he would never drinke hard in company, and was wont to say that, he would not play the goodfellow in any man's company in whose hands he would not trust his life. He had not a generall acquaintance. . . . He kept bottles of wine at his lodge-

6. See Jonathan Goldberg's discussion of "The Nymph Complaining" in *Voice Terminal Echo: Postmodernism and English Renaissance Texts* (New York and London: Methuen, 1986), 14–37.

ing, and many times he would drinke liberally by himselfe to refresh
his spirits, and exalt his Muse."[7] This image of Marvell, festive yet
solitary, loving wine yet fearing public intoxication, cautious in company yet liberal with wine and words when alone, is I think directly
related to the delectable evasiveness of nearly every sentence that
flows from his pen. Unlike Ben Jonson, whose indignation against
political and poetic opportunism Marvell ventriloquizes in "Tom May's
Death," Marvell cannot imagine a "tribe" of like-minded individuals
among whom he could drink freely and speak unguardedly. Rather, for
Marvell, the self becomes its own best audience, as well as its only
trustworthy drinking companion.

I would like to claim, then, that the peculiar social conduct Aubrey
describes is, like the poems we so value, a defensive response to the
immense pressures placed upon behavior and speech in an age of
political turmoil. In the Introduction to the *Second Part* of *The Rehearsal
Transpros'd*, Marvell refers explicitly to these pressures, suggesting that
because of the suspicion with which all utterance is received, "not to
Write at all is much the safer course of life." Yet this seems to be a course
he was unable to maintain. He did, though, largely avoid publishing,
an activity he likens to preparing for war: "whosoever he be that comes
in Print whereas he might have sate at home in quiet, does either make
a Treat[y], or send a Chalenge to all Readers; in which cases, the first, it
concerns him to have no scarcity of Provisions, and in the other to be
compleatly Arm'd."[8] Unable to stop writing, Marvell nevertheless preferred to compose "at home in quiet" rather than to mobilize for the
wars of publishing.

The recurring motif of the garden seems to offer Marvell a haven
from such violence. Yet the natural order of these gardens is precarious,
vulnerable, always in danger of espionage or violence from the world
they try to exclude. "The Nymph Complaining for the Death of Her
Faun" lives a life of blissful retreat until huntsmen invade her grove and
kill her fawn. Marvell's mowers bear the wounds of their encounters
with others, and transfer them to the landscape they assault. But in
"The Garden," the speaker finds what he had mistakenly and naively
sought "In busie Companies of men"—"Fair quiet," "Innocence," and
a "delicious solitude" to which "Society is all but rude." As in Aubrey's
portrait of Marvell drinking liberally but alone, release is made possible
only when one is isolated from a treacherous social world:

7. *Aubrey's Brief Lives*, ed. Oliver Lawson Dick (Harmondsworth: Penguin, 1962),
268.
8. *The Rehearsal Transpros'd and The Rehearsal Transpros'd: The Second Part*, ed.
D. I. B. Smith (Oxford: Clarendon Press, 1971), 159–60, 160.

> The Luscious Clusters of the Vine
> Upon my Mouth do crush their Wine;
> The Nectaren, and curious Peach,
> Into my hands themselves do reach;
> Stumbling on Melons, as I pass,
> Insnar'd with Flow'rs, I fall on Grass.
>
> (35–40)

Drunken abandonment to a festive vegetable love is possible only in the secure solitude the garden represents; the *felix culpa* is reinscribed as an absolutely asocial experience. Unlike Milton's Adam, who regretfully concedes to Eve that "solitude sometimes is best society," Marvell finds the Ciceronian preference for solitude to be not only a mode of misogyny—"Two paradises 'twere in one / To live in Paradise alone"—but also a principle of political survival.

In "Upon Appleton House," Marvell makes so much of the estate's origins in a convent not only because of the anti-Catholicism it allows him to vent but also because the nuns' desire for religious retirement and internal freedom is so uncomfortably close to his own. One of the "Suttle Nunns" tells Isabella Thwaites that "These Walls restrain the World without, / But hedge out Liberty about" (94, 99–100). The estate likewise offers Marvell the chance to "retir[e] from the Flood, [and] / Take Sanctuary in the Wood" (481–82). The woods are so dense they seem to present a solid front, providing him with just the kind of refuge from the world for which he castigates the nuns:

> How safe, methinks, and strong behind
> These Trees have I incamp'd my Mind;
> . . . .
> 			where the World no certain Shot
> Can make, or me it toucheth not.
> But I on it securely play,
> And gaul its Horsemen all the Day.
>
> (601–2, 605–8)

As the subtle nun suggests to Isabella Thwaites, freedom is possible only by means of exclusion. Protected from the artillery of a bellicose world, Marvell can engage in the ostensibly free play of the mind.

This isolationist impulse imbues Marvell's work on a personal and national level. Fairfax's estate offers at once a microcosm of and a retreat from England, "The Garden of the World." Like the estate, England is blessed with geographical security from outside attack; heaven, "to exclude the World, did guard / With watry if not flaming

Sword" this "dear and happy Isle" (321–26). The Civil War, however, was no *felix culpa*; rather, it was a fall from the grace of isolation into the grisly realm of politics. Before the War, militaristic tendencies were absorbed by natural processes; then

> Gardens only had their Towrs,
> And all the Garrisons were Flowrs,
> When Roses only Arms might bear,
> And Men did rosie Garlands wear[.]
> Tulips, in several Colours barr'd,
> Were then the *Switzers* of our *Guard*.
>
> (331–36)

But the War despoils this delicate order, bending these horticultural energies to the purposes of fortification; now "We Ordinance Plant and Powder sow" (344). As the "Unhappy Birds" who "build below the Grasses Root" discover, even keeping a low profile offers no sure refuge from its butchery. The careless scythe of the "tawny Mowers" despoils their nest, driving home the message that "Lowness is unsafe as Hight" (409–11).

These imminent dangers imprint not only Marvell's overtly political utterances but also his most ethereal lyrics. "On a Drop of Dew" seems to record, with a requisite circumspection, the desire to escape the pressures tenuously excluded from "Upon Appleton House" and "The Garden." The globe of water, Marvell tells us, "Round in its self incloses," it "Scarce touch[es] where it lyes," it restless "roules and unsecure, / Trembling lest it grow impure." It has "pure and circling thoughts" and manages to exclude the world around it while "Yet receiving in the Day." By shutting out the world whose contamination it fears, the drop achieves the secrecy and self-containment idealized in Marvell's translation of the second chorus from Seneca's *Thyestes*—

> Climb at *Court* for me that wil,
> Tott'ring favor's Pinacle;
> All I seek is to lye still.
> Settled in some secret Nest
> In calm Leisure let me rest;
> And far of the publick Stage
> Pass away my silent Age.
> Thus when without noise, unknown,
> I have liv'd out all my span,
> I shall dye, without a groan,
> An old honest Country man.
>
> (1–11)

The drop, then, functions as an analogue not only for the heaven-seeking religious soul but also for the security-seeking political self. The mercurial ambiguity that characterizes such occasional utterances as the "Horatian Ode" supplies the lyrical equivalent of the slipperiness and instability idealized in "On a Drop of Dew." If one cannot sustain the silence recommended in the translation from Seneca, one can at least achieve the prophylactic self-enclosure depicted in "On a Drop of Dew."

Marvell's lyrics, then, are difficult to stabilize because they purposefully occlude the interiority they purport to exhibit. Even when they promise self-disclosure, Marvell's personae recoil from the vulnerability such exposure entails. The speaker of "The Gallery," for example, invites his beloved to "come view my Soul," but when she looks inside all she sees are portraits of herself. We tend to organize our discourse about seventeenth-century literature by separating out private from public concerns, meditative from occasional motives. But Marvell defies these dichotomies, composing poems on public subjects for private consumption (for example, the "Horatian Ode"), and depicting in his paeans to retirement the processes by which the pressures of politics continue to trespass on the territory of the self. In "To His Noble Friend Mr. Richard Lovelace, upon His Poems," Marvell complains that "Our wits have drawne th'infection of our times." The antithesis of a poetry of confession, Marvell's is a poetry of concealment, cultivating detachment and evasion as a necessary protection against the contagions of a treacherous political world.

Marvell, then, could not stop singing but also could not bear the risk of being overheard. We depend upon the posthumous folio edition of the *Miscellaneous Poems* (1681) for the texts of most of the poems we value. Ironically, the pressures that pervade and produce the poems very nearly preclude their entry into the public domain. In "The Mower against Gardens," Marvell contrasts an exotic plant, the "*Marvel of Peru*," to the "Forbidden mixtures" that are "enforc'd" by the "Tyrant[s]" of contemporaneous horticulture. The extraordinary achievement of that exotic plant we call the Marvell of Hull was to thrive despite the oppression of another kind of "tyrant," to avoid the "forbidden mixtures" of apostasy in an age when it was nearly impossible to do so, and to cultivate in the greenhouse of the self flowers of remarkable delicacy, complexity, and beauty.

Notes on the Contributors

DIANA TREVIÑO BENET teaches at New York University. She is the author of *Secretary of Praise: The Poetic Vocation of George Herbert* and *Something to Love: The Novels of Barbara Pym,* as well as numerous essays.

DOUGLAS D. C. CHAMBERS is an associate professor in the Department of English at Trinity College in the University of Toronto. He has written on Milton and John Evelyn and has just published an edition of the poems from Thomas Traherne's recently discovered manuscript, *Commentaries of Heaven.* He is also a garden historian and an associate editor of *Journal of Garden History.*

ANN BAYNES COIRO is Associate Professor of English at Rutgers University. She is author of *Robert Herrick's "Hesperides" and the Epigram Book Tradition.*

EUGENE R. CUNNAR is Associate Professor of English at New Mexico State University. He has published articles on Donne, Herbert, Milton, Crashaw, Vermeer, and Zurbaran. His current research explores the relationships between Renaissance art and literature.

M. L. DONNELLY is Associate Professor of English at Kansas State University. A contributor to *A Milton Encyclopedia* and *The Spenser Encyclopedia,* he has presented papers on a wide variety of Renaissance figures and topics. He is currently engaged in further work on panegyric modes and political mythology in the seventeenth century and on the cultural and psychological tensions in Milton's early work.

BARBARA L. ESTRIN, Professor of English at Stonehill College, is author of *The Raven and the Lark: Lost Children in Literature of the English Renaissance* and numerous articles on Renaissance and modern topics. Currently she is working on a book-length study, "Discovered by Desire: 'Youing' the 'I' in Wyatt, Donne and Marvell."

DONALD M. FRIEDMAN is Professor of English at the University of California, Berkeley. He is author of *Marvell's Pastoral Art* and of essays on Shakespeare, Wyatt, Milton, Donne, and Spenser. His current projects include a book on the representation of sense experience in seventeenth-century poetry and a study of Shakespearean "playing."

JOAN HARTWIG is Professor of English at the University of Kentucky. She has published two books on Shakespeare, essays on Marvell and Shakespeare, and is currently working on two book-length studies: one on the horse in English Renaissance literature and the other on the use of metaphor in Shakespeare, Donne, and Marvell.

JOHN KLAUSE teaches at Hofstra University. He is author of *The Unfortunate Fall: Theodicy and the Moral Imagination of Andrew Marvell.*

TED-LARRY PEBWORTH is William E. Stirton Professor in the Humanities and Professor of English at the University of Michigan–Dearborn. He is author of *Owen Felltham;* co-author of *Ben Jonson;* and co-editor of *The Poems of Owen Felltham* and of collections of essays on Herbert, on Jonson and the Sons of Ben, on Donne, on the seventeenth-century religious lyric, and on poetry and politics in the seventeenth century. A recent president of the John Donne Society of America, he is author or co-author of numerous critical and bibliographical articles and serves as a member of the advisory board and as a textual editor of *The Variorum Edition of the Poetry of John Donne.*

DALE B. J. RANDALL is Professor of English at Duke University. Among his publications are *"The Golden Tapestry": A Critical Survey of Non-chivalric Spanish Fiction in English Translation (1543–1657); Joseph Conrad and Warrington Dawson: The Record of a Friendship; Jonson's Gypsies Unmasked: Background and Theme of "The Gypsies Metamorphos'd"; Gentle Flame: The Life and Verse of Dudley, Fourth Lord North (1602–1677);* and *"Theatres of Greatness": A Revisionary View of Ford's "Perkin Warbeck."*

STELLA P. REVARD is Professor of English at Southern Illinois University, Edwardsville, where she teaches courses in both English literature and Greek. Her book *The War in Heaven: "Paradise Lost" and the Tradition of Satan's Rebellion* received the James Holly Hanford Award of the Milton Society of America. She is currently completing a book on the influence of Pindar on sixteeth- and seventeenth-century English poetry.

JOHN ROGERS, formerly a Mellon Fellow at the Society of Fellows in the Humanities at Columbia University, is Assistant Professor of English at Yale University. He has completed a book entitled *The Matter of Dissent: The Poetics of History in the Age of Milton.*

MICHAEL C. SCHOENFELDT is Associate Professor of English at the University of Michigan–Ann Arbor. He is author of essays on Donne, Jonson, and Herbert, and of *Prayer and Power: George Herbert and Renaissance Courtship.*

PAUL R. SELLIN is Professor of English and Anglo–Dutch Relations, University of California, Los Angeles, and *oudhoogleraar,* English Literature since 1500, at the Free University of Amsterdam, The Netherlands. In addition to *Daniel Heinsius and Stuart England, John Donne and 'Calvinist' Views of Grace,* and *So Doth, So Is Religion: John Donne and Diplomatic Contexts in the Reformed Netherlands, 1619–1620,* he has published essays, monographs, and translations on such subjects as Donne, Milton, Anglo–Dutch relations, and Renaissance–Neo-Latin criticism.

CLAUDE J. SUMMERS, William E. Stirton Professor in the Humanities and Professor of English at the University of Michigan–Dearborn, is author of books on Christopher Marlowe, Christopher Isherwood, and E. M. Forster; co-author of *Ben Jonson;* and co-editor of *The Poems of Owen Felltham* and of collections of essays on Herbert, on Jonson and the Sons of Ben, on Donne, on the seventeenth-century religious lyric, and on poetry and politics in the seventeenth century. Past President of the John Donne Society of America, he has published essays on Marlowe, Shakespeare, Donne, Herbert, Herrick, Vaughan, Forster, Auden, Isherwood, and others. His most recent books are *Gay Fictions: Wilde to Stonewall* and *E. M. Forster: A Guide to Research.*

RICHARD TODD is Associate Professor and Reader in English at the Free University Amsterdam, and in 1988–1989 was Visiting Netherlands Professor at the University of Michigan–Ann Arbor. His publications include *Iris Murdock: The Shakespearian Interest, Iris Murdock,* and *The Opacity of Signs: Acts of Interpretation in George Herbert's "The Temple."* His other publications include articles, review articles, and reviews in sixteenth-, seventeenth-, and twentieth-century literature in scholarly journals in both the United States and Europe.

Index

This index includes only primary works. Lengthy titles are abbreviated, and anonymous works are alphabetized by title.